D1475103

A History of Charisma

A History of Charisma

John Potts
Associate Professor, Macquarie University, Australia

First published 2009 by
PALGRAVE MACMILLAN

Palgrave Macmillan in the UK is an imprint of Macmillan Publishers Limited, registered in England, company number 785998, of Houndmills, Basingstoke, Hampshire RG21 6XS.

Palgrave Macmillan in the US is a division of St Martin's Press LLC, 175 Fifth Avenue, New York, NY 10010.

Palgrave Macmillan is the global academic imprint of the above companies and has companies and representatives throughout the world.

Palgrave® and Macmillan® are registered trademarks in the United States, the United Kingdom, Europe and other countries

ISBN-13: 978-0-230-55153-4   hardback
ISBN-10: 0-230-55153-X   hardback

This book is printed on paper suitable for recycling and made from fully managed and sustained forest sources. Logging, pulping and manufacturing processes are expected to conform to the environmental regulations of the country of origin.

A catalogue record for this book is available from the British Library.

A catalog record for this book is available from the Library of Congress.

10   9   8   7   6   5   4   3   2   1
18   17   16   15   14   13   12   11   10   09

Printed and bound in Great Britain by
CPI Antony Rowe, Chippenham and Eastbourne

Contents

Illustrations

Acknowledgements

This book could not have been written without the assistance of many people. I wish to thank Michael Strang, History Publisher at Palgrave Macmillan, who supported this project when it was only at proposal stage, and guided me through the long process of realising it as a book. Our periodical discussions over coffee at the British Library, whenever I made it to London, were enjoyable staging posts on the journey. My thanks also to Ruth Ireland at Palgrave Macmillan, who was ever ready to provide assistance and encouragement as the book began taking shape.

A project such as this is informed by many perspectives, and takes form as a result of dialogue. I have been fortunate to draw on the advice of several individuals well placed to engage with the trajectory of my study of charisma. The following have been conversants with whom I have discussed issues large and small during the writing of this book: Mitchell Dean, Marnie Hughes-Warrington, Christopher Forbes, Charles Merewether and Edwin Judge. As a result of these conversations, I refined my views, clarified my approach, discovered new angles and, on at least one occasion, changed course. This is what one would hope for from stimulating dialogue. I am very grateful to each of these conversants for the time and intellectual energy they contributed to this work.

Once the book was in progress and draft chapters were produced, I needed thorough criticism from expert readers. This I received from James Harrison, Mark Evans, Marnie Hughes-Warrington, Mitchell Dean and Noel King. The constructive criticism offered by these readers was essential to the development of the book. Errors were corrected, interpretations modified, alternative perspectives proposed. I thank each of these readers for the time they took to contribute their specialist knowledge to the improvement of my work. Similarly, I received expert advice from other scholars pertaining to specific sections of the history. My thanks to Stuart Piggin, Ken Parry, Doris McIlwain and Eduardo de la Fuente for the benefit of their invaluable suggestions and commentary.

Many other individuals provided assistance in a variety of ways: solutions to theoretical or technical problems, suggestions for fruitful directions in research, the checking of statements and assertions. I extend my gratitude for their kind contributions, with apologies to anyone inadvertently omitted: Daniel Kane, Halyna Koscharsky, Andrew Siedlecki, Peter Forshaw, Ian Hunter, Kevin Killeen, Agnieska Steckowicz, Bernard Zuel, Gordon McMullan, David Matthews, Alex Munt, Steve Collins, Kathryn Millard, Sherman Young, Greg Fox, David Mitchell, Greg Levine, Amen Gakavian, Christine Dudley, Annette Hamilton and Robyn Clark.

I gratefully acknowledge the financial assistance of the Media Department and the Division of Society, Culture, Media and Philosophy at Macquarie University, Australia.

Finally, my special appreciation to Sophie Forbat for her encouragement, support and inspiration during the writing of this book.

1
The History of a Word

This book is a history of the word 'charisma', and the meanings associated with that word, over a duration spanning the first century AD to the twenty-first. In a severely brief outline, this history is as follows: the term 'charisma' emerged in the early Christian church of the first century; charisma was eclipsed as a religious concept within the church by the end of the third century; it lay submerged for many centuries, with intermittent appearances; charisma was reinvented in Max Weber's sociology in the early twentieth century; the word is widely used in contemporary Western culture, in media, academic scholarship and popular discourse. My analysis of the history of this term – its invention, eclipse, reappearance and transformation – explores its shifting cultural role over two millennia.

This schematic overview signals both the type of history assayed in this book and the kind of book it is not. I have not attempted a chronological history of charismatic individuals or of those world figures deemed to possess charisma. This approach, while no doubt colourful, would be dependent on subjective judgement, and would follow a universalist definition of charisma that is alien to my method in this work. Likewise, I have not conducted a transcultural survey of charisma and its equivalents or near equivalents in other cultures, such as the Melanesian *mana* or the Sufi *barakah*. Each of these terms is generated from specific belief systems; none is exactly equivalent; none has the particular sense and associations of charisma; none has undergone the trajectory of the term 'charisma': that is, a transformation from religious idea to sociological concept to general usage. Rather than attempting the enormous task of assembling the global equivalents of the charismatic, I have restricted myself to charting a history of the specific word charisma, and its shifting meanings across time.

1

One advantage of this approach is its sensitivity to anachronistic interpretations of the word. Charisma as defined by the sociologist Max Weber in the early twentieth century is markedly different to charisma as defined by the apostle Paul in the middle of the first century. Yet many writers, including historians of religion, have blurred the two senses of the word when analysing – to take one example – charismatic authority and leadership in the early Christian world. This is to impose Weber's reinvention of charisma onto the historical setting in which the word was first employed and defined. The various forms of charisma identified by Paul do not include leadership or authority; indeed such notions of domination by an individual are entirely foreign to the original meaning of charisma.

The Weberian theory of charismatic authority has been so influential and has become so prevalent across contemporary cultures that it is very difficult not to impose it retrospectively and universally. This book resists that temptation, aiming instead to trace the specific meanings of charisma as they have been generated from widely divergent historical contexts. 'Charisma' has meant different things at different times and in different cultures; the careful study of the word's role in these varying environments produces a historicised account, avoiding anachronism. Such an approach also lays the groundwork for one of the ambitions of this book, which is to determine how much (or how little) of the word's previous meanings endure in the twenty-first-century usage of the word charisma.

What is charisma?

The contemporary meaning of charisma is broadly understood as a special innate quality that sets certain individuals apart and draws others to them. I have composed this definition following extensive study of the word's usage not only in recent media, particularly newspapers, magazines and websites, but also in the discourse of various academic disciplines, including sociology, psychology, management theory, media studies and cultural studies. The definition offered here derives largely from Weber, attesting to the power of his formulation of the concept of charismatic leadership. However, the current meaning has shifted away from the restricted range of charismatic authority elaborated in Weber's sociology. Charisma in contemporary culture is thought to reside in a wide range of special individuals, including entertainers and celebrities, whereas Weber was concerned primarily with religious and political leaders.

Contemporary charisma maintains, however, the irreducible character ascribed to it by Weber: it retains a mysterious, elusive quality. Media commentators regularly describe charisma as the 'X-factor'. This aspect of charisma suggests its debt to Weberian theory, which proposed an irrational force – charismatic authority – challenging the 'iron cage' of rationalisation built in twentieth-century modernity. The enigmatic character of charisma also suggests a connection – at least to some degree – to the earliest manifestation of charisma as a spiritual gift. Charisma was invented as a religious concept referring to extraordinary gifts of the spirit; this belief within the very early Christian church was the inspiration for Weber's theory of charisma. A word widely used in today's secular Western societies thus had its origin as an ancient religious idea, reshaped much later by a social theorist concerned with the disenchantment of the modern world. The history of this word – incorporating shifts, breaks, ellipses and mutations of its meaning over a span of 2000 years – illuminates aspects of the word's meaning active even in contemporary culture.

Does charisma exist?

Yet the objection may already be raised: Does charisma even exist? Could the word signify nothing more than a chimera born in the wishful thinking of Max Weber, who dreamed up an alternative to traditional and bureaucratic authority and named it 'charisma'? Or again, perhaps the vagueness and lack of precision associated with the word betray its fanciful nature. Perhaps it is nothing more than an inherited form of mysticism, removed from its original religious framework and loosely applied to any exceptional individual. There have been sceptical figures, within a number of disciplines, prepared to mount such a critique.

The critical sociology of Pierre Bourdieu is antagonistic to Weber's 'naive' notion of charisma as 'a mysterious quality inherent in a person'.[1] Bourdieu, who focuses on relations of power rather than on the intrinsic qualities of individuals, charges Weber with inventing a justification for domination. In this sharp appraisal, charisma represents nothing more than a theoretical construct, justifying certain forms of power relations. In the field of management theory, John Kotter – widely regarded as a leading authority on business organisation and management – is dismissive of the role of charisma in effective leadership. Kotter asserts that there is nothing 'mystical' about leadership: it 'has nothing to do with having "charisma" or other exotic personality traits'.[2] In psychology, psychometric testing of 11 allegedly charismatic leaders by Len Oakes revealed nothing extraordinary about them apart from traits of narcissism,[3] which, given the obsessive need for followers displayed by cult leaders, gurus and other individuals commonly deemed charismatic, may be a more useful descriptor of their personalities.

These are but three critiques of charisma as a concept; there have been many other criticisms and modifications of Weber's theory since translations from the original German became widely available in the middle of the twentieth century. However, stringent critiques or rejection of the very notion of charisma have constituted a tiny minority in the discourses concerning this term. Weber's theory of charismatic authority is generally considered a 'classic' work within sociology; it has been accepted within that discipline and within psychology, political theory and other academic pursuits as a persuasive model of authority, leadership and group dynamics. Scholarship since Weber has been primarily concerned with adjusting or modifying the model, by focusing, for example, on the role of the followers of the charismatic leader. Other studies have analysed the political consequences of charismatic leadership, or the settings in which charismatic leaders may function (ranging from the world of self-help gurus to academia). The many scholarly works on the topic take Weber as the starting point; despite the three dissident voices cited earlier, his theory of charisma is adopted as the framework within which enquiry may operate. John Kotter may declare that charisma is irrelevant to good leadership in business, but there are many other management theorists and leadership gurus writing (and selling) books on the vital importance of that mysterious ingredient known as charisma.

Beyond the academic disciplines of sociology, psychology or management theory, charisma has a secure place in everyday discourse. I take the prevalent position of charisma in popular media – particularly magazines, television, radio and websites – as a reliable indicator of the word's currency in popular usage. Charisma is consistently used to refer to exceptional individuals in a broad range of endeavours. Politicians are frequently assessed on their charisma factor: even if they are thought to lack charisma completely, this lack is considered worthy of comment. In an age where popular culture is seemingly fascinated with celebrity, media discourse reserves a special role for the quality of charisma. As reality TV shows generate growing numbers of minor celebrities, and as prominent individuals augment their celebrity status by scandalous behaviour, the charisma factor is widely considered a gauge by which to judge such individuals. Charisma is believed to be an innate quality, whereas celebrity is increasingly viewed as fabricated. Charisma is thought to be a gift that cannot be simulated; many celebrities have been accused of lacking charisma altogether. The 'gift' of charisma functions in contemporary culture as a guarantor of the genuine in an age of celebrity manufacture. The relationship with celebrity is only one of the functions performed by charisma in contemporary Western culture. Given the frequency and consistency with which the word is used, the critique by Bourdieu is largely impotent. Very few politicians, commentators, critics or members of the public ever question in the media the existence of charisma. It has a currency within the culture; its meaning is commonly understood. The pertinent question is not whether charisma actually exists, but why it exists. Contemporary popular discourse maintains a role for this word; there is a cultural need for it. Charisma cannot be replaced by other words such as 'glamour', 'fame', 'prestige', 'aura' or 'celebrity'. Its 'X-factor' quality distinguishes it from these and other commonly used words. To grasp the functions of charisma in contemporary culture may also be to understand why it persists in that culture.

A first-century Greek word

Few of those experts, commentators and members of the public who deploy 'charisma' so freely may be aware that they are using an ancient Greek word which first appeared in written form in the middle of the first century. Many will be unaware that when the term was initially used in Christian circles in the first century, it conveyed attributes, including miraculous spiritual powers, ranging from prophecy to healing and speaking in tongues. χάρισμα first appears in the epistles of Paul, written in the period of about AD 50–62. Paul used the word charisma to mean 'the gift of God's grace'; it is usually translated as 'spiritual gift'. The intended audiences of Paul's letters were the fledgling Christian communities in urban centres such as Corinth, Rome and Colossus; the letters' inclusion in the New Testament has given them a much wider, and much later, readership.

Generations of Christian revivalists have turned to Paul's letters for inspiration, finding there his description of the charismata – the plural form of charisma. The charismatic movement of the 1960s was founded explicitly on Pauline charisma – but by then the secular meaning attributed to charisma in Weber's sociology had also become current in Western societies. One of the objectives of this book is to consider the relationship between these two versions – religious and secular – of charisma.

Paul's letters were written in Greek; his definition of the word charisma drew on aspects of its root Greek word *charis*, broadly meaning grace or favour. Christian theologians writing in Latin in the second century transliterated χάρισμα into the Roman alphabet, resulting in 'charisma'. The Latin 'charisma' persisted in Catholic theology for a short time, before it was generally replaced by other Latin terms: *donum* (gift) or *gratia* (grace). χάρισμα maintained a presence in liturgy in the Greek Orthodox church tradition. Charisma became 'charism' in English language theological scholarship, before reverting to 'charisma' in the nineteenth century (the Anglicised 'charism' is still used in some theological works). Weber adopted the word from late nineteenth-century German theology, which had become interested in the early church. When Weber's theory of charismatic authority was published in the 1920s, however, charisma was a very rare word outside theological circles. Its emergence into common usage in the second half of the twentieth century is directly attributable to the spread of interest in Weber's theory. Charisma was then transliterated into many non-Latin-based languages, often with a direct phonetic translation. This spread of the word across languages also reveals the singular nature of charisma: several languages simply use the Latin-based word, suggesting that no equivalent for the idea of charisma had existed in those cultures.

This sketch of the passage of 'charisma' from its first-century origin in Greek, through its various linguistic transformations, provides some indication of the remarkable journey undertaken by this rather peculiar word. I have not attempted, at this introductory stage, to sketch the constitutive factors involved in the word's original meaning, nor the social and political factors that contributed to its semantic shifts over time. Paul's charisma owed something to Greek intellectual culture that can be traced back to Homer; it also incorporated facets of Jewish tradition as expressed in the Old Testament. The fate of charisma in Christian theology is part of a complex narrative embracing the institutionalisation of the church and theological debates – including matters of heresy – on the role of the Spirit. I have devoted Chapters 2, 3, 4 and 5 of the book to tracing the path of charisma from its ancient roots through centuries of Christian history. When charisma was secularised and popularised in the twentieth century, that process was merely one more stage in the word's history: a transformation from within secular modernity of an ancient religious term.

Remarks on method

My history of charisma takes its place alongside other 'word histories', including book-length studies of the histories – or sections of histories – of the words 'enthusiasm', 'image', 'curiosity' and 'imagination'.[4] In her study of 'enthusiasm', Susie Tucker charts the word's semantic change from the seventeenth century to the twentieth. Her aim is to examine the word in history, to deduce its historically given definitions and to note attempts to restrict or control the word's reference.[5] The scope of the historical period under review reveals the late appearance of older senses, so that this particular study of semantic shift could almost equally well be termed a 'semantic see-saw'.[6] Other studies in political theory have pointed to the radical changes in meaning associated with certain key words. Terence Ball has highlighted the fundamental semantic shifts undergone by such words as 'ideology', 'patriot', 'rights', 'state' and 'revolution'. 'Ideology', for example, referred in the eighteenth century to the systematic study of the origins of ideas; a 'patriot' was once a citizen who for the sake of his *patria* dared to criticise his government. Ball concludes that 'words do not change, but concepts and meanings do'.[7]

A dynamics of semantic change is integral to my method in this book, as is attention to the social contexts in which the word 'charisma' has circulated. Individual words, in common with the ordered aggregations of words known as texts, are 'worldly', in the manner described by Edward Said: they are 'enmeshed in circumstance, time, place and society'.[8] The word charisma – in its original Greek form – denoted a religious idea in the first-century world of the early Christian communities; that idea was subject to various pressures within the intellectual climate of the church over the next few centuries. As a result, the idea became less prominent in Christian thought, and the word itself lapsed from use for long periods. When the word charisma was revived by Weber in the twentieth century, this revival took place in an entirely different setting. The word – its Latin version incorporated into German – was now enmeshed within secular modernity, in a particular theoretical framework operating within that environment. A new meaning was generated from this context: charisma came to denote a concept within a theory of leadership.

Contextualisation is vital in explaining the transformations undergone by ideas in different historical periods. An idea may change, lapse or be revived, as its social and cultural context changes. These shifts in meaning may occur to meet specific social needs; they may reflect competing cultural interests waging a contest over meaning or status. This has been the case with the meanings associated with charisma. The word has remained the same, in transliterated versions, but it has been subject to contests over its status within the regime of Christian thought, so that it all but disappeared as a word and idea. Invented and reinvented in different circumstances, it has signified different ideas in different contexts. As worlds change, so do meanings.

If meaning resides in context, a history of a word and its meanings must be immersed in those distinctive contexts to avoid 'anachronistic misreadings', as David Spadafora has claimed in his study of 'progress' in the eighteenth century.[9] Spadafora contends that only the social context can yield a comprehension of the dynamics of an idea, 'the human source of its birth and development' and the consequences of its uses.[10] This is necessarily an imperfect enterprise, as Spadafora acknowledges: the socio-cultural character of a previous period will always remain elusive to some extent. But it is also true that historical scholarship is not an individual adventure: each new historical study makes use of previous scholarship focused on the relevant period.[11] Such scholarship is particularly valuable when considering the genesis of charisma as a term first used in the early Christian environment. That environment was conditioned by the prevailing Graeco-Roman culture and the Jewish intellectual tradition. This particular milieu contained several characteristics which bore directly on the invention of charisma as a religious concept: one of those characteristics was the widespread belief in miracles, prophecies and other supernatural phenomena. It is impossible to grasp the meanings initially associated with the word charisma without a careful consideration of the cultural milieu from which the word emerged.

Much recent work in intellectual history follows the contextualist approach; however, studies spanning long historical periods are rare. Even the word-histories cited earlier tend to examine semantic shift over restricted durations, of one or two centuries. The reluctance to expand historical analysis is partly a result of the severe critiques levelled at earlier models of the history of ideas, such as the long-span histories of 'unit-ideas' developed by A. O. Lovejoy in the 1930s.[12] This approach assumed an identity of word and meaning in the 'unit-idea' persisting across long experiences of time. Such assumptions attracted criticism from a number of quarters and on a number of grounds; notable attacks were delivered by Michel Foucault and Quentin Skinner among many others.[13] The history of ideas of this type was reproached for its abstraction of ideas from their social formation, and for its imposition of false continuities across historical epochs. As a result of the methodological difficulties exposed by these critiques, it is no longer tenable to propose the unchanging continuity of great ideas as they traverse vast expanses of time. In the wake of Foucault in particular, intellectual history focuses on the historical determination of knowledge, and the contingencies which uniquely shape knowledge in different historical periods.

More recently, postmodern and post-structuralist critical thought has declared an aversion to grand narratives of any kind, along with all other forms of totalising discourse. Cultural and intellectual history conducted in this domain operates under the sign of historical discontinuity, emphasising epistemological breaks, ruptures and paradigm shifts in the history of thought, as derived from the 1960s works of Foucault and Thomas Kuhn. Most intellectual historians now mine narrow patches of historical territory, with a tight historical focus and specificity. In the zone of critical and cultural theory, a deep suspicion of long historical narratives persists, and the *longue durée* remains largely unGoogled.

My history of charisma, then, operates against the backdrop of these critical theories. Accordingly, I do not propose a grand narrative of the good ship Charisma, sailing unchanged and unharried through the oceans of time. As the brief outline in this opening chapter already indicates, the journey of 'charisma' has been far from smooth. It has sunk at least once, and if it had not been dredged up by Weber, it may have remained forgotten by all except a few historians and scholars. It is true that 'charisma' has endured for almost two millennia, but it is by no means clear that it is the same ship, after those 20 centuries, as first set sail around AD 50.

My study of charisma, in other words, is attentive to change and disjuncture in the history of this word and its meanings. Charisma begins as a term denoting a technical religious concept, but it later takes on other meanings. The vicissitudes of charisma are as pertinent as its endurance. Its history cannot blithely be traced as a noble idea in continuous progress from ancient origin to the present. That history is rather the identification of the mutations, breaks, twists and turns undergone by this word as its meanings shift according to historical and cultural circumstances.

There remain two brief points to be made concerning method. My investigation of charisma in the first century is focused on the writings of Paul; in the twentieth century, the writings of Weber are of crucial interest. In this concentration on the contributions of individual authors, my analysis deviates from the methodology of Foucault, which favours discursive systems over human agency. Foucault's emphasis on the constitutive role of discourse at the expense of authorial agents has justifiably been criticised as resembling 'a laboratory without a scientist in it'.[14] A sensible history of charisma cannot be written without extensive focus on the two chief scientists: Paul of Tarsus and Max Weber. Without the ingenuity demonstrated by Paul in his letters, 'charisma' may never have come into widespread usage; without the invention displayed by Weber, we may not include 'charisma' in our current vocabulary. The creative role of these two individual authors is paramount. At the same time, however, they were two individual agents shaped by their circumstances: their works were generated from within specific, historically determined, formations of knowledge.[15]

The final methodological point relates to the body of scholarship on which I must draw in excavating first-century charisma. The study of the early Christian period, and of Paul's role in that world, has undergone enormous change over many centuries. Exegesis of Paul's letters was available in the second century; debate over the meaning of his works has waged since then. More recently, Paul's texts have been scrutinised by modern scholarship informed by contemporary values, including feminism and postcolonialism. Lengthy biographies have assessed Paul in a 'critical' manner as a historical figure. As a result of two millennia of commentary and interpretation, Paul has been construed as a prophet, a mystic, a shaman, a social conservative, a misogynist, a theologian and a religious genius. This is by no means a definitive list.

Rather than delve into the many debates within biblical scholarship, I make use of those studies of Paul's epistles relevant to my present concern: that of establishing a social and cultural context for Paul's construction of charisma. In this endeavour I have found most useful the social historical approach to early Christian studies, which has developed since the 1970s.[16] Situating Paul firmly in his socio-cultural environment will insulate analysis from the 'many fleeting spectres of Paul which either disappear or reappear with each new generation of scholars'.[17] This modern perspective on Christian antiquity no doubt carries its own set of assumptions and biases – as does any theoretical model – yet it has proved of great benefit in illuminating the setting in which 'charisma' emerged. The detailed analysis of Paul's writings, set against what is known of his milieu, has allowed scholars to grasp – as much as is possible – something of the motivation, intention, meaning and reception of Paul's letters. The original meaning of charisma is situated within this purview.

Continuity or discontinuity?

As I have sketched earlier, the history of charisma incorporates various forms of discontinuity. This relates to the radical difference between historical periods in which the word is used; it also refers to durations in which the word is seldom found or disappears altogether. From one perspective, the change in the word's meaning from the first century to the twenty-first may be so fundamental that its passage could be accorded the paradoxical description of a 'discontinuous history'. Paul's charisma was a strictly religious idea generated within the collectivist spirit of the early church; twenty-first-century charisma is a secular entity and distinctly individualistic in temper. As circumstance has changed radically, so perhaps has charisma.

And yet there is an element of continuity: the word has endured, despite all its vicissitudes, for 2000 years. A continuist view inquires: Is there more in common between first and twenty-first-century charisma than the word they share? Are they really so different? Perhaps the current meaning of charisma retains a mystical, if not religious, hue. The contemporary usage of charisma may indicate the persistence – in however modified a form – of mystical thought, even within technologised and rationalised societies. In such an event, the thread of continuity stretching two millennia may not have been broken. I return to this question, following the investigation of the invention and reinvention of charisma, in the final chapter.

2
The Roots of Charisma

The word 'charisma' did not appear until the first century AD, generated within an environment informed by Jewish and Graeco-Roman cultures. While 'charisma' was a late Greek word, it is possible to trace its roots – as term and concept – back several centuries, on two registers: the range of meanings associated with the root Greek word *charis*, and the precedents in ancient cultures for the idea of spiritual gifts. These meanings and usages, operating in different cultural settings, eventually coalesced in the term 'charisma' as developed by Paul in the middle of the first century. They also resurfaced, much later, in various alignments and emphases in the differing uses of 'charisma' in the twentieth century.

Charis in Greek and Hellenistic culture

Charis was a remarkable word in Greek culture, encompassing a broad range of meanings. The English word most suited to conveying the breadth and diversity of nuances contained in charis is 'grace' – but only if grace is understood to incorporate, at the very least, 'attractiveness', 'favour', 'gratitude' and 'charm', as well as 'gift'. The primary meanings attached to charis before Paul's appropriation of the word were 'grace, beauty, charm, favor, goodwill, free benevolence, gift, benefit, gratitude'.[1] These connotations derived from three branches of significance associated with its primary meaning of 'grace': grace in the sense of personal beauty or charm; in the sense of favour or love; in the sense of benefit or gift, offered out of one's goodness.[2] Charis accumulated its extraordinary richness of meaning through its role in a succession of different discourses: the mythology and epic poetry of ancient Greece; the discourse of classical philosophy; the political theory of reciprocity; and general usage in Hellenistic and Graeco-Roman culture.

Charis features in the mythology detailed by Homer and Hesiod in the eighth century BC. In the *Iliad*, Charis is a 'lovely' goddess with a 'shining veil', outstanding in the realm of deities due to her beauty: she is 'shining among divinities' (18, 382–8).[3] In plural form (number unspecified in Homer, identified as three in Hesiod), the *Charites* or Graces confer all grace, even the favour of Victory in the Games.[4] In the *Odyssey*, the goddess Athene bestows charis on a favoured mortal, Odysseus's son Telemachus:

> Athene endowed him with such supernatural grace [*charis*] that all eyes were turned on him in admiration when he came up.
>
> (2, 11)[5]

This Homeric reference contains two elements that will appear – in a transformed state – in Paul: that charis is bestowed by a divine agency, and that it results in a special quality in certain humans. Charis in Homer also contains the sense that a special individual's outward grace is the result of being well favoured. The primary Classical Greek meaning of grace as physical loveliness covers attractiveness of speech and physical beauty,[6] as well as the notion that such outward grace is the result of bestowal by the gods.

The gracious act of bestowal, as represented in Athene's endowment of grace upon a mortal, is an important component of the network of meanings contained within charis. Grace was understood as a favour, connecting giver and recipient in a binding relationship. For the giver, charis meant graciousness and goodwill to the one receiving the act of kindness. For the recipient, charis meant the favour received and the gratitude resulting from this favour. The acknowledgement of gratitude was an important social act: it could be expressed in a return gift, or in acknowledging that the recipient was beholden to the giver. This ethos of reciprocity features in Homer, particularly in the counter-gift that connects benefactor and recipient in a system of obligation and honour.[7] The social convention of favour and its implications was an early statement of the reciprocity system which became a pervasive social doctrine in the Hellenistic world.

Philosophers from the Classical period to the Graeco-Roman era engaged with the social regulations governing charis. In general, Greek philosophers endorsed the 'civic-minded' honour system of benefaction and gratitude, while at times questioning whether such a system articulated true benevolence. Aristotle considered that charis (act of favour) had a 'prized status as an act deserving of gratitude', but only if the benefactor had the right motives: that is, beyond self-interest.[8] Because charis could be bestowed by both divine and human benefactors, the acknowledgement of the gods' favour was an integral part of Greek religion. Plutarch, writing in the first century AD, stated that since charis provided by deities was a principal agent of transformation, humans should be profoundly thankful for the gods' munificence. It was imperative to show gratitude with 'correct ritual and motivation'.[9] In the Graeco-Roman world, the obligations proceeding from an act of charis encompassed relations with all manner of benefactor, from gift giver to wealthy patron to Emperor to god.

Apart from the sense of charis as a grace or power distributed by the gods, the term's general usage in Greek culture had no religious dimension. Charis was largely associated with the domain of attraction, pleasure and love. Charis could mean a person's charm, in the sense of 'charming': an attractive inner quality that shone out from individuals. Objects such as jewels could exhibit this shining quality; in a related sense, charis could denote a magic charm. It could also mean any gift or favour from one person to another, or the delight or gratitude associated with such a favour.[10] To be favoured with grace, as in the Homeric example of Telemachus, made an individual exceptionally attractive, in the literal sense of attracting others. Once endowed with grace, Telemachus has extraordinary appeal: 'all eyes were turned on him in admiration when he came up'.

Grace in Hebrew culture

The concept of divine grace was conveyed in Jewish culture by the root *hnn* ('favour, grace') used throughout the Old Testament. When the Hebrew Bible was translated into Greek in the third century BC, *hen* became *charis*; the two terms conveyed similar meanings. The *hnn* group signified in particular the giving of grace, whether by God or righteous humans. This involves the 'gifted initiation of relationship',[11] whereby God grants favour to individuals; many psalms and liturgical compositions in the Hebrew Bible are intense appeals to God to bestow such relationships of grace (also rendered as favour or mercy).

Charis in the Greek version of the Hebrew Bible incorporated the complex set of nuances described earlier: it could mean both the endowing of favour or kindness and the finding of favour in the eyes of God or a superior.[12] If God responded to pleas and supplications, the beneficient act was described as charis, referring to 'God's gracious and compassionate disposition'. In the book of Zechariah, God makes a gracious promise:

> And I will pour out on the house of David and the inhabitants of Jerusalem a spirit of compassion and supplication.
>
> (Zech 12: 10)[13]

The Greek words used to express this divine gift – *pneuma charitos* – convey 'spirit of grace and compassion'.[14] This phrase is a precursor to the notion of 'spiritual gift' – charisma – defined and elaborated by Paul in his epistles. Jewish culture in Graeco-Roman territory, first century AD, possessed a notion of charis that embraced both the range of meanings found in Greek culture and the spiritual connotation expressed in the Hebrew Bible. Paul's invention of charisma as a religious concept was rooted in this legacy of fused cultures.

Proto-charisma: The notion of the Holy Spirit

If it is possible to identify a form of proto-charisma, it is found in the idea – expressed in the Old Testament – of the holy spirit infusing certain individuals. By proto-charisma I mean a precursor to charisma as enunciated by Paul, containing some of the qualities of charisma, yet lacking the specific attributes and functions associated with charisma in Paul's definition. Paul found it necessary to use the term 'charisma' to explain his notion of the spiritual gift: more familiar terms such as *pneuma* (spirit), *charis* (grace or favour) or even their combination *pneuma charitos* were inadequate for his specific purposes. Yet several of the factors informing charisma as propounded by Paul are evident in the Old Testament: the notion of a holy spirit suffusing all creation; the enhanced spiritual grace and power that could ensue from this spirit; and the manifestation of spirit in certain individuals, imbuing them with extraordinary abilities. In the Old Testament the power of the spirit is visited on special individuals, who become as a result great religious leaders. Manifestations of spirit are also evident in the ancient prophets, whose ability flows from direct divine revelation.

In the book of Isaiah, it is prophesied in Isaiah's vision that 'a shoot from the stump of Jesse' will be especially favoured with spiritual attributes:

> And the Spirit of the Lord shall rest upon him, the spirit of wisdom and understanding, the spirit of counsel and might, the spirit of knowledge and the fear of the Lord.
>
> (Isaiah 11: 2)

According to the prophecy, the spiritually blessed 'root of Jesse' will become a righteous and merciful leader, standing as 'an ensign to the peoples' of Judah (11: 10). These six endowments of the Spirit – wisdom, understanding, counsel, might, knowledge and fear of God – may be regarded as an antecedent to the forms of charisma outlined by Paul in his letters. However, none of these six spiritual forms corresponds to the diverse spiritual gifts described by Paul as variants of charisma. In addition, whereas Isaiah depicts one individual as recipient of multiple gifts from the Spirit, in Paul the different types of charisma are distributed throughout the congregation, so that each individual is differently gifted.

Another Old Testament instance of divine inspiration visiting gifts on an individual is found in Exodus. Moses is assured by God that a tradesman named Bez'alel has been filled 'with the Spirit of God, with ability and intelligence, with knowledge and all craftsmanship' to construct the necessary buildings and furnishings for worship. In addition, other craftsmen have been given 'ability' by the Spirit to work with Bez'alel (Exodus 31: 1–6). This endowment of craftsmen with abilities by the Spirit supplements the Old Testament tradition of divinely inspired leaders and prophets, and is a precursor to the bestowal of spiritual gifts to ordinary members of the Christian community, as detailed by Paul in his epistles.

Despite the differences between the Old and New Testaments concerning the endowment of spiritual gifts, Christian theologians – including Paul – regarded spiritual power as the link between the ancient Jewish prophecies and the contemporary Christian church. The later Hebrew prophets, with their visions of the future outpouring of spirit in a messianic age, were said to be vindicated in the person of Jesus, and in the spiritually empowered apostles. The one force linking the Hebrew scriptures, the Old Testament prophets, Jesus, the apostles and the institution of the church was thought to be Spirit. This notion was expressed in the earliest Christian literature, becoming a central feature of Christian theology. In the early third century, Hippolytus, Bishop of Rome, wrote of this unifying power of the Spirit in his *Discourse on the Holy Theophany*, supporting his claim with quotations from Old and New Testaments:

This is the Spirit that at the beginning 'moved upon the face of the waters'; by whom the world moves; by whom creation consists, and all things have life; who also wrought mightily in the prophets, and descended in flight upon Christ. This was the Spirit that was given to the apostles in the form of fiery tongues ... By this Spirit the rock of the church was stabilised.

(Ch 9 86–7)[15]

Thus Spirit was believed to extend across time, granting spiritual gifts and enabling institutions. From this idea of blessings of the spirit, noted in the Old Testament, flowed the notion of charisma in the teaching of the apostle Paul.

The Old Testament prophets

Prophets come in many forms in the Old Testament, reflecting both the long historical passage conveyed in the scriptures and the multifarious nature of prophecy itself. Some prophets spoke in an ecstatic or frenzied state; some were credited with miraculous powers, including the ability to raise the dead; others served as military advisers to kings.[16] The one attribute linking such disparate activity was the belief that prophets were the recipients of divine messages, whether conveyed in dream, ecstasy, or direct aural and visual communication. Some were thought to answer a 'call' from God, who imbued them with a visionary quality to be placed at the service of their community. The Hebrew term *nabi*, meaning 'one who is called', was the most common term for prophet in the Hebrew scriptures;[17] *nabi* was later translated as the Greek *prophetes*, meaning one who speaks for a god.

The earliest-known Israelite prophets were itinerants operating in the eleventh century BC. These prophets wore their own distinctive costume, moved around freely, subsisted on offerings from the peoples they served, and combined the characteristics of 'the holy man, the sage, the miracle-worker, and the soothsayer'.[18] Contrasting with these wandering prophets were those stipended in official and permanent advisory positions, as court prophets. Their role included the delivery of oracles, advice to the king concerning the waging of war and the prediction of outcomes.[19] Later prophets of the seventh and eighth centuries addressed themselves not only to kings but also to all peoples, and began to prophesy the destruction of the nation as punishment for sin.[20] Prophets active after the exile of the Israelites (from the sixth century BC) foretold national restoration, the coming Kingdom of God or the advent of a messianic figure. These eschatological prophets were expected to have supernatural power such as miracle working as an expression of their authority; they preached repentance in preparation for the imminent day of Yahweh, the God of Israel.[21]

An insight into beliefs concerning prophecy in the Graeco-Roman period is found in the writings of Philo (c. 20 BC to AD 50), a Jewish philosopher and contemporary of Paul. Philo's synthesis of Platonic philosophy with Judaism included a role for prophecy, understood as divine possession affording extraordinary visions. Commenting on the ecstasy of Abraham recorded in Genesis 15: 12, Philo defines a prophet as

> the vocal instrument of God, smitten and played by his invisible hand ... The mind is evicted at the arrival of the divine Spirit, but when that departs the mind returns to its tenancy ... The prophet, even when he seems to be speaking, really holds his peace, and his organs of speech, mouth and tongue, are wholly in the employ of Another, to show forth what he wills. Unseen by us that Other beats on the chords with the skill of a master-hand.
>
> *(Quis Rerum Divinarum Heres* 259–66)[22]

Philo claimed to have had prophetic experiences of his own, including possession and frenzy leading to 'ideas' and the 'keenest vision'.[23]

One belief connecting prophets from the ancient Israelites of the eleventh century BC to the philosophy of Philo in the first century AD was the idea that direct inspiration ensued from a revelatory trance.[24] The prophet Hosea called himself 'man of spirit' (Hos 9: 7), expressing the common belief that the Spirit of God caused the prophet's revelatory trance.[25] The Holy Spirit could impose itself on individuals whether they were seeking inspiration or not: in 1 Samuel, messengers sent by Saul to capture David are diverted by the Spirit, which causes them instead to prophesy (1 Sam 19: 20–1). Prophets were considered holy men who had learnt how to control the various forms of spiritual trance repeatedly visited on them. In this regard, they represented a link to the belief in spiritual powers found in many cultures, generally embodied in the figure of the shaman.

The shamanic tradition

Shamanism is an ancient and widespread religious system, in which the shaman is considered a specialist or exceptional individual, capable of entering a trance to communicate with the spirits on behalf of the community.[26] It has been argued that shamanism was humankind's first form of religion, and that it served as the basis for all later religious systems.[27] The shaman was a universal feature of nomadic hunter-gatherer societies, functioning as the 'magico-religious practitioner' in such social groupings.[28] In later forms of society, shamans were thought to possess a number of skills and powers, varying across cultures. Shamans were considered to have a mastery of the spirit world, which made them capable of magical feats, including healing, sorcery, spirit travelling and prophecy. The shaman was in many instances also a storyteller, keeper of the community's knowledge and identity through oral tradition. All these capacities were thought to be inspired: that is, endowed by the spirits.

Recent studies in the structures of consciousness have contended that shamanism ensues from universal neurological structures in the human brain. One of the results of the fundamental operations of the brain is that all human cultures have 'animated the world with human qualities', understood as spirits.[29] According to this theoretical approach, shamanism's engagement with the spirit world – including the sense of a spirit detached from the body – reflects invariant aspects of human consciousness.[30] However, it is not necessary to embrace this speculative theoretical model to examine the influence of shamanism on Old Testament prophecy, and, by extension, on the emergence of charisma as a religious concept. Whether or not shamanism has proliferated as a universal condition, it is possible to trace a line of direct contact in the ancient world, linking various inflections of the shaman role.

David Aune notes that the first Israelite prophets, in the eleventh century BC, had much in common with prophets in other near eastern cultures. He describes these earliest Hebrew prophets as 'shamanistic', due to characteristics they shared with shamans in other societies, including the combination of functions in the one holy man figure (prophet-priest-healer-miracle-worker).[31] James Dunn points to the 'ecstatic frenzy' of these early prophets,[32] as recounted in 1 Samuel. The 'company of prophets' presided over by Samuel 'lay naked all that day and all that night' prophesying, when imbued by the Spirit (1 Sam 19: 20–4).

A shamanic impulse has also been discerned in ancient Greek culture. Herodotus described the function of shamans – part soothsayers, part healers, part sorcerers – of the nomadic Scythian peoples in Book IV of his *Histories*. In his study of the irrational in ancient Greece, E. R. Dodds traced a 'tentative line of descent' of the shaman impulse which

> starts in Scythia, crosses the Hellespont into Asiatic Greece, is perhaps combined with some remnants of Minoan tradition in Crete, emigrates to the Far West with Pythagoras, and has its last outstanding representative in the Sicilian Empedeocles.[33]

According to this account, Pythagoras, a semi-legendary figure – mathematician, philosopher, mystic – from the sixth century BC, displays aspects of the shaman function in his purported mastery of the spirit world. Pythagoras was credited by his followers with the powers usually attributed to shamans: prophecy, magical healing, travel to the spirit world and bilocation (the ability to appear in two places at once).[34] The religious order founded by Pythagoras believed in the transmigration of souls, a belief perpetuated by philosopher Empedeocles in the fifth century. Dodds identified in Empedeocles the synthesis of many strains of thought and belief, including shamanism; Pythagoras and Empedeocles exhibited the 'still undifferentiated functions of magician and naturalist, poet and philosopher, preacher, healer, and public counsellor'.[35] After Empedeocles, these attributes splintered across disparate pursuits and disciplines.

The shaman is an important figure in the prehistory of charisma, which was understood in the first century as 'spiritual gift'. The shaman, master of the spirit world, was thought to receive exceptional abilities and powers from those spirits. More than one commentator has remarked that the shaman 'receives a supernatural gift from the spirit world'.[36] Accepted by his or her people as a spiritually enhanced individual, the shaman is precursor to later figures such as prophets, healers, soothsayers and even apostles, thought to be possessed or gifted by the spirits.

Religious figures later termed 'charismatic'

Recent historians of religion have placed emphasis on shamanism as an early manifestation of charismatic religious authority. When Weber reinvented the idea of charisma as part of his sociological theory of authority in the early twentieth century, he mentioned shamans as instances of charismatic religious figures. Many theologians and religious historians writing in the second half of the twentieth century simply followed Weber's lead. I. M. Lewis, for example, has described the shaman as the 'very epitome of charismatic authority'.[37] Elucidations of the shaman's social function have focused on the relationship between shaman and society in a way reminiscent of Weber's theorisation of the charismatic leader and followers. John Ashton, in Weberian mode, remarks that 'the shaman's authority depends upon an ability to persuade other people of his or her exceptional gifts'.[38]

It is often a difficult task to disentangle the Weberian model of charisma from the first definition of the term, which emerged in the first century AD. A prudent approach is to resist the Weberian call that would conscript the shaman as the first charismatic; the analysis of shamans, prophets and religious leaders as 'charismatic' is strictly anachronistic, in that it describes ancient figures in Weber's terms, before the word 'charisma' was even available. The shaman, like the prophet and leader, was for Weber a figure of religious authority; yet 'charisma', in its first usage, does not refer to leaders, religious or otherwise, as bearers of authority. For the purposes of a history of the word charisma, we must guard against the retroactive use of the term. Suitably alerted, however, we can explore the roots of charisma – as 'spiritual gift' – with reference to historical figures who, much later, were described as charismatic.

In his book *The Charismatic Leader and His Followers*, originally published in German in 1968, Martin Hengel applied Weber's definition of charismatic leadership to Jesus and earlier religious leaders. Hengel placed Jesus in the historical context of previous Jewish and Hellenistic charismatic leaders, including the eschatological Jewish prophets such as Elijah. His Hellenistic examples were teachers who were at the same time charismatics, like Pythagoras and Empedeocles. Hengel notes that first-century Palestine was 'particularly fruitful soil for prophetic-charismatic movements of an eschatological stamp',[39] identifying among other figures Judas of Galilee, founder of the Jewish Zealot movement. For Hengel, the Jewish line of tradition – stretching back to the ancient prophets and including John the Baptist and Jesus – has the conviction that God bestows charisma on the prophets, and that the people are called to conversion through the mouths of those prophets. This process is distinct from the idea in Greek philosophy of a divine quality inherent in individuals: the mechanisms of bestowing and calling convey the belief that divine qualities are imparted to individuals, who must make themselves willing to receive the divine.[40] Paul is the heir of this tradition: this belief is an integral component in Paul's construction of charisma as a gift of divine grace, bestowed on individuals who have opened themselves to receive a spiritual gift.

Other religious historians have looked elsewhere for lineages of the charismatic. From another perspective, a line of Galilean Hasid charismatics, including Honi the Circle-Drawer and Hanina ben Dosa – known as miracle-workers from rabbinic literature – is seen to culminate in Jesus of Galilee.[41] However, such comparative studies are inherently hazardous, in that they attempt to match the Weberian model with historical figures to whom certain 'charismatic' attributes have been ascribed, but whose social roles were quite dissimilar to that of the charismatic leader as described by Weber. The shortcomings of this comparative approach are revealed when rival interpretations contest their Weberian credentials. A mere nature miracle-worker, for instance, may be dismissed as lacking true charisma, whereas an ancient prophet may be upheld as 'not just any old charismatic', but the revolutionary leader of a new religious movement, thereby fulfilling Weber's prescription.[42]

The entanglements and confusions encountered in this comparative approach derive from its ahistorical nature. Holy men and miracle-workers in various cultures at different times performed divergent social roles: some may have been leaders, and others were regarded as sages, counsellors, storytellers, healers. The indiscriminate labelling of these individuals as charismatic in Weber's sense wrenches them from their cultures and their historical periods. For our purposes, it is enough to note that these figures and their social roles were not called 'charismatic' in their own time. Nevertheless many of them were considered by their peers to possess certain – and varied – spiritual attributes. And the spiritual abilities thought to reside in shamans, prophets and religious leaders eventually found expression, in a transformed state, and in a particular time and place, as the various forms of charisma. That particular time and place was occupied by the Christian apostle Paul. It is to Paul's invention of charisma as a religious term that we now turn.

3
Paul Invents Charisma

The meaning of charisma as a special quality or gift within certain individuals derives from the New Testament writings of Paul. In his epistles, written in Greek in the period c. AD 50–62, Paul endowed the word with a religious significance: he used 'charisma' to mean 'the gift of God's grace'. The term is strongly linked to the older Greek word *charis*, which occupies a crucial role in Pauline theology as the grace of God offering salvation. Paul utilised the word 'charisma' to signify the various 'gifts' – including spiritual and supernatural abilities – ensuing from this divine grace.[1]

In considering the role of charisma within Paul's theology, we are fortunate in being able to situate its genesis in its social, cultural and intellectual context. Enough is known of the milieu within which Paul moved – the Graeco-Roman communities of Greece and Asia Minor in the middle of the first century – to provide an explanatory framework for Paul's writings. Many factors contribute to the social and cultural setting bearing on Paul's invention of charisma as a religious concept. These include the blend of Greek philosophy and Judaism informing Paul's intellectual milieu; the political system of the Roman Empire; and the character of the early Christian church, to which Paul's letters were addressed. Another significant element is the prevalent belief in miraculous feats performed by spiritually empowered individuals, whether prophets or magicians; this belief provided part of the background for Paul's definition of charisma. The individual circumstances of Paul himself – the zealous protector of Jewish Law turned advocate of the redeeming power of Spirit – are also relevant. A consideration of these factors will assist our inquiry into the original meaning of charisma. Specifically, why did Paul feel the need to adopt this obscure term, imbuing it with religious significance and granting it importance within the fledgling Christian communities?

The early Christian church

The earliest Christians were Jews whose mother church was at Jerusalem. They differed from other Jews in their conviction that Jesus of Nazareth was the Christ (a Greek translation of the Hebrew 'Messiah') as foretold by the Jewish prophets. They were called 'Nazarenes' because of this belief; the term 'Christian' was later applied to them by pagans in Syria once the faith had reached that far. The Christians held to a continuity with Judaism, regarding Jesus as the fulfilment of God's promise. Early converts came from Jewish sects such as the Pharisees, as well as from gentiles – but it was the relationship with Judaism that most occupied the early Christians.

From Judaism the Christians took the act of baptism as an initiating rite, as well as the symbolism attached to bread and wine in the Passover ceremony. An ethic of chastity, respect for family and acts of charity were also adopted from Judaism. The Christians accepted the Jewish scriptures as a holy book, used in the version known as the Septuagint (made by 70 translators from Hebrew to Greek in the third century BC). Unlike the Jews, however, the Christians interpreted the prophecies within the Septuagint as divine predictions that had been vindicated in the person of Jesus. The early Christians had no texts of their own until the epistles of Paul and other apostles. Christian gatherings were sustained by an oral tradition, recounting the time of Jesus and his disciples (the four gospels of the New Testament were not written until the period c. AD 65–100).

The Greek word used in the New Testament, translated as 'church' or 'congregation', was *ecclesia*. This word literally meant 'assembly' or 'meeting', which more accurately conveys the gatherings of Christians at the time of Paul. The Christian communities had no public buildings in which to congregate: enduring public churches were not built until after Emperor Constantine's conversion in 312. The early Christians met in rooms in private homes or in private residencies converted into 'church houses'. Sunday was adopted as their day of worship; the ritual of eucharist (literally 'thanksgiving') involved the sacred meal of bread and wine for those baptised into the faith. A strong communal spirit was evident in the early Christian congregations; class distinctions were overridden by the communal focus of the ritual and by the notion that all had entered the faith through the same conversion process.

The contentious issue which helped define the Christians as more than another Jewish sect concerned the conversion of gentiles. Some of the Jewish Christians argued that all converts should abide by Jewish custom, including boundary-markers such as circumcision and food laws – the prohibition against 'unclean' foods. This view was overruled at a Council in Jerusalem around AD 50, recounted in the Acts of the Apostles (written by the author of the Gospel of Luke around AD 80). The prevailing policy at this conference was an inclusive perspective, which allowed for gentiles to be converted in the ritual of baptism but without the necessity of the Jewish prohibitions and customs (Acts 15: 1–21).[2] The underlying significance of this decision was that the Law of Moses as upheld by Judaism was usurped in Christian faith by the idea of divine mercy, or Grace. This meant, as Henry Chadwick remarks, that the Christians were freed from the Law of Moses.[3] It also meant that Paul was free to embark on his mission of converting gentiles within the Roman world, a mission that included Rome itself. Jerusalem remained in Paul's time the mother-church, but Paul took the new faith – a universal church open to Jews and gentiles alike – westward.

Paul was the leading figure in the church's 'Apostolic age', which lasted until around AD 70. Other apostles included the original disciples – notably Peter, the 'rock' on which the church was to be built; and James, the 'Lord's brother', president of the Jerusalem church until martyred in 62. Acts provides an account of the apostles and the early church; it links, in theological terms, the apostles both with the life of Jesus and with the Old Testament prophets. In this respect, the attribution to the apostles of spirit-endowed powers – including healing, ecstatic utterance and prophecy – inscribes the apostles within the tradition of divinely inspired holy men. It also provides a setting for Paul's definition of the term 'charisma': as an apostle, he himself is considered in Acts to possess these powers, which he will later include within the spiritual gifts – 'charismata' – available to all within the Christian faith.

From the beginning, Acts associates the apostles with spiritual power and miraculous abilities. At the first Pentecost following Jesus' crucifixion, the 12 apostles (with newcomer Matthias replacing Judas) are visited by a mighty wind of divine origin:

> And there appeared to them tongues as of fire, distributed and resting on each of them. And they were all filled with the Holy Spirit and began to speak in tongues, as the Spirit gave them utterance.
>
> (Acts 2: 4)

Acts records that 'many wonders and signs were done through the apostles' (2: 43), and that this miracle-working was regarded by Peter as fulfilment of the prophet Jo'el's prediction of visions and prophecies 'in the last days' (2: 16–20). Peter declared that any Jew baptised in the name of Jesus 'shall receive the gift of the Holy Spirit' (2: 38), yet the miraculous powers of the Spirit seem to be reserved for the apostles or those directly imbued by them. Peter is described healing the lame and sick (3: 6 and 4: 16) and having a vision (11: 5); his miracle-working extends to the ability to revive the dead (9: 40–1). Stephen, one of seven followers especially empowered by the apostles through prayer and laying on of hands, becomes 'full of grace and power', allowing him to perform 'great wonders and signs among the people' (6: 1–8).

Spiritual power in Acts encompasses both the miraculous and the less wondrous inspiration to preach. On trial after his arrest, Peter delivers a speech while 'filled with the Holy Spirit' that so impresses with its boldness that he is freed (5: 8–13); elsewhere, galvanising delivery of sermons is considered a sign of the Spirit. The one instance in Acts of the Spirit visiting extraordinary powers on ordinary individuals occurs when Peter preaches to an audience of both Jews and gentiles. The Holy Spirit 'fell on all who heard the word', amazing the Christian Jews because

> the gift of the Holy Spirit had been poured out even on the Gentiles. For they heard them speaking in tongues and extolling God.
>
> (10: 44–5)

The glossolalia performed by the gentiles is held as evidence by Peter that they have received the Spirit and therefore should be baptised; Acts records that Peter uses this instance to persuade the church in Jerusalem of the right to evangelise gentiles as well as Jews.

Acts describes a Christian personnel of apostles, prophets and teachers spreading the faith following the council in Jerusalem. Prophets are credited with the ability not only to foretell the Kingdom of God but also to predict earthly circumstances. Disciples send food relief to Christians in Judaea in response to a prediction of famine by a prophet called Agabus (11: 27–30). But it is the apostles who are the main custodians of Spirit – with all its attributes – in Acts. Following his conversion, Paul is depicted as exhibiting miraculous powers during his missions. While in Ephesus, he performs 'extraordinary miracles' of healing and exorcism:

> Handkerchiefs or aprons were carried away from his body to the sick, and diseases left them and the evil spirits came out of them.
>
> (19: 11–12)

Like Peter, Paul possesses the supreme gift of revivifying the dead (20: 9–12). Paul also has the power to impart Spirit to those he has baptised:

> And when Paul laid his hands upon them, the Holy Spirit came on them; and they spoke with tongues and prophesied.
>
> (19: 6)

Paul, a convert rather than original disciple, had no direct contact with Jesus. Nevertheless in Acts his miraculous powers are the equal to Peter and the other original apostles. Paul became the most influential apostle due to the range and energy of his mission, and due to the lasting impact of his epistles, 13 of which were later adopted as a major component of the New Testament canon.

Paul in context

It has been remarked that Paul's socio-cultural context was in fact three contexts – or three 'worlds' – in constant interaction.[4] The first was his Jewish heritage: Paul was educated in Jerusalem and later asserted his membership of his 'native' culture: the Jews of Palestine. The second was the prevailing Graeco-Roman culture: Paul was born in the Hellenistic city Tarsus in Asia Minor; his writings exhibit the influence of Greek philosophical thought, particularly Stoicism. The third was Roman rule, which was experienced by Paul not as a form of oppression but as an opportunity: Paul was a dual citizen of Tarsus and Rome who moved freely throughout the Roman Empire.[5]

The Romans considered their assimilation of all religions within their Empire as a sign of strength; the Roman government tolerated Judaism despite the Jews' rejection of pagan gods and practices. The Jewish community in Palestine was split between a conservative faction intent on collaboration with the Roman rulers and the nationalist Zealots, who advocated revolt against Rome. The early Christians did not support the Zealots' cause; they hoped instead to convert the gentiles within the Roman Empire. A significant factor within the early Christian communities was a radical pacifism derived from Jesus' teachings. In his mission to the gentiles, Paul advocated not subversion of the state but the maintenance of stability and order, which would allow the Empire to serve as a vehicle for the spread of the Christian religion. Nevertheless Christians suffered periodic persecution by Roman authorities. Popular suspicion that the Christian cult practised black magic, even incest and cannibalism, was prompted by the Christians' private nocturnal meetings,[6] while Emperors could always capitalise on this suspicion if in need of a public scapegoat. This was the case following the great fire in Rome of 64: Emperor Nero blamed the Christians and had Paul and Peter executed around 65–67.

The towns and cities of the Roman Empire were culturally pluralistic: Tarsus was a cosmopolitan city infused with a diversity of religious and philosophical thought. Prominent Stoic philosophers were influential in the city, while numerous mystery religions flourished (the latter included the cults of Isis and Mithras and featured rituals – often re-enactments of a deity's drama and suffering – thought to effect spiritual change in initiates). Throughout the Graeco-Roman world, all manners of belief – including magical practices, divination, astrology, mysticisms, philosophies and religious cults – jostled for attention.

An age of miracles

One striking aspect of this social milieu is that members of the early Christian communities firmly believed in the reality of visions, possession, miracles and ecstatic powers, including speaking in tongues. In the twenty-first century, we may interpret the psychological states associated with visions, religious conversions and glossolalia in neuropsychiatric terms – as symptoms of epilepsy, schizophrenia or auto-suggestion.[7] In the first century, however, these ecstatic states were ascribed to religion or magic, with a hazy boundary between these two realms.

There was a widespread belief throughout the Graeco-Roman world in magical feats and miracle-working, conducted in the name of divergent sources of spiritual power. Magicians were thought to have similar talents in this regard to holy men. Miraculous control of the weather was attributed to exceptional individuals, including rabbis; ancient historians, including Livy, documented reports of miracles and supernatural exploits, including flying and walking on water; Roman emperors, including Augustus, were considered immortal and the possessors of supernatural powers. There were also many varieties of spiritual possession and ecstatic utterance, found in prophets and oracles. In the Greek religion, oracles were believed to deliver the word of the gods while in a trance, resulting in the often enigmatic nature of these divine messages; Socrates referred to the 'divine madness' of prophecy and ecstatic speech.[8] Oracle cults and mystery cults had a strong presence, their practices stretching back to archaic Greece.[9]

Acts 14: 8–13 describes the reaction of a crowd in Lystra to a miracle performed by Paul: the supernatural feat was interpreted in terms familiar to the local Greek religion. Paul and his companion Barnabas are assumed to be Hermes and Zeus in human form; the priest of Zeus brings oxen before them to sacrifice. On the island of Paphos, Paul must match his supernatural powers with those of a magician who opposes the Christian faith. Acts 13: 6–11 records Paul's victory in this supernatural battle, as he strikes the magician blind, thus demonstrating to the local proconsul the superiority of his faith.

The common belief in supernatural powers in Paul's time is important in the genesis of charisma, which incorporated mystical powers for the benefit of the Christian community. In the Graeco-Roman culture, spirits were thought to operate as causal agents in a ubiquitous manner: gods, demons and spirits were widely considered to be unseen instigators of events.[10] Paula Friedriksen remarks that healing and miracle-working were so common in the early first century that the perceived ability to perform miracles 'would confer no unique distinction' on an individual, including Jesus: these abilities would need to be supplemented with a strong moral message within preaching.[11]

The significance of this cultural belief has been downplayed by recent scholarship, which often has been concerned with defining Paul as a historical figure, supported by as much empirical accuracy as possible. This has imposed a perspective determined by contemporary beliefs and biases: sceptical, rationalist, dependent on verifiable documentary evidence. The 'critical' biography of Paul by Jerome Murphy-O'Connor, for example, follows the methodological principle that Paul's letters must always take precedence over Acts, which is largely dismissed as the work of a 'tendentious theologian'.[12] The result evident in the accounts of Murphy-O'Connor and similar recent books is that the depiction in Acts of Paul's miracle-working is entirely absent, while Paul's own references to his miraculous powers, as in 1 and 2 Corinthians, are also neglected or quickly passed over. Instances of exorcism and other supernatural abilities described in the New Testament are ignored in such scholarly accounts, or dismissed as fanciful or embarrassing to a contemporary Christian.[13]

There has been criticism, however, of the narrowness induced by this perspective. John Ashton declares that it is impossible to attain 'any real understanding of the religious Paul whilst wearing blinkers that shut out the sight of the spiritual and demonic world in which he lived'.[14] If our aim is to situate the genesis of charisma – as invented and defined by Paul – within its social and cultural context, we cannot ignore the belief in the supernatural prevalent at the time. Paul was familiar with the schools of Greek philosophical thought, but he also openly referred to his miraculous powers. His auditors in the various Christian congregations knew the outline of the Christian faith, but they had also absorbed belief in demons, magic and supernatural feats, drawn from a myriad of magical and religious systems. Mystical belief – including an acceptance of miracles, exorcisms and other supernatural exploits – is an integral part of Paul's cultural environment.

From Pharisee to apostle, from law to grace

Paul's education included training in rhetoric, while he was also exposed in the synagogue to the Jewish Hellenistic philosophy of Philo.[15] His initial response to his hybrid cultural environment was conditioned by his education in Judaism: he became a prominent member of the Pharisees, an order dedicated to the upholding of Jewish Law. The Pharisees sought to resist Hellenistic influences on Judaism through a strict observance of the Law of Moses, as inscribed in the Bible and as interpreted by specialist scribes. Paul's zealous devotion to doctrinal Law motivated his hostility to Christianity; his journey to Damascus was in pursuit of Jewish Christians. Acts gives a vivid portrait of the passionate persecution of Christians practised by Saul, as he was known before his conversion:

> But Saul, still breathing threats and murder against the disciples of the Lord, went to the high priest and asked him for letters to the synagogues at Damascus, so that if he found any belonging to the Way, men or women, he might bring them bound to Jerusalem.
>
> (9: 1–2)

So effective was Saul in causing 'havoc' to the early Christians, that he was greeted with fear and suspicion by them even after he converted to their faith (9: 21, 26). His famous conversion on the road to Damascus, inspired by a vision of Jesus appearing to him, set the tone for his Christian theology, which emphasised faith and divine grace. The act of conversion itself, as recounted in Acts, has an extreme physical aspect:

> [S]uddenly a light from heaven flashed about him. And he fell to the ground and heard a voice saying to him, 'Saul, Saul, why do you

persecute me?' ... Saul arose from the ground; and when his eyes were opened, he could see nothing ... And for three days he was without sight, and neither ate nor drank.

(Acts 9: 3–9)

This intense experience has been deciphered by modern commentators, in accordance with a rationalist sensibility, as, variously, a lightning strike, hallucination or epileptic seizure. Chris McGillion notes that Paul's conversion experience included a number of factors – sudden bright light, temporary blindness and the inability to eat or drink for three days – now understood as symptoms of epileptic fits.[16] The event was experienced by Paul as a violent spiritual transformation, prompting a radical change of course. Recent commentators focusing on the spiritual intensity of this event have likened it to the call received by the ancient Hebrew prophets, and even to the traumatic experience initially undergone by shamans, after which they assume their spiritual powers.[17]

Paul switched from a persecutor of Christians to a Christian mission-ary, from a zealot of religious law to an advocate of spiritual grace. He recognised that his conversion occurred *despite* his knowledge of the Law, not because of it; he therefore argued in his Christian teaching that faith, not adherence to received doctrine, was the basis of salvation. Paul later wrote in Galatians 2: 16 that salvation was to be obtained not 'by works of the law but through faith in Jesus Christ, because by works of the law shall no one be justified'. His own spiritual transformation, experienced as an intensely visceral and emotional event, was the basis of his conviction that individuals must open themselves to God's Spirit, which bestowed spiritual renewal and salvation in an act of freely given love. The unsolicited nature of Paul's conversion event was also a deter-minative influence on his conception of God's grace as a unilateral force of mercy and compassion.

Paul's missionary work took him, courtesy of the Roman road system, to the important cities of Greece and Asia Minor. His strategy was to found churches in major centres which he would later revisit. His epis-tles were written to advise these new Christian communities on matters both spiritual and practical, sometimes in response to questions sent to him by those communities. These letters were an efficient way for Paul to communicate instruction to a range of communities; writing was also the medium that most suited his communication abilities. Paul acknowl-edged that he was a poor public speaker and had an unimpressive physi-cal presence (2 Cor 11: 6), but his rhetorical skills found an outlet in his

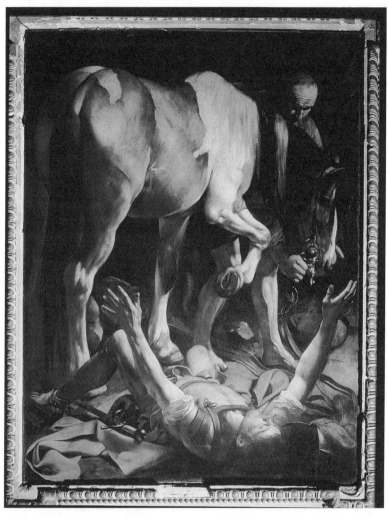

Figure 3.1 Caravaggio, *The Conversion of St Paul*, 1601. Caravaggio conveys the intensity of Paul's conversion, experienced as a visceral and emotional event. This experience set the tone for Paul's belief in the transforming power of *charis* or divine grace.

letters, which were read aloud to congregations. Even his opponents, who were eager to highlight his shortcomings – 'his bodily presence is weak, and his speech of no account' – acknowledged the skill and persuasive power of his writing: his letters 'are weighty and strong'

(2 Cor 10: 10). The Christian communities of Paul's time consisted of both affluent, well-educated citizens – who provided financial support to the church – and slaves, who comprised a significant portion of worshippers. To this mix of social classes, with its diversity of educational standards, religious and cultural backgrounds, Paul addressed his epistles.

Paul's transformation of charis

We are now in a position to consider Paul's transformation of the term 'charis', along with his use of the related term 'charisma'. Paul's letters were written in the Koine (or common) Greek, which at the time prevailed over a large territory encompassing both East and West. Paul's auditors would have readily understood his epistles, which were composed in a language closer to the everyday Koine than to the elevated literary form favoured by many Hellenistic philosophers and historians.[18] However, the diversity of religious and cultural backgrounds encountered by Paul in his missionary work could create difficulties in comprehension and interpretation. Paul's education and conditioning were Jewish, whereas the gentile Christians hearing his letters had pagan backgrounds.[19] This necessitated a degree of invention on Paul's part, by which older terms – whether Jewish or secular – were appropriated and endowed with new Christian meanings.

'Charis' was such a term. Ceslas Spicq comments that this secular Greek word was 'suited for taking on a theological meaning' and that 'its nuances made sense to new converts' to Christianity.[20] In Paul's time charis possessed a remarkable 'semantic versatility',[21] encompassing favour, grace, thanks, gratitude and the acts of bestowing or receiving gifts. Paul adopted and adapted the term for his own purposes. While he used the Greek word, Paul's notion of grace was influenced by the Hebrew concept denoted by the root *hnn* (the giving of favour or grace) used throughout the Old Testament, translated as 'charis' in the Septuagint. Yet Paul transformed charis (and by implication its Hebrew equivalent) by emphasising the free gift of God's grace. He moved God's 'initiative of relationship' to such a prominence that seeking God's favour – as in the Hebrew Bible – faded;[22] he expanded its significance to that of salvation in response to divine grace.

The centrality of grace to Paul's theology has been recognised by many scholars: Pauline theology has been described as 'charitocentric', with grace the 'fundamental concept' through which the 'event of salvation' is expressed.[23] For Paul, divine grace – including its gift of salvation – has the character of an act.[24] Friedrich observes that Pauline grace has a sense 'midway between force and magic'.[25] Grace is the act of God in the present, a transforming power that is experienced by the believer: James Dunn remarks that grace is experienced by the recipient emotionally as much as it is believed in.[26]

In his letters, Paul tailored his religious concept of charis to the social environment informing his listeners. In first-century Graeco-Roman culture, charis could refer to both the ritual of giving and that of receiving. The earlier Homeric ethic of the counter-gift survived in a broader civic context as a complex system of conventions governing reciprocity. This system could apply to the relation between a wealthy benefactor and his city or community, within a domestic household, between the Caesars and local political associations, and between states. Charis was 'the central leitmotiv of the Hellenistic reciprocity system', in relationships of benefaction involving both human and divine agents.[27] This convention, governing the roles of giver and receiver, was so strong that it was described by Seneca as 'the chief bond of human society'.[28] Paul's letters would have been interpreted by his listeners in the setting of this reciprocity system; his use of charis was even attuned to specific local contexts, varying across city states.

In Rome, for example, the immediate context for charis was the grace of the Caesars. Roman listeners had already experienced the Augustan 'age of grace', in which the Emperor's acts of beneficence had assumed a 'cosmological status':[29] his gifts included the establishment of peace, while he was regarded as a 'divine father' and 'Saviour'. James Harrison considers it likely that these themes 'resonated within the minds of Paul's auditors as they heard about Christ's reign of grace'. Paul presented his theology of grace within these 'first-century cultural codes', which he in part preserved, while also engaging with them and transforming them. Paul 'democratised' benefaction in that the Christian has 'continual access' to the 'favour of the divine Benefactor'.[30]

Paul's concept of charis differed in one other respect to that version contained within the Graeco-Roman reciprocity system. In his letters to the Romans and the Corinthians, Paul emphasised love, both of God and man, in the dispensing of charis or grace. This enabled Paul to redefine the conventions of beneficence, which was now motivated by divine grace establishing fellowship, not reciprocity. Harrison identifies a 'new vision of social relationships' in Paul's theology of grace,[31] which has a radical social aspect. The old Homeric code of gift and counter-gift is displaced, as is the hierarchical structure perpetuated by the Graeco-Roman reciprocity system. In Pauline theology, beneficence is not motivated by obligation to return favour; a social superior does not give with the expectation of binding the recipient in obligation. The honour owed to the wealthy is redirected to God as the 'cosmic benefactor', and to those socially marginalised in the community. The pervasiveness of benefaction allowed Paul to communicate the 'gospel of grace attractively at a theological and social level', while undermining the prevailing social reciprocity system: divine grace becomes 'the great social leveller'[32] within the Christian community.

Paul's invention of charisma

There are only very few instances of the word 'charisma' in extant Greek texts before the writings of Paul, and those instances are subject to scholarly dispute. 'Charisma' appears twice in the whole of the Septuagint, and only in variant manuscript versions, replacing the 'charis' of most versions, conveying a meaning of favour between men rather than divine grace.[33] The philosopher Philo (c. 20 BC to AD 40) uses 'charisma' twice in his *Legum Allegoria*, yet many scholars do not accept that the original text contained the word.[34] It is likely that 'charisma' was added to Philo's text by a later editor; even if the usage is accepted, 'charisma' in Philo is ill-defined. Friedrich comments that in Philo charisma is 'interchangeable with charis': charisma appears to denote the result of charis, but it is given 'no sharp distinction from this term'.[35] Most scholars accept that Paul's use of the term 'charisma' was original. Certainly he endowed it with a meaning not evident in Philo, and he defined the term in a detailed and complex treatment in his letters. It is not disputed that Paul produced 'the most extended and original use of χάρισμα in antiquity',[36] nor that the use of the term in its Christian context was 'uniquely Paul's contribution'.[37] James Dunn concludes that charisma is 'a concept which we owe almost entirely to Paul'.[38]

Given the limits of our understanding of the cultural intricacies of the period, we can only speculate on the genesis of the word in Paul. One line of speculation is that Paul adapted the term charisma from the colloquial language of his time, with the meaning of 'gift' or 'present'.[39] Siegfried Schatzmann notes the relationship with the verb *charisomai*, 'to give' or 'to act kindly', suggesting that the word charisma has the form of a 'verbal noun'. The *-ma* suffix in Greek designated the result of an act: charisma would denote the 'concrete result of a bestowal'.[40] Charisma thus has the meaning of 'the result of the gift of grace', or more succinctly, 'grace-thing'.[41] The construction of the word produces several semantic effects: it links charisma to charis while simultaneously distinguishing it from its root term; it denotes the relationship between the two such that charisma is understood as the result or product of charis; and it establishes the 'thing-ness' of charisma, removing it from abstraction and expressing its concrete or specific characteristics.

For Paul, charisma is the gift offered by divine grace. Charisma could refer to the gift of redemption itself; it also refers to specific divine gifts assigned to the early Christians by God's grace. There is a clear distinction between charisma and charis: charisma is the direct result of divine charis or grace. God's grace generates a wide variety of gifting within the church, which Paul enumerates. He uses the plural *charismata* to designate these diverse attributes, which include miraculous powers such as speaking in tongues and healing. These gifts are manifestations of the Spirit resulting in ecstatic behaviour and extraordinary abilities.

For Friedrich, charisma is linked with charis on one side and *pneuma* ('spirit') on the other, 'to the degree that spiritual manifestations are called *charismata*'.[42] The spiritual aspect of charisma is evident whether Paul is referring to the spiritual possession of the believer (*charisma pneumatikon*) – in Romans 1: 11 – or the special non-material gifts (charismata) bestowed by the grace of God on individual Christians. Yet the specific nature of the various charismata also conveys the sense of the 'concrete expression of grace'.[43] Other scholars have proposed similar definitions of Pauline charisma: 'God's grace finding particular and concrete actualisation' (John Goldingay); 'concretion and individuation of one and the same Spirit' (Schulz); 'the experience of grace and power in a *particular instance*' (Dunn).[44] Dunn adds an emphasis on the divine origins of charisma: it is 'an event, the gracious activity of God through a man', and never confused in the Pauline letters with human talent or natural ability.[45]

There is a degree of scholarly consensus on the distinctive use of the term charisma by Paul. Prior to Paul, charisma was a 'little-known Greek concept'[46] which has left only very meagre traces in Judaic and secular Greek texts. Paul took this obscure Greek word and endowed it with original meaning within the framework of his theology. Paul, the 'apostle of grace' in Harrison's words, used charisma as his 'preferred term for giftedness'[47] – that is, giftedness bestowed by God. In his letters, Paul deploys charisma as a remarkably flexible term, assigning to it a range of attributes according to context. The originality and versatility evident in Paul's deployment of the word offer, for Schatzmann, a 'unique example of the apostle's linguistic ability'.[48] The appropriate means of examining the construction of the term by Paul is to consider its function in his letters, while situating those letters themselves in their specific cultural settings.

Paul refers to charisma 16 times (there is only one other mention of charisma in the New Testament – in 1 Peter – its single instance prompting scholars to describe it as an 'echo' of Paul).[49] Apart from three individual references – in 1 Timothy 4: 14, 2 Timothy 1: 6 and 2 Cor 1: 11 – Paul elaborates his conception of *charisma* and *charismata* primarily in his epistles to the Romans (six references) and 1 Corinthians (seven references). Both epistles affirm the divine origin of these spiritual gifts; both counsel the Christian community on how to utilise them.

Charisma of the Corinthians

1 Corinthians is dated around the year 54,[50] which means it was the first epistle to mention charisma. As well as being Paul's inaugural statement on the theme of charisma, this epistle has the most detailed exposition of the various forms of charismata. It also offers significant insight into the circumstances of the fledgling Christian communities 20 years after the death of Jesus.

The wide differences in social class and educational attainment within those communities could produce problems, as was the case in Corinth. The immediate context of Paul's letter to the Corinthians concerns discord within the congregation in that city. 1 Corinthians is Paul's response to reports of trouble in Corinth, and to questions that members of the congregation had conveyed to him. The most pressing difficulty faced by Paul was the presence of a spiritual elite at Corinth, to whom he refers as 'spirit people' (*pneumatikoi*). This elite considered themselves spiritually mature or complete, superior to their brethren, and the masters of supernatural gifts, of which they valued glossolalia most highly. This gift was understood as the ability of speaking in 'tongues' or languages – human or heavenly – that the speaker had not learnt.[51] These 'spirit people' also believed that their spiritual superiority freed them from moral constraints on the earthly plain. Paul's ambition in this letter is to re-establish harmony in the congregation; this entails deflating the claims of the spiritual aristocracy, establishing a communal sensibility and enforcing his own spiritual authority. Murphy-O'Connor believes that the better educated in this community found Paul's preaching 'anti-intellectual'. They claimed for themselves a special spiritual knowledge (*gnosis*) more attuned to the writings of Philo – with its distinction between 'heavenly man' and 'earthly man' – than Paul's theology.[52] Glossolalia was celebrated by this group as a manifestation of their *gnosis*; Paul opposed this direction, and the fragmentation of the community appearing in its wake. He mocked these individuals for their arrogance, directing them to abandon their self-importance for a communal spirit based on love: 'Knowledge [*gnosis*] puffs up, but love builds up' (1 Corinthians 8: 1). In the twelfth chapter of 1 Corinthians, Paul deploys his concept of charisma to engage directly with the problems of this challenging environment. Leading up to this passage, he introduces the term and frames its meaning.

Near the beginning of 1 Corinthians, after the salutation to the church at Corinth, Paul uses *charisma* for the first time. After emphasising the enriching grace of God that has been bestowed on the Corinthian church, he informs the Corinthians: 'you are not lacking in any spiritual gift [charismata], as you wait for the revealing of our Lord Jesus Christ' (1 Corinthians 1: 7). The plural 'charismata' suggests that Paul is referring to the wide range of gifts, including those of a supernatural nature, evident in the Corinthian community. This first reference to charisma is notable for the theological context in which Paul encases the spiritual gifts: they are to be understood as ensuing directly from divine grace; and they are to be regarded not as an end in themselves, but as abilities to be used in the period leading to the eschatological event of the Return. This framing of the charismata by a future divine event undermines the fervour and pride with which some Corinthians had revelled in their supernatural gifts. Paul has placed limits on the spiritual gifts at the same time as celebrating them.

The next mention of charisma occurs as Paul answers a question from the Corinthians concerning the relative merits of marriage and celibacy. Paul states that individuals should marry to avoid immoral temptations, but wishes that 'all were as I myself am' (celibate) (1 Cor 7: 7). Acknowledging that this cannot be the case, he observes that 'each has his own special gift [charisma] from God, one of one kind and one of another' (7: 7). While commentators have argued over whether in this passage Paul is claiming celibacy in general, or even marriage, as a charisma, it is most likely that he is referring to his own celibacy, which he regards as part of his charismatic function as itinerant apostle. Celibacy is part of his spiritual gift in that it removes him from carnal temptation and does not impede his ministry.[53]

1 Corinthians 12 is Paul's most detailed account of charisma. It is significant that when, at the opening of this chapter, Paul refers to 'spiritual gifts', he uses the term *pneumatika* (literally 'spiritual things'): 'Now concerning spiritual gifts [pneumatika], brethren, I do not want you to be uninformed' (12: 1). 'Pneumatika' is presumably the

term used by the spiritual elite at Corinth to describe their own gifts. Paul then connects this term with the pagan past of the Corinthians: 'when you were heathens, you were led astray to dumb idols, however you may have been moved' (12: 2). The ecstatic expression of 'spiritual gifts' celebrated by the Corinthians is thereby associated with the pre-Christian past. Yet Paul does not reject the spiritual gifts; rather, he redefines them, using the new word *charismata* to replace *pneumatika*: 'Now there are varieties of gifts [charismata], but the same Spirit' (12: 4). The shift in terminology, in the space of four brief verses, signals Paul's intent to his Corinthian auditors. His new term for spiritual gifts emphasises the divine grace by which they have been bestowed, rather than the spirit which had been thought to privilege some Corinthians over others. The word meaning 'spiritual gift' has been replaced by one meaning 'grace gift'.[54] Paul maintains an emphasis on spiritual powers, but locates these strictly within a Christian framework, that is of the Holy Spirit. In his elaboration of the charismata he emphasises the communal nature of these gifts, which are available to all in the congregation:

> To each is given the manifestation of the Spirit for the common good. To one is given through the Spirit the utterance of wisdom, and to another the utterance of knowledge according to the same Spirit, to another faith by the same Spirit, to another gifts of healing by the one Spirit, to another the working of miracles, to another prophecy, to another the ability to distinguish between spirits, to another various kinds of tongues, to another the interpretation of tongues. All these are inspired by one and the same Spirit, who apportions to each one individually as he wills.
>
> (12: 4–11)

There are nine diverse charismata listed here, combining supernatural powers ensuing from divine inspiration – healing, miracle working, prophecy, glossolalia, utterance of spiritual wisdom and knowledge – with less spectacular abilities whose function is to support the ecstatic or miraculous gifts: faith, the skill of distinguishing spirits, the interpretation of glossolalia. This wide range of spiritual gifts, encompassing abilities of differing intensity, allows for charisma to be spread throughout the Christian community in many forms. Paul's emphasis on the 'one Spirit' generating these disparate charismata is sustained throughout a lengthy section in which individual members of the community are enjoined to consider themselves part of the one body sustained by the one Spirit. To this communal sensibility is later added a hierarchy of spiritual gifts, which also serves as a hierarchy of church office:

> Now you are the body of Christ and individually members of it. And God has appointed in the church first apostles, second prophets, third teachers, then workers of miracles, then healers, helpers, administrators, speakers in various kinds of tongues.
>
> (12: 27–28)

This passage is notable for a number of reasons. First, it sets a hierarchy within the mid-century church as decreed by Paul: apostles occupy the pre-eminent position, followed by prophets, then teachers. Of these first three positions, the apostles and prophets are understood to possess charismatic powers, including healing, ecstatic speech and prophecy. The teachers presumably possess more worldly skills, but are installed by Paul within the top rankings. Prophecy is understood as inspired speech when spontaneously empowered by God, revealing new truths to the community; teaching is below it in the hierarchy because it imparts knowledge and instruction already revealed to the church.[55]

Second, the list of eight roles contains a mix of charismatic abilities – healing, glossolalia, miracle working, prophecy – and the more mundane occupations of helper and administrator. All, however, are considered worthy and divinely appointed. Third, Paul relegates speaking in tongues to the bottom of this hierarchy; his reason for assigning glossolalia the lowest position is revealed in the following passages.

Paul advises the Corinthians that no one can expect to possess all these spiritual powers: 'Are all apostles? Are all prophets? Are all teachers?' (12: 29). However, he also urges them to 'earnestly desire the higher gifts [charismata]' (12: 31). By this he means prophecy, but only when supplemented by the 'still more excellent way' of love. Paul contrasts the selfless nature of love with behaviour he terms jealous, boastful, arrogant, rude and resentful (13: 4–6). He then proceeds to link such self-centred behaviour with the practice of speaking in tongues:

> For one who speaks in a tongue speaks not to men but to God; for no one understands him, but he utters mysteries in the Spirit.
>
> (14: 2)

This restricted spiritual communication is contrasted with the greater communal benefit flowing from prophecy:

> he who prophesies speaks to men for their upbuilding and encouragement and consolation. He who speaks in a tongue edifies himself, but he who prophesies edifies the church.
>
> (14: 3–5)

Paul's motivation for ranking prophecy so much higher than glossolalia is made clear:

> He who prophesies is greater than he who speaks in tongues, unless someone interprets, so that the church may be edified.
>
> (14: 5)

The charisma of glossolalia, then, is of limited benefit to the church, unless complemented by another charisma: 'the interpretation of tongues'. Glossolalia operating without interpretation offers no 'edification' for the community beyond the self-esteem of the speaker who, without the aid of an interpreter, speaks 'into the air' (14: 10). Paul acknowledges that the Corinthian congregation is 'eager for manifestations of the Spirit', but urges that such spiritual abilities should be used 'in building up the church' (14: 12). He recommends that glossolalia should always be accompanied by interpretation: 'he who speaks in tongues should pray for the power to interpret' (14: 13). He even advocates limits to be placed on glossolalia in church services:

> If any speak in a tongue, let there be only two or at most three, and each in turn; and let one interpret. But if there is no one to interpret, let each of them keep silence in church and speak to himself and to God.
>
> (14: 27–8)

This restriction on glossolalia activity serves the dual function of curbing the self-importance of speakers in tongues and preventing church services descending into confusion (Paul also recommends that no more than two or three prophets should speak at a service).

Paul's critical comments on the charisma of glossolalia in 1 Corinthians are modified by two statements on the topic. First, he declares that he himself possesses this gift, to a supreme degree: 'I thank God that I speak in tongues more than you all' (14: 18). This self-proclaimed ability also functions to assert his authority as an apostle in the face of criticism or scepticism from the Corinthian spiritual elite. From his declared position of eminence in this charisma, he states his own preference concerning ecstatic utterance and knowledge:

> [I]n church I would rather speak five words with my mind, in order to instruct others, than ten thousand words in a tongue.
>
> (14.19)

He then concludes this section on the spiritual gifts with a final instruction to the Corinthians:

> So, my brethren, earnestly desire to speak in prophesy, and do not forbid speaking in tongues; but all things should be done decently and in order.
>
> (14: 39–40)

He is not prepared to ban glossolalia, even though it provokes inflated self-esteem and a divisiveness that may endanger community concord. Despite these concerns, Paul is prepared to permit the practice, within the restraints he recommends, and with the understanding that it occupies the lowest rank of the charismata.

The criterion for the ranking of spiritual gifts is community benefit. Prophecy is ranked the highest charisma because it more than any other upbuilds the community, strengthening faith and humbling believers before divine revelation.[56] The nine charismata identified by Paul in 1 Corinthians 12 are distributed throughout the congregation in interlocking ways, as with the power to interpret, which supplements – and validates – glossolalia. This dispersal of charisma operates as a spiritual layer on the communal basis of the church emphasised throughout Paul's letters. 1 Corinthians implies that all in the community have access to a charisma, although the precise nature of that charisma will vary. It should also be noted that leadership is not listed as one of the charismata: the Pauline emphasis is strictly aimed at community, not leadership.

Paul recommends that individuals should 'pray for the power to interpret' or should 'earnestly desire to prophesy': even the highest charisma of prophecy, it seems, is not out of reach of any individual. Such prayer or desire may not be granted, however, and an individual may instead be gifted with one of the other charismata. Paul exhorts every individual to be satisfied with the charisma he or she may possess, as it has been granted by divine will and is intended to serve the greater good: the Spirit 'apportions to each one individually as he wills'.

His metaphor of the community as body, composed of many parts of differing dimension, is designed to illustrate the importance of all gifts, whether of the highest register (prophecy), lowest (glossolalia) or the seemingly mundane (interpretation, administration). Just as the head cannot dismiss the feet, so the charismata that may seem 'weaker' or 'less honourable' are nevertheless 'indispensable' for the community (13: 21–3). The problems at Corinth had derived from the divisive aspect of the *pneumatika*: those claiming the spiritual gift of glossolalia had set themselves above the rest of the community. Paul's charismata are no less spiritual and no less supernatural – but as grace-gifts, their purpose is to create unity, to strengthen community and to build the church.

Charisma of the Romans

Paul develops a similar theme in Romans, dated around 56.[57] He exhorts the Romans to live harmoniously and to eschew pride; he employs the body metaphor and details the various charismata and their functions, as in 1 Corinthians. Yet there are subtle differences between the letters and their treatment of charisma, reflecting the dissimilar contexts of Corinth and Rome.

Paul introduces the Romans to his concept of charisma at 1: 11, when he writes that he longs to see them, 'so that I may impart to you some spiritual gift [charisma pneumatikon] to strengthen you'. The inclusion of the adjective meaning 'spiritual' is presumably to emphasise the nature of the charisma or gift, and to avoid confusion concerning its origin: although it is imparted by the apostle, it emanates from the Spirit. Paul's association of charisma with 'strengthening' signifies the empowering force of the otherwise unspecified spiritual gift; the communal nature of this empowering is suggested by the following phrase: 'that we may be mutually encouraged by each other's faith' (1: 12). The notion of charisma as a spiritual force that enhances or builds community is thus conveyed to the Romans early in the epistle.

When Paul next uses the term, at 5: 15–16, it is to serve a different function. It features in a passage contrasting Adam, as the man who introduced sin and death to humanity, with Jesus:

But the free gift [charisma] is not like the trespass. For if many died through one man's trespass, much more have the grace of God and the free gift in the grace of that one man Jesus Christ abounded for many. And the free gift is not like the effect of that one man's sin. For the judgement following one trespass brought condemnation, but the free gift following many trespasses brings justification.

(5: 15–16)

This rather convoluted passage connects charisma closely with charis or divine grace. It has been suggested that the meaning of the first verse could be more effectively rendered by the translation of charisma as 'work of grace', in that charisma here ensues from God's grace – with the express function of overcoming the Fall.[58] Divine grace has bestowed on humanity a gift which, in its most fundamental expression, delivers 'justification' or redemption from sin and death. This aspect of charisma is made clearer at Romans 6: 23: 'the free gift [charisma] of God is eternal life in Christ Jesus, our Lord'. Salvation is declared the 'foundational charisma'[59] without which none of the other charismata is possible.

Romans 11: 29 refers to the charismata of the Israelites: 'For the gifts [charismata] and the call of God are irrevocable'. This is the first instance in which charisma is given a historical perspective: it refers to the gifts of grace that have previously been bestowed on the Israelites as a chosen people. Paul informs his gentile Roman audience that despite its divine blessing, 'Israel failed to obtain what it sought' (11: 7), and now 'salvation has come to the Gentiles, so as to make Israel jealous' (11: 11). Paul tells the Romans that 'a hardening has come upon part of Israel' (11: 25), so that if his ministry makes his 'fellow Jews jealous' it will have the beneficial effect of saving 'some of them' (11: 14). Israel will be restored to its status of 'election' if it once again heeds the call and bestowal of charisma previously granted it.

Romans 12: 6–8 contains a list of specific charismata that the Romans exercise. Paul prefigures this account with recourse to the body metaphor, emphasising the need for cooperation within the community: 'so we, though many, are one body in Christ, and individually members one of another' (12: 5). The charismata and their functions are detailed in this context:

Having gifts that differ according to the grace given to us, let us use them: if prophecy, in proportion to our faith; if service, in our serving; he who teaches, in his teaching; he who exhorts, in his exhortation; he who contributes, in his liberality; he who gives aid, with zeal; he who does acts of mercy, with cheerfulness.

(12: 6–8)

Paul stipulates seven charismata here – prophecy, teaching, exhorting, encouraging, giving aid, showing mercy – compared to the nine
he enumerated for the Corinthians. This elaboration of the gifts of
grace differs from that given in 1 Corinthians in that it does not
rank the charismata (although prophecy maintains its pre-eminence
as the first gift mentioned), and in its emphasis on worldly abilities:
service, teaching, aid, mercy. Prophecy is the only supernatural gift
described here, reflecting the differences between the Corinthian and
Roman communities. Whereas Paul made strenuous efforts to down-
play the relative importance of miraculous gifts to the Corinthians,
whose spiritual elite had overvalued the supernatural, in Rome he is
more concerned to counter individual pride and foster a sense of community. Paul exhorts the community to live 'in harmony with one
another' (12: 16), rejecting pride and embracing humility: 'do not be
haughty, but associate with the lowly' (16).

Other mentions of charisma

There are only three other references to charisma in Paul's letters, all
of them brief. The first occurs in 2 Corinthians, written around 56. At
2 Cor 1: 11, Paul refers to his escape from life-threatening circumstance,
which he attributes to the prayers of the Corinthians. He implores them
to continue prayer, 'so that many will give thanks on our behalf for the
blessing [charisma] granted us in answer to many prayers'. Charisma
here does not relate to the specific charismata detailed in 1 Corinthians
or Romans; it has a more general sense of 'gift of grace' or 'blessing'.

The other two references are in the two letters to Timothy, written
in the period 62–7.[60] At 1 Timothy 4: 14, Paul writes: 'Do not neglect
the gift [charisma] you have, which was given you by prophetic utterance when the council of elders laid their hands upon you'. At 2
Timothy 1: 6, he writes: 'Hence I remind you to rekindle the gift of God
[charisma] that is within you through the laying on of my hands'.

As these letters were written later than 1 Corinthians and Romans,
there has been scholarly speculation that these two references indicate a
shift in the charisma concept from 'gift of grace' to 'office', as laid on by
the hands of Paul or church elders. It has been claimed that in these late
letters, charisma has already been institutionalised as a form of office.[61]
But Schatzmann is no doubt correct when he points out that the laying
on of hands to confer ministry as well as spiritual powers was recorded
in Acts as a practice of the early church, including the dedication of
Paul himself.[62] Paul makes clear to Timothy that his gift is from God, as

were the charismata outlined for the Corinthians. There is no evidence for the conclusion that 1 and 2 Timothy signal a transfer of charisma to church office; indeed, Paul's intention seems to be to urge Timothy not to waste his own charisma.

There are no other mentions of charisma or charismata in the New Testament. There is a parallel reference to *donata* (gifts) to the church in Paul's letter to the Ephesians. This epistle is of uncertain authorship and date, and may have been written later than AD 70; the use of 'donata' may indicate a different emphasis. Yet the elaboration of the gifts in this letter echoes that of the charismata in 1 Corinthians and Romans:

> And his gifts were that some should be apostles, some prophets, some evangelists, some pastors and teachers, to equip the saints for the work of ministry, for building up the body of Christ.
>
> (Ephesisans 4: 11)

Charisma, authority and community

These then are the characteristics of Pauline charisma. Charisma is the gift of God's grace; the specific gifts (charismata) are to be used for the benefit of the community rather than for personal prestige. Paul's vision entails a church unified by charis while enjoying the diversity of the charismata.[63] There are several contextual factors influencing Paul's construction of charisma as a spiritual gift understood in communal terms. Paul's advocacy of a collective deployment of charisma served the political function of maintaining social harmony, while also preserving the authority of his own teaching. A harmonious Christian community was less likely to attract the attention of Roman authorities, particularly given the rumours circulating within the Graeco-Roman world concerning the unsavoury practices of the Christian cult. Acts describes several instances of over-exuberant gatherings 'in danger of being charged with rioting'[64] by the local authorities. Pauline charisma works smoothly within an internal social network, and is unlikely to draw attention to itself.

On the other hand, there is a radical aspect to the collectivist notion of Pauline charisma. Paul's exhortations to the Corinthians and the Romans promote a spiritual unity within Christian communities, which in many respects challenged the hierarchical ordering of Hellenistic society. To assert that each member of the Christian community is 'uniquely gifted' and therefore indispensable to the health of that community is, for Harrison, to overturn the prevailing social and political ideas within the Roman empire.[65] The spiritual democracy enabled by the communal nature of Pauline charisma also came to propose difficulties, in the second century, for the church as it developed an institutional framework.

While the collectivist ethos of charisma is insistent and consistent through Paul's letters, there remains the issue of the relation between charisma and authority. Several scholars have sought to connect Weber's notion of charismatic authority with the Pauline charismata articulated in 1 Corinthians and Romans. John Howard Schütz casts the first century in a Weberian hue when he asserts that the '[a]scription of charisma is really the ascription of authority'.[66] However, there is no support whatsoever for this position in Paul's epistles. In Paul's detailing of the charismata in all their variety, none is related to leadership or authority. It is true that Paul ranks the position of apostle highly, and considers himself empowered to instruct the Christian communities, but the apostle is understood as an itinerant role, with no permanent place in any community. Paul's letters aim not to establish himself as the authority, but rather to encourage a communal approach within the congregations. He never addresses individual leaders or leadership groups: the community is expected to make its own assessments and decisions.[67] This corporate sensibility respects the divergent functions of the charismata, shifting the focus of authority 'from the few to the whole'.[68] Paul's criticism of the spiritual elite at Corinth is motivated by his concern at their attribution of authority and superiority to themselves, based on their gift of glossolalia. For Paul, such presumed authority fails the community test, hence his relegation of this gift to the least of the charismata. Authority is to be exercised by the community as a whole, and is not invested in any charismatic function, whether apostle or speaker in tongues.

A more circumspect application of Weber's theory of charisma to the early church is made by Bengt Holmberg, who regards the 'Primitive Church' as manifesting the 'routinization of charisma' theorised by Weber.[69] Holmberg resists the ascription of pure charismatic authority to Paul, noting that no individual in the early church holds such a position: in that sense, 'Jesus has no successor'.[70] Paul set limits to his own authority, which was bound by the tradition of the gospel, unlike the messianic charismatic authority of Jesus. Holmberg concludes that authority in the early church cannot be characterised as charismatic in Weberian terms, but is 'mixed with traditional and rational elements'.[71] Holmberg also proposes that the institutionalisation of the church was already active in Paul's time, but adds that Paul's presence was a retarding factor in this process due to his emphasis on the pneumatic: '[a]s long as Paul is present or active in his churches the local offices remain undeveloped'.[72]

A detailed study of the Pauline idea of community – and within it the roles of charisma and authority – has been made by Robert Banks. Banks observes that the spirit with which the charismata are distributed is democratic, but not egalitarian: democratic in that each member of the community receives a charisma, but unegalitarian in that certain gifts are ranked higher than others. There is a degree of flexibility involved in the distribution, however: Paul encourages members of the congregation to seek the higher gifts, which are apparently not out of reach. Banks makes the further point that the charismata are so diverse and so interlocking that they 'encompass every aspect of the community's life',[73] taking on an everyday quality. This centrality of the charismata in the functioning of the Christian communities enters into greater relief when we consider how much of conventional religious activity is omitted by Paul in his letters. Paul provides no instruction concerning religious code, liturgy, clerical structure or leadership.[74] There is no division between holy men and followers; indeed there is scant reference to priests or specific church offices. Even in those rare instances when Paul refers to church officers, such as his greeting to bishops and deacons in 1 Philippians (c. 58), these seem general descriptions of pastoral roles – synonymous with 'overseer' – rather than technical positions of office.[75]

Reflecting on Paul's idea of community, Banks finds some precedent in the 'commonwealth of reason' envisaged by the Stoic philosophers, the Judaic notion of 'an international theocracy',[76] and the membership of cults. Yet Banks, like several other commentators, is struck by the distinctiveness of Paul's 'revolutionary' vision of community. A religious congregation without a book or a rite, the Pauline community was united by its focus on 'a set of relationships',[77] Paul's constant emphasis on harmony and the subordination of individual pride to the greater good is in service of this principle of unity in diversity. Race, class and gender distinctions within Graeco-Roman society are overcome in the Pauline community, in part because all await the Last Days on an equal footing, but also because all are thought to be baptised by the one Spirit.[78]

The charismata are integral to this levelling process: everyone in the community is infused with the Spirit, each has a spiritual gift. Supernatural abilities were well known in the Graeco-Roman world, but were always associated with extraordinary individuals: miracle-workers, prophets, magicians. As Banks notes, the Greek vocabulary incorporated words to describe these feats and states: *ekstatsis, enthusiamos* and the *pneumata* addressed by Paul at Corinth.[79] Paul's innovation was to transform these feats of special individuals into a collective experience: charismata for all within the community. As a result, the miraculous suffuses the group, and spiritual leadership is 'a corporate affair devolving in some measure upon all who participate in the community's gatherings'.[80] Dunn makes a similar conclusion, referring to the Pauline 'charismatic community', unified by the shared conversion experience of the Spirit of all members.[81] Authority within this community is dynamic, dependent on interaction between charismatic individuals and on self-restraint concerning individual authority or pride. Paul's accentuation of the communal good is so strong that it forms part of his definition of charisma itself. His articulation of the roles of the charismata in 1 Corinthians and Romans is always in the terms of community benefit. Schatzmann, noting this connection between charisma and service, proposes that Pauline charisma 'functioned for the purpose of the upbuilding of the church', so that 'charismatic endowment' was for Paul 'integrally linked with service in and for the community'.[82] Above all, a charisma was a spiritual gift that should be used responsibly, for the common good.

One final contextual factor relates to the supernatural character of some of the charismata. The miraculous and ecstatic powers referred to by Paul as specific gifts of God's grace could easily have been interpreted in other ways. Cities such as Corinth were suffused with magical beliefs in many forms – miracles, healings, ecstatic speech and behaviour, prophecies, visions, demonic possessions. Early in his first letter to the Corinthians, Paul addresses any 'misunderstanding' concerning the ecstatic charismata. For Paul the Corinthians' excited embrace of ecstatic powers was potentially dangerous not just for the hubristic tendency of the spiritual elite but also because of these powers' proximity to practices associated with magic and pagan cults. Paul transformed the concept of spirit which had, in previous formulations, emphasised the spectacular; instead he accentuated the role of spirit in building up the community. His conflict with the Corinthian elite concerned their recalcitrance in celebrating the 'miraculous' manifestations of spirit.[83] Paul's attribution of the supernatural gifts to God's grace, his inscription of them into a communal framework, his counselling of humility regarding their use, and his relegation of glossolalia to the lowest rung of the Christian spiritual hierarchy, may all be interpreted as his attempts to control the fervour surrounding the supernatural charismata.

Paul mobilised the obscure term 'charisma' to provide an explanation for abilities that could otherwise have been attributed to magic, *gnosis* or the ecstatic manifestations associated with cults. The miracle-working and prophecy conducted by the early Christians were in competition and conflict with the magical practices prevalent in the Graeco-Roman world; Forbes remarks that the Christians, led by Paul in this regard, were at pains to differentiate their beliefs from their competitors.[84] Christian prophecy – revelation direct from the Spirit – was considered different to the cryptic practices of Greek oracular prophecy; Christian glossolalia – understood as a form of praise and revelation – was considered different to the frenzied 'ecstatic' states experienced in Greek religion or mystery cults. Christian glossolalia also required the interlocking gift of interpretation for it to offer any value to the community. The concept of charisma, which defined these and the other abilities as 'gifts of God's grace', secured for these gifts a specifically Christian explanation.

4
Charisma Eclipsed

Paul may have been the leading Christian missionary of the period and his writings may constitute a significant portion of the New Testament, but the legacy of his thought and preaching was mixed. Even in the first and second centuries, his thought was not the dominant influence in the developing church. While some of his emphases – such as the importance of divine grace – were accepted into mainstream Christian theology, others – including his concept of charisma – were not. While charisma in Paul's most general sense – the gift of God's grace offering salvation – was acceptable, the ecstatic spiritual powers associated with the charismata were not encouraged by later church authorities. The significance of the supernatural gifts described by Paul was marginalised in the church, and with it much of the sense of charisma as a special or extraordinary quality. The eclipse of the Pauline notion of charisma was effected with remarkable speed.

Paul himself anticipated the expiry of the charismatic gifts. In his first letter to the Corinthians, he followed his veneration of love as the 'excellent way' with the declaration:

> Love never ends; as for prophecies, they will pass away; as for tongues, they will cease; as for knowledge, it will pass away. For our knowledge is imperfect and our prophecy is imperfect; but when the perfect comes, the imperfect will pass away.
>
> (1 Cor: 8–10)

Several scholars have claimed that this prediction looks forward to the imminent end of the early Apostolic period of Christianity, and its replacement by a church authority based on a canon of scripture; but it is much more likely that Paul is referring to the return of Christ, when all will be rendered 'perfect'.[1] Yet Paul's reckoning of the charismata as part of a transitional phase was later echoed by authorities within the church; the effect was to seal off the charismatic gifts within the earliest stages of Christian history.

Changes within the church

When Paul wrote his epistle to the Corinthians in the early 50s, he addressed a community revelling in its various spiritual gifts, including speaking in tongues, miracle working and prophecy. Paul's own stated hierarchy of spiritual abilities placed prophets in second place, below only the rank held by Paul himself, apostle. Paul's letters describe early churches defined by a strong communal sensibility, in which individuals contributed their own specific charismata to the local Christian community. Within 60 years, the church had changed significantly. Around 110, Ignatius, the Bishop of Antioch, described the hierarchy of church ministry as bishop, presbyter, deacon. As has been noted,[2] apostles and prophets are missing from this list.

Paul's vision of the Christian church as a charismatic community was such a radical – and idealistic – notion that it could not be expected to survive intact as the church developed. Dunn is perhaps too severe when he states that Paul's vision of the communal church did not outlive him;[3] yet in a technical sense he is correct in observing that the characteristically Pauline concept of charisma 'is almost completely lost' after Paul.[4] Paul's faith in the spiritually empowered community was so insistent that he placed no emphasis on the offices or apparatus of the church. Yet the major transition that occurred within the church's 'sub-Apostolic age' (c. 70–140) was the installation of a formal structure of office and hierarchy. The vitality and spiritual conviction of Paul's generation gave way to succeeding Christian generations whose religious experience began 'to harden into set forms'.[5]

A key factor in the development of a stable church structure in the second century was the need to defeat the many competing interpretations of Christian theology, as propounded most notably by the Gnostic sects. As the church increasingly defined itself against the mystical tenor of these and other versions of Christianity, charismatic gifts came to be regarded as problematic within Christian communities. In place of the disparate supernatural gifts bestowed by the Spirit, the church erected an edifice based on scriptures, doctrine, sacrament (ceremony) and the authority of bishops. The church preferred to invest its ministers with a power derived from the institution itself, rather than from a Spirit that may endow any Christian individual with special gifts.

The charismata did not disappear from the Christian communities immediately: there are references to charisma in Christian texts through the second century and into the third. In his detailed analysis of Christian literature from c. 90 to 320, Ronald Kydd concludes that the sources reveal a church still 'strongly charismatic up until A. D. 200'.[6] Yet there is a sharp decline in the third century, when charismatic gifts fade in significance and are met with altered attitudes. From around 260, Kydd remarks, 'there is no more evidence of charismatic experience' in the Christian communities.[7] In this chapter, I trace the process, within the late first and second centuries, by which charisma was eclipsed within Christianity, before examining more closely the third and fourth centuries for surviving traces of charisma within the church.

The rise of bishops, the demise of prophets

The transition from the rather free-wheeling Christian communities of Paul's time to the structured ministry of the second-century church was swift; unfortunately, the transition is also obscure. Historical sources offer merely fleeting glimpses of the process. We can only compare the situation as described in Paul's letters with later church documents of the late first and second centuries. Those documents are, regrettably, few, and subject to a degree of dispute among scholars.

The first of these texts is the *Didache* ('Teaching of the Twelve Apostles'), an anonymous church document probably from the second half of the first century. This short work contains instructions for Christian communities on the procedures for baptism and eucharist, as well as advice concerning the local and itinerant ministry. The date of the document is contested, with most scholars opting for the period AD 70–90;[8] several aspects of the text are ambiguous and inconsistent, suggesting multiple authorship drawing on an oral tradition.[9] It is plausible to regard the *Didache* as a notation of oral instructions circulating and evolving in one community, possibly in Syria[10] from as early as mid-century: the genesis of the work in oral transmission over a period of time would account for the inconsistencies and omissions evident in the text.

The value of the *Didache* for our purposes is that it deals directly with the issue of charismatic abilities, as possessed by prophets. The word 'charisma' is used once in the *Didache*, at 1: 5:

> for the Father wants people to share with everyone the gifts [*charismata*] that have been freely granted to them.[11]

Yet the *Didache* is concerned not with charisma as general spiritual gift, but with the specific role of prophets within the newly formed Christian communities. Chapter 11 of the text provides instructions on how to receive the three types of itinerants visiting the community: teachers, apostles and prophets (a personnel consistent with that recounted in Acts' account of the early missionary period). The apostles are accorded high rank: 'Let every apostle who comes to you be received as the Lord' (11: 4). This acclamation suggests that the honour extended to the apostles is linked to the status of the original disciples of Jesus. However, the *Didache* makes no mention of the 12 apostles, other than in its title, nor does it refer to the later apostles such as Paul. The only other explicit reference to apostles is in the next instruction:

> He shall stay [only] one day, or, if need be, another day too. If he stays three days, he is a false prophet. When the apostle leaves, let him receive nothing but [enough] bread [to see him through] until he finds lodging. If he asks for money, he is a false prophet.
>
> (11: 5–6)

After this brief and rather curt directive, the *Didache* then focuses its attention on the prophets, who are privileged as the leading priests, deserving of material reward:

> So when you take any firstfruits of what is produced by the wine press and the threshing floor, by cows and by sheep, you shall give the firstfruits to the prophets, for they are your high priests.
>
> (13: 3)

The prophets come from outside the community, but if they wish to stay, they should be welcomed: 'Every true prophet who wants to settle in with you deserves his food' (13: 1). Prophets are esteemed because they are divinely inspired: their gift is to 'speak in spirit' and because of this gift they should not be doubted or disrespected:

> Do not test any prophet who speaks in spirit, and do not judge him, for every [other] sin will be forgiven, but this sin will not be forgiven. Not everyone who speaks in spirit is a prophet but only those whose behaviour is the Lord's. So the false prophet and the prophet will be recognised by their behaviour.
>
> (11: 7–8)

The true prophet is to be given liberties within the community, 'for his judgement is with God. The ancient prophets acted in the same way' (11: 11). The text seems to imply that these wandering prophets infused with the Spirit may behave in unconventional ways, but this very behaviour is to be respected as part of a continuity with the Old Testament prophets.

While the *Didache* emphasises the status and rights of the 'true prophets', it also expresses concern over inauthentic itinerants. The text provides specific means of detecting false prophets seeking to enrich themselves by exploiting the Christians' generosity:

> Any prophet who gives orders for a table [i.e., a meal] in spirit shall not eat of it; if he does, he is a false prophet. If any prophet teaching the truth does not do what he teaches, he is a false prophet ... You shall not listen to anyone who says in spirit, 'Give me money, or something'.
>
> (11: 9–12)

The *Didache* also warns against other impostors seeking to exploit the community by fraudulently using the Lord's name: the term used to describe these charlatans – 'Christemporos' (12: 5) – has been translated as 'Christ-peddler' and 'Christ-monger'.[12] But the greatest concern is reserved for the false prophets, who have a role in the *Didache*'s final apocalyptic chapter:

> For in the final days false prophets and corruptors will be multiplied, and the sheep will turn into wolves, and love will turn into hate. As lawlessness increases, they will hate and persecute and betray one another, and at that time the one who leads the world astray will appear.
>
> (16: 3–4)

In this apocalypse, false prophets are seen as precursors of an anti-Christ figure whose reign will herald the coming of the Lord. As the *Didache* considers these events imminent – 'be ready, for you do not know the hour at which our Lord is coming' (16: 1) – the prevalence of false prophets, who may or may not be speaking in spirit, is more disturbing than the appearance of mercenary 'Christ-mongers', who may be seeking nothing more than free food and accommodation.

On this point of true and false prophets, the *Didache* is echoed by one other early Christian text, known as *The Shepherd* by Hermas of Rome. The date of this text and the role of Hermas within the Roman Christian community are both contentious issues, but it is likely that *The Shepherd* was composed in the first half of the second century.[13] In a section on prophecy, Hermas counsels the community on detecting the false prophet: such a 'bold and shameless' individual will ask for payment, will shun 'an assembly of righteous men' while prophesying to the gullible 'in a corner', offering up prophecies 'in an empty manner' reflecting the desires of his auditors (43: 12–13).[14] The true prophet, by contrast, is gentle and 'humble' and does not prophesy on demand; but will speak to a righteous assembly only when 'filled by the holy Spirit', thereby allowing the divine will to be known by the congregation (43: 8–10). *The Shepherd* of Hermas supports the account given within the *Didache* on several grounds: that at least in some Christian communities, prophecy maintained an integral role into at least the early second century; that false prophets seeking to exploit those communities abounded; and that the community itself was deemed responsible for maintaining the veracity of the prophetic experience.

The other significant feature of the *Didache* is the attention it gives in Chapter 15 to the ministry drawn from the community itself:

> Select, then, for yourselves bishops and deacons worthy of the Lord, mild tempered men who are not greedy, who are honest and have proved themselves, for they too perform the functions of prophets and teachers for you. So do not disregard them, for they are the persons who hold a place of honour among you, together with the prophets and the teachers.
>
> (15: 1–2)

The admonition not to disregard the locally appointed ministers indicates that at this stage the community has afforded more esteem to the itinerant prophets and teachers than to its local representatives. The text asserts that locally appointed bishops and deacons should be no less deserving of honour, and that they are equally capable of performing functions, presumably the eucharist rite as prescribed in the *Didache*. Another instruction, however, directs that the prophets be allowed 'to give thanks as much as they like' at the eucharist (10: 7), permitting prophets a licence not extended to others. The language used to describe the ideal bishops and deacons – 'mild tempered', 'not greedy', 'honest' – betrays a preference for a stable, even stolid, ministry. Humble service is valued as a counterpoint to the more flamboyant, perhaps erratic, effusions of the travelling prophets. Given the repeated warnings in the *Didache* of false prophets and other impostors, it should occasion no surprise that honesty and modesty feature highly in the job description for local officers of the church.

The *Didache* offers a tantalising glimpse into a transitional period. The text describes a community in which the missionary practices of Paul's time coexist with a nascent church authority structure. The nominal positions of bishop and deacon already existed within the church during Paul's ministry, even if his reference to these roles – as in the letter to the Philippians – is to a general pastoral function rather than to specific offices. The churches founded by missionaries evidently appointed local clergy, who remained subject for a time to the authority of the travelling apostles and prophets. Yet the *Didache* reveals some of the tensions within the still fluid church congregations of the period. The sensibility is of a small local group looking with some apprehension to the outside. Those Christian authorities visiting the community – apostles, prophets and teachers – are greeted with as much suspicion as reverence. Fraudulent 'Christ-mongering' must have been rife for the *Didache* to devote so much space to arming the community with means of detecting it. Within this dynamic of inside and outside, local ministry and mobile charismatics, it is possible to glean something of the fate of the apostles and prophets within the developing church.

The first issue relates to the apostles, who were the founding authorities of the early church, but who barely figure in church documents even in the second century.[15] The *Didache* accords them honourable status in Chapter 11, but after that point they disappear from the text, which is concerned only with prophets, teachers, bishops and deacons. Even when they are mentioned, it is with a restricted enthusiasm: the community is directed to permit apostles to stay for only one day, a maximum of two, before they are sent on the way with nothing more than bread. Such a short visit would curtail, if not eliminate, the preaching role of the apostles, reducing their function to little more than roving ambassador.

There is a startling contrast between the pre-eminent role – complete with spectacular charismatic powers – accorded to the apostles in Acts and by Paul, and the diminished function evident in the *Didache*. The perception may have been that the foundational role of apostles was no longer needed once a community was established. Another factor seems to have been the irritation of charlatans masquerading as apostles. Historical events also overtook the function of apostle. The early missionaries such as Paul set out from the mother-church in Jerusalem carrying authorisation of their mission. The destruction of Jerusalem in 70, following a four-year war waged against Jewish nationalists by the Romans, removed this source of authority, effectively rendering the office of apostle obsolete.

If we accept that the *Didache* was composed over a period of years, we may reasonably trace the demise of the apostle function in the text. The brief instruction regarding apostles reflects a time when they were still arriving at the community – but even then they were to be granted only limited welcome and could not receive money for their mission. For Jonathan Draper, these instructions 'sound the death knoll' for the apostle, emasculating the 'prestigious charismatic office' to that of a barely tolerated visitor.[16] The sections of text on church offices, in which apostles are not mentioned at all, were probably composed at a later date (Patterson suggests late in the first century or even early second), reflecting a time when apostles have stopped coming and 'apostilicity would have long since passed from the scene'.[17] Apostles did not disappear entirely: wandering missionaries took the Christian message to the East, where they are noted in the second and third centuries in Palestine and Syria.[18] But they pass from view almost entirely in the West by the early second century, their usefulness and influence exhausted. Certainly when the *Didache* offers instructions on wandering charismatics, it is concerned not with apostles but with prophets.

The lifestyle of the prophet is evident from the *Didache*: homeless, itinerant, penniless. There are also hints concerning the prophets' unconventional behaviour and appearance. The *Didache* exalts true prophets as 'high priests', instructing the community not to test or judge a prophet when he 'speaks in spirit'. The prophets' ecstatic utterances could be channelled into the eucharist rite, at which the prophets were allowed free rein; this suggests that the charismatic prayers lasted as long as divine inspiration possessed the prophet. It is likely that a significant portion of the prophets' declamations were eschatological, given the temper of the *Didache*, as well as the text's association of these contemporary prophets with the 'ancient' or Old Testament prophets.

Even the eucharist ritual phrases prescribed in Chapter 10 are redolent of the End of Days and the second coming:

> May grace [charis] come, and may this world pass by ...
> Our Lord, come! Amen.
>
> (10: 6)

The prophets, in the tradition of their Old Testament forbears, may have expanded on the theme of the impending Kingdom of God within their thanksgiving prayers, with a greater intensity than practised by the rest of the community.

The charismatic powers of the true prophet are highly valued and unquestioned in the *Didache*, but the text also provides some clues as to the decline of prophets within the Christian church. The prophets come from elsewhere, imbued with a charismatic ability; but the community makes no provision to train or produce new prophets. Indeed, it is understood that the innate charisma cannot be passed on:

> No prophet ... who does not teach [others] to do everything that he himself does, shall be judged by you, for his judgement is with God.
>
> (11: 11)

Furthermore, prophets – unlike apostles – are to be welcomed and provided for if they choose to settle in the community. Prophets, then, could choose to abandon the itinerant life, with its hardships and suffering, and live in a community where they are privileged as high priests and awarded the first-fruits of produce. We can assume that this opportunity was taken up by more than a few prophets.

When a prophet ceases to wander, his lifestyle changes, as does his social function. There is no suffering in isolation, no hunger, no visions generated from ordeal; he no longer makes a vivid impression when he wanders in to new communities. Living as a settled member of a community, even his charismatic prayers would come to conform to the structured pattern of rites. As more time passes, and the prophesied End of Days does not arrive, apocalyptic fervour would subside, replaced by the repetitive comforts of orthodox ritual. It is unlikely that the composers of the *Didache* intended the taming of prophets as one of the consequences of their instructions: there is evident respect for their charismatic powers. Yet the prophets' domestication meant that the *Didache* community 'appears to attract, absorb, and in the end dissolve the prophetic spirit itself'.[19]

The prophets' demise is closely related to the changing status of the locally appointed ministry. The office of bishop in the very early church did not enjoy the prestige it would later acquire: bishops were leaders or elders of the local community in a role probably modelled on the synagogue. Deacons performed the role of assistant or administrator. The initial function of these positions is reflected in the words' etymologies: 'bishop' literally meant 'overseer' or 'shepherd'; 'deacon' was literally 'servant'.[20] Since there is no mention in the *Didache* of bishops speaking 'in spirit' or prophecy, it is reasonable to infer a distinction between charismatic and non-charismatic leadership within the community.[21] Indeed, it is recommended that 'mild tempered' and dependable locals be appointed bishops; they are not expected to attain the fervent abandon achieved by the prophets. The exhortation to the community to trust and respect their own appointed clergy seems in part to have derived from a need to build local authority as a reliable base for the church, thus lessening the need to depend on travelling prophets who may or may not be genuine. While the authors of the *Didache* may have been concerned at the lack of respect accorded to the bishops and deacons, it did not take long for the bishops to overtake the prophets as central authority figures within the church.

Oral to literate

This shift of power coincides with the transition from an oral transmission of the Christian message to the establishment of authoritative written texts. The very early Christian communities had little or nothing in the way of Christian texts (even Paul's epistles were read aloud to congregations). The diverse charismata described by Paul functioned in this oral environment: individuals prophesied, spoke in tongues, interpreted prophecies, taught the Christian message, performed miracles. None of these spiritual gifts was associated with written texts; each was performative and depended on an immediate audience. As Draper remarks, a predominantly oral culture affords 'the charismatic, oral performer immense power'.[22] The prophets, as described in the *Didache*, are master oral performers: spellbinding speakers offering visionary declamation in an inspired state. They are like the 'ancient prophets' presumably because they preach the coming of the Kingdom of God, but also because they are skilled exponents of an oral tradition which they are able to adapt to new circumstances.[23] The *Didache* testifies to their spiritual authority and the respect they command in a predominantly oral culture, where training in the Christian ways has been delivered by spoken means.[24]

But the very existence of the *Didache* as a written text testifies to a significant change. When the prayers and instructions within the *Didache* were committed to literary form, the first step was taken in this community to establish a written canon. Written texts differ profoundly from oral delivery, generating new organisations of knowledge with new emphases. The performative mode of the prophet entails improvisation, as the individual speaker inflects the material in idiosyncratic ways. Indeed, the intensity expected of prophets in their ecstatic state must have permitted marked variations on the narrative material, drawn from the oral account of Jesus, the predictions of the End of Days and ancient prophecies. Oral performance allows for the injection of the teller into the tale. Information encoded in literate form allows for no such variation. When a text is accepted as definitive, it does not change. A document is fixed; the teachings within it become accepted as doctrine. The custodians of this literate mode practise interpretation of the text rather than the creative improvisation of the prophets. Part of this custodial role entails judging of texts for their authenticity and value: the fixing of the canon itself. Another is determining and promulgating the orthodox interpretation of texts. Once scriptures have become canonised, another step away from charismatic revelation has been taken: further revelation is not necessary, as the history of God's revelation to humanity is now enshrined in the authorised scriptures.

In its final instruction before the apocalyptic conclusion, the *Didache* alludes to the literalisation of Christian teaching: 'Perform your prayers and your almsgiving and all that you undertake as you have it [written] in the gospel of our Lord' (15: 4).[25] The accumulation of the four Gospels as a corpus of written Christian works gathered pace from the end of the first century. This corpus became the centre of Christian knowledge, replacing the oral performances of the prophets. Prophets are eclipsed as spiritual custodians by those better placed to preserve and interpret the textual tradition: bishops and deacons.[26] Before long, in a church increasingly aligned to its newly developed literature, there is no role left at all for the prophets. Their charisma has become redundant.

'Prophet-Bishops': Church office in the early second century

As the prophets either settled down or declined in influence, the bishops' authority within the church rose. This process can be gleaned from several letters written by bishops around 100. In approximately 96, the church at Corinth – which had troubled Paul almost half a century earlier – again proved volatile by ejecting its clergy and replacing them with new leaders. In response, Clement of Rome wrote a long counselling letter to the Corinthians. Clement is recorded elsewhere as the fourth bishop of Rome,[27] although he does not refer to himself with that title. In describing the church leaders at Corinth, he uses the term presbyter – literally 'elder' – as synonymous with bishop; presumably church leadership at the time comprised a number of presbyters or bishops. The hierarchy observed by the Romans of Clement's time is, therefore, still the basic structure described in the *Didache*: bishop or presbyter, supported by deacon. Clement's letter also reveals a stage in another transition: the development of Christian literature. He quotes copiously from the Old Testament, and refers to the letters of Paul, including Corinthians; yet his knowledge of Christ's own message seems to derive from the oral Gospel tradition, as there is no quotation from the written Gospels.

Clement's letter is a plea for harmony within the congregation, to heal the 'odious and unholy breach of unity' provoked by 'a few hot-headed and unruly individuals' (Ch 1).[28] Clement implores the Corinthians to overcome their discord by treating each other with mildness, kindliness and humility, avoiding the 'glorification of self' (Ch 35) that can incite enmity. In this, as in several other respects, Clement's letter to the Corinthians echoes Paul's. Where it differs is in its entreaty to respect the office of bishop, which is held to be divinely sanctioned. In Chapter 42, Clement delineates the sacred authority: 'Christ received His commission from God, and the Apostles theirs from Christ'. The apostles then set out on their mission, appointing those converts successfully tested 'by the Spirit' to be 'bishops and deacons for the believers of the future'. Clement can then decree that due to this divine line of command, opposition to God's ministers is 'impious'. He concludes by enjoining the rebels in Corinth to 'accept correction' and learn to 'subordinate' themselves before their leaders (Ch 57).

The pious and obedient community advocated by Clement does not appear to leave provision for the supernatural charismatic gifts as articulated by Paul. Clement briefly mentions prophecy in Chapter 17, yet in a manner tailored to fit his general theme of humility. According to Clement, the Old Testament prophets were humble before God; even Moses 'never indulged in high-flown speeches' but saw himself as an unworthy vessel of the divine: 'I am but smoke from a pot'. Clement's characterisation of the prophetic function is far removed from the feats of the wandering charismatics afforded such respect in the *Didache*.

When Clement praises the 'marvellous' gifts of God in Chapter 35, he refers to immortal life, righteousness, faith and chastity. To attain these gifts, individuals must renounce their wickedness, including greed and promotion of self.

In Chapter 38, Clement makes specific mention of 'spiritual gifts' (charismata) in a passage strongly reminiscent of Paul. The Corinthians are urged to think of themselves as parts of one large body, each with its own contribution to the whole: 'with each of us giving way to his neighbour in proportion to our spiritual gifts'. Yet these spiritual gifts are decidedly mundane: the strong and the weak should respect each other, as should the rich and poor; a wise man should act wisely; a modest man should not speak of himself; a chaste person should not boast of chastity, because 'the ability to control his desires has been given him by Another'. There is no mention of the miraculous gifts outlined by Paul in 1 Corinthians: for Clement, spiritual gifts have value only if they further his programme of humility and righteous behaviour.

Clement's epistle was representative of more than his own views: it was addressed to the Corinthians from 'the Church of God at Rome'. It embodied a successful strategy to curb dissent within Christian communities by underlining the divine authority of the church ministry. Within this ministry, there is no role for charismatic powers. 'High-flown speeches' of prophetic intensity are to be avoided. The spiritual gifts bestowed on community members are modest traits to be employed modestly: there is nothing remotely supernatural about them. Any more potent or grand a gift is likely, in Clement's judgement, to induce 'glorification of self' and is therefore not to be encouraged. Even Paul had cautioned the Corinthians that the gift of glossolalia was potentially divisive, and had relegated it to the bottom of the charisma hierarchy as a precaution. Clement's letter repeats Paul's warnings against divisiveness, but adds a sub-Apostolic reverence for the church ministry. The bishops have succeeded the apostles as divinely sanctioned officers of authority. With this spiritual regime in place, Clement can afford to omit altogether the function of prophet and the diverse spiritual gifts described by Paul.

The slightly later letters of Ignatius, Bishop of Antioch (died some time before 117), offer further perspective on this transitional period. Ignatius was condemned under the reign of Emperor Trajan and transported to Rome where he was to be executed. On this journey, he wrote letters to the congregations of seven churches, in which he enthusiastically anticipated his martyrdom. The letters reveal a further stage in the development of the church ministry: Ignatius refers to a three-tiered hierarchy of church office, in which a single bishop presides over a number of presbyters, while deacons provide assistance. This extended hierarchy strengthened the role of bishop; indeed, Ignatius's letters repeatedly place the bishop at the very centre of the church. He directs the Ephesians to 'regard the bishop as the Lord himself' (Ephesians 6);[29] to the Magnesians he orders that the bishop should be 'set over you in the place of God' (Magnesians 6), and condemns as invalid a dissident faction meeting without a bishop. In his letter to the Smyrnaeans, the word 'catholic' (meaning whole or universal) is applied for the first time to the Church: 'Wherever the bishop appears, there let the congregation be; just as wherever Jesus Christ is, there is the whole [catholic] church' (Smyrnaeans 8: 2). Ignatius emphasises – as had Paul and Clement – the need for harmony within the congregation, but privileges the bishop as indispensable to this concord. His plea for harmony is mediated through the agency of bishop: 'your worthily reputed presbytery', he tells the Ephesians, 'is attuned to the bishop like strings to a cithara' (4: 1). To dispute this arrangement is to violate the community's harmonious functioning.

Ignatius's advocacy of the bishop as lynchpin of the church is insistent and unvarying throughout his letters. He makes no mention of prophets or apostles except as historical figures: the presbyters are to assume 'the place of the council of apostles' within church services (Magnesians 6). When Ignatius refers to prophets, they are always of the Old Testament variety, inspired individuals who served as prelude to the coming of Christ. Indeed, Ignatius gives the impression that the ancient prophets were fulfilled only through Christ. 'For the most divine prophets lived according to Jesus Christ', he tells the Magnesians (8: 1); the prophets 'were disciples in the spirit, him to whom they looked forward as their teacher' (9: 2).

If Ignatius consigns the prophets to the pre-Christian past, the charismatic function is not entirely occluded in his letters. He writes of inspired utterance – as practised by himself. In his letter to the Philadelphians, Ignatius justifies his outburst at a previous meeting with them as prompted by the Spirit:

> [T]he Spirit, which is from God, is not deceived; for it knows whence it comes and whither it goes, and it exposes hidden things. I cried out while among you, I spoke with a loud voice – the voice of God: 'Attend to the bishop and the presbytery and the deacons'.
>
> (7: 1)

Ignatius has appropriated the prophetic function to himself in his role of bishop. He speaks in Spirit, unpredictably, as had the prophets of the *Didache* community or the prophets recounted in Acts and Paul. His inspired utterance is to be understood as the divine voice speaking through him – yet the content of this particular outburst is markedly prosaic. It is, indeed, the constant refrain of obedience to ministry found throughout Ignatius's letters. The charismatic gift of prophecy is now in the hands of bishops, who – at least in this instance – deploy it to support the ministry, and their pre-eminent role within the hierarchy. Ignatius describes his divine revelations in other letters: to the Ephesians, he promises 'explanation of the divine plan ... particularly if the Lord reveals anything to me' (20: 1–2). Kydd, following other scholars, finds ample evidence in these letters that Ignatius considered himself a 'prophet-bishop'.[30]

Ignatius uses the term 'charisma' in two places. To the Ephesians, he addresses the question: 'Why do we foolishly perish, being ignorant of the gift [charisma] which the Lord has truly sent?' (17: 2). Ignatius's letter to Polycarp, a fellow bishop, is more revealing in its exhortation: 'ask that things unseen be revealed, so that you may lack nothing and abound in every gift [charisma]' (2: 2). This address echoes Paul's encouragement of the Corinthians to desire the spiritual gifts, especially the higher ones; yet in this context, the encouragement is of a bishop by a fellow bishop. Kydd remarks that Ignatius's letters, addressing a large geographical area, indicate that spiritual gifts were familiar to Christians in Syria and Asia Minor.[31] The other significant factor emerging from the letters is that when Ignatius refers to the charismatic abilities – especially prophecy – it is with regard to his own possession of this gift, or as encouragement to a colleague to become a prophet-bishop.

As for the other charismatic abilities, Ignatius, like Clement before him, prefers to emphasise not individual gifts of God's grace, but the divine Grace residing in the sacraments of the church itself. For Ignatius, the divine spirit infuses the office of bishop; therefore, Christian communities are suffused with God's grace if they observe the central authority of the bishop. Ignatius's writings reflect the shift in the church in the early second century, whereby spiritual power is invested in the office of bishop and, to a lesser extent, in the supporting positions of church office. This investiture comes at the expense of the Pauline notion of the dispersal of spiritual gifts throughout the Christian community. If prophecy were to endure in any form within the church, it was according to the model embodied by Ignatius: safeguarded within the person of the authorised bishop.

The persistence of charismatic prophecy: The Montanist crisis

Yet if the church was moving to cement a centralised and formal authority, the more widespread charismatic spiritual expression was not entirely lost. There is evidence that the charismata as defined by Paul were still known and appreciated, at least in some quarters, in the middle of the second century. The philosopher Justin Martyr, who was a Christian apologist in Rome and was martyred in the 160s, referred to contemporary Christians receiving gifts. In a passage on converts from Judaism, he notes that some of these 'are also receiving gifts'. He then provides a short list of these gifts, in a passage echoing 1 Corinthians 12:

> For one receives the spirit of understanding, another of counsel, another of strength, another of healing, another of foreknowledge, another of teaching, and another of the fear of God.
>
> (Dialogue Chapter 39)[32]

This list, like that provided by Paul, mingles supernatural powers – healing, foreknowledge – with more mundane abilities – counsel, teaching; Justin adds gifts not found in Paul: strength, fear of God. The most revealing line in this text, however, comes later, when Justin declares: 'For the prophetical gifts [*prophetika charismata*] remain with us, even to the present time' (Ch 82). He later confirms this observation: 'It is possible to see amongst us women and men who possess gifts of the Spirit of God' (Ch 87). Justin's account of the Christian worship he experienced in Rome is considered reliable by modern scholars;[33] his remarks indicate that the Pauline charismata survived as part of worship – at least in the Roman church as experienced by Justin – in the middle of the second century.

In the second half of that century, the 'prophetical gifts' mentioned by Justin Martyr assumed a central place in a turbulent – and defining – dispute within Christianity. From the 170s, virulent debate was waged on the relative merits of direct inspired utterance and the developing church orthodoxy. Was the church to remain true to its origins in the Apostolic age, valuing the spiritual gifts bestowed on individuals in the Pauline manner? Or was it to become a rigid apparatus, heavily codified in doctrine, and hierarchical in its veneration of the bishops? The focal point of this debate was the Montanist crisis of the 170s.

Montanus of Phyrigia and two women, Prisca and Maximilla, delivered prophecies in an ecstatic state, predicting the imminent second coming in Phyrigia. Their supporters, known as Montanists, claimed that the three prophets were directly inspired by the Holy Spirit and that to reject them was blasphemous. Montansim has been characterised as a 'prophetic renewal movement informed by the Holy Spirit';[34] its emphasis on direct inspiration touching individuals connected it more closely with the charisma described by Paul than with the institutionalised church. The Montanism movement was both charismatic and ascetic; the image we have of it, derived largely from the theologian Tertullian, is of a revivalist movement, accentuating ecstatic utterance and spiritual infusion, while practising a rather austere form of purism. Montanists claimed direct inspiration not from bishops or the church, but from the Paraclete (a term for the Holy Spirit used in the Gospel of John). The emphasis on the Spirit and spiritual gifts could claim affinity with the teaching of Paul; but in the late second century, such an emphasis antagonised the orthodox church and its authority figures: the bishops. Indeed, the Montanists' belief in direct spiritual visitation rejected the authority of bishops. The church initially vacillated on this issue, yet its eventual response articulated an orthodoxy that would be refined in opposition to a succession of heresies.

The church valued uniformity of creed, which it upheld against the divisiveness of the Montanists and the many Gnostic sects. In rejecting the alternatives suggested by the 'New Prophecy' of Montanism, the leading Christian theologians propounded a doctrine that moved beyond the Pauline notion of charisma. More specifically, the orthodox view absorbed a general concept of the spiritual gift, while marginalising the specific and diverse charismata described by Paul. The Montanists' claim of direct authorisation by the Spirit intensified the resolve of the orthodox theologians to defend their position. One element of this defence was the establishment of a definitive set of scriptures, or New Testament canon. Irenaeus (c. 130–202), Bishop of Lyons, asserted a canon which corresponds to the accepted New Testament (although it was not formally approved by the church until the fourth century). In his *Against Heresies*, a work in five books written in Latin over a number of years around 180, Irenaeus expounds the first large-scale and systematic treatise of Christian theology.[35] His twin defences for the church against all heresies are the authority of the scriptures and the unbroken power of church tradition. Irenaeus is resolute regarding the scriptures, which he considers 'perfect' and 'the ground and pillar of our faith' (*Against Heresies* 2.28.2 and 3.1.1).[36] Irenaeus quotes or uses every New Testament book except three minor epistles: he holds all these texts as divinely inspired, therefore without error and speaking the Word of God.

The benefit of a fixed canon for the defenders of the orthodox faith was that religious observation now became a matter of interpretation of authoritative texts, rather than the eliciting of direct visitation from the Spirit. A closed canon implies that no documents after a certain date may be accepted as divinely inspired. In addition, the role of the bishop as interpreter of God's word, as deposited in the canon of scriptures, is enhanced. The contemporary role of prophecy, and other divine inspiration, is correspondingly diminished. If the New Testament was the official account of Jesus as foretold by the ancient prophets, there is no purpose to further prophecies. The interpretation of scripture in religious service becomes a matter of reinforcement of doctrine, rather than one of surprise or novel spiritual developments.

Irenaeus treated Christian tradition as an even greater source of authority than scripture. Although scripture is divine, heretics may assert that its meaning is ambiguous, requiring interpretation (3.2.1). Irenaeus argues that scripture is ultimately dependent on the doctrine of the church, which is supported by the power of tradition. He defines a very strict lineage of Christian tradition and power, designed to eliminate as heretical any alternative interpretation. Tradition is first derived from the apostles, who were 'invested with power from on high when the Holy Spirit came down [upon them]', delivering them 'perfect knowledge' (3.1.1). From this divine authority flows a succession of bishops instituted by apostles and continuing 'to our own times' (3.3.1). This means that every church in the world teaches the same doctrine built on the same foundations:

> [T]he church throughout all the world, having its origins firm from the apostles, perseveres in one and the same opinion with regard to God and His Son.
>
> (3.7)

Irenaeus adds another source of authority, 'the universally known church founded and organised at Rome by the two most glorious apostles'. For Irenaeus,

> It is a matter of necessity that every church should agree with this church, on account of its pre-eminent authority.
>
> (3.3.2)

The church at Rome had assumed a more commanding position following the complete destruction of Jerusalem by the Roman Empire in 135; Irenaeus entrenches its position by installing it at the centre of Christian doctrine and authority.

Irenaeus does not condemn charismatic gifts as heretical; he refers to the charisma of prophecy, transliterated into Latin as *'propheticis ... charismatibus'* (3.11.9). He acknowledges the existence of 'prophetic gifts and speaking through the Spirit in all tongues' within the contemporary church (5.6.1), and accepts Paul's view that such 'spiritual' individuals use their gifts within the congregation for the 'common good'.[37] Irenaeus also refers to *charisma veritatis*, or the divine gift of knowledge.[38] But he rejects the Montanists as 'wretched men indeed' because they have chosen to operate outside the universal church. He disparages them as 'pseudo-prophets' because they 'set aside the gift of prophecy from the church' (3.11.9). Irenaeus uses Paul's letter to the Corinthians – potentially a support for the unorthodox celebration of spiritual power – against the Montanists. He notes that in 1 Corinthians Paul 'speaks expressly of prophetical gifts, and recognises men and women prophesying in the church'. The argument is that Paul inscribed prophecy within the church; therefore, for the Montanists to acclaim prophecy only outside the church must mean that 'they cannot admit the Apostle Paul'. Irenaeus's core case against Montanism and all other heresies is that the church is the only repository of spiritual grace and power, and that to prophesy or preach outside this institution is to abandon Christian authority. For Irenaeus, the Montanists' sin is to 'hold themselves aloof from the communion of the brethren' (3.11.9): to refuse the sacraments of the church, and its doctrine, is to refuse Christianity itself. Irenaeus is adamant that spiritual power is not to be found in contemporary charismatics and 'pseudo-prophets' but within the edifice of the church.

Hippolytus (170–235), Bishop of Rome and a follower of Ireneaus, included in his 'Doctrine of Truth', with which he concludes his *Refutation of All Heresies*, the observation that the time for prophets has passed. For Hippolytus, the ancient prophets received their gifts from the Logos of God, so that their words were 'uttered by divine power'. But God then incarnated the Logos in the form of Jesus, which for Hippolytus superseded the function of prophets. The Logos need no longer 'speak by a prophet', which had entailed the disadvantage of being 'obscurely proclaimed' and becoming 'the subject of mere conjecture' (*Refutation* Bk X Chapter 29).[39] The consequence of Hippolytus's theological writings is the elevation of the supreme Gift of conversion above the quest for miraculous gifts.[40]

Charisma becomes abstracted in the theology of Irenaeus and of Hippolytus: every Christian has access to the gifts of Spirit. For Irenaeus, the 'gift of God has been entrusted to the church ... that all the members receiving it may be vivified'. The Holy Spirit is 'distributed' through the church, so that the Spirit 'and every kind of grace' are synonymous with the church itself (3.24.1). It is therefore unnecessary to indulge in ecstatic utterance, prophecy or miracle-working; indeed these supernatural practices can induce pride or generate division within the congregation. For Hippolytus, the Spirit pervades the church sacraments and ministry, as supervised by the bishops. The charismata are superfluous, even dangerous, given that the supreme charisma is generalised within the church and is available to all Christians through the normal rituals of devotion.

Charisma inside and outside the church: Tertullian

If this had become the orthodox perspective by the end of the second century, it was by no means uncontested. One vociferous critic of the orthodoxy was Tertullian (160–220), Bishop of Carthage. Tertullian followed Irenaeus in many respects, vigorously defending the church against Gnostic heresies. Like Iranaeus, he did not dispute the existence of spiritual gifts; in the early phase of his career, he asserted that those gifts could only be realised within the church. In his work *Against Marcion* (c. 200, concerning the heretic Marcion), Tertullian refers to those 'free gifts [*donativa*] which we call *charismata*' (5. 8.5).[41] Tertullian has preserved the Pauline term charismata, transliterated into Latin, to refer to the spiritual gifts experienced within the church. The Latin *donum* (gift) presumably lacks the weight in Tertullian's eyes to convey the force of charisma, hence his use of *donativum*. This word designated the sum of money given by the Roman emperor to soldiers at a time of public rejoicing, such as the emperor's accession. Tertullian lists those gifts (*dona*) that Marcion claims issue from 'his god': prophecy, visions, tongues, interpretation of tongues. Tertullian counters that 'all such proofs are more readily put in evidence by me': that is, from within the church to which Tertullian belongs, 'in full accord with the rules and ordinances and regulations of the Creator' (5.8.12).

In a slightly later work, Tertullian honours two martyrs, Perpetua and Felicitas, by noting their prophetic and visionary powers. He adds:

> We also regard the rest of the powers of the Holy Spirit as tools of the Church to whom the Spirit was sent, administering all of the outstandingly impressive gifts [*donativa*] to everyone just as the Lord distributes to each.
>
> (*Passio S. Perpetuae*, 1)[42]

The 'distribution' of gifts echoes the list of assorted charismata in 1 Corinthians 12; Tertullian evidently strongly believed in the persistence of these gifts as 'tools' of the church. He again uses the word *donativa*, translated by Kydd as 'outstandingly impressive gifts', to emphasise their exalted character.

Yet in later life Tertullian supported the Montanists, and quarrelled sharply with the church as a result. While he accepted the right of bishops to administer Christian rites such as baptism, he was outspokenly critical of bishops who based their authority solely on their office, rather than on their spiritual qualities and resolve. Tertullian revived the opposition between Spirit and Law which had animated Pauline theology a century and a half earlier. He asserted this perspective most forcefully in *De pudicitia* (translated as 'On Modesty' or 'On Purity') written after his break from the church in 212, when he allied himself with the Montanists.

This treatise was triggered by an edict that the church would pardon serious sins, issued by an authority derided by Tertullian as 'bishop of bishops' (thought to be either the bishop of Rome or of Carthage). Tertullian, as puritanical as he is vitriolic, condemns this ruling as a violation of Christian purity; he extends his critique to a rejection of the authority of the bishops themselves. He builds his argument by referring to the apostles, who, he declares, derived their authority not from the doctrine or teaching they received from God, but from the divine power (*potestas*) bestowed on them:

> Doctrine gives direction to a man; power marks him out with a special character. The power of the Spirit is a thing apart, for the Spirit is God.
>
> (Ch 21)[43]

According to Tertullian, doctrine is a body of teaching transmitted by the apostles to their successors in the church: the bishops. But power of the Spirit is a charisma – imbuing 'a special character' – which is non-transferable. It cannot be transmitted through the office of bishop or through the institution of the church. Tertullian emphasises this distinction by addressing a contemporary church leader, mockingly:

> Now then, apostolic man, show me samples of your prophetic works so that I may recognise your divine authorization: after this, claim for yourself the power to forgive such sins. If, however, you

have been entrusted with no office beyond that of teaching moral doctrine ... then who do you think you are ...? ... You show yourself neither prophet nor apostle; therefore you lack the power in virtue of which pardon is granted.

(21)

Tertullian here wilfully breaks the structure founded on the succession of bishops, which had been carefully constructed by theologians from Ignatius to Irenaeus. He even questions the authority of the church as an institution, if it has come to neglect the Spirit. Resuming his one-sided dialogue with the orthodox church-man, he adds:

'But the Church', you say, 'has power to forgive sins'. I know this better than you do and I regulate it better, because I have the Paraclete Himself saying in the person of the new prophets.

(21)

This refers to the oracles of the Montanist prophets, considered by followers to be a direct communication of the Spirit, and equal in status to the holy scriptures. In Tertullian's view, the church has erred drastically in rejecting the new prophecy, leaving itself potentially bereft of spirit. For Tertullian, the church proper does not consist 'of a number of bishops'; it is rather 'the Spirit Himself'. Power belongs not to the institution and those at the top of its hierarchy, but 'to those who have the Spirit – to an apostle or a prophet'.

Tertullian does not consign prophecy and other charismatic gifts to the past: he recognises the new prophecy and other current manifestations of the spirit. Tertullian uses the Latin term *charismatici* to designate those in the church empowered by the Spirit with special gifts.[44] It is clear from this text that Tertullian does not expect charismatic power to be vested in the bishops. Such power is invested in the contemporary prophets and other spiritually blessed leaders. Accordingly, Tertullian decrees that

from this time on, any number of persons at all joined in this faith, is recognised as the Church by Him who founded and consecrated it [the Spirit].

This edict justifies, for Tertullian, not only the Montanist movement, but other unorthodox sects claiming the authority of the Spirit. In his view, the true church is above all a spiritual entity. In a final barb at the

Catholic church, he declares that the right to make theological decrees 'belongs to God Himself, not to a priest'.

As a Montanist heretic, Tertullian lived the last years of his life outside the Catholic church; as a result, he was never canonised, despite the enduring influence on Christian theology of his earlier writings. There is evidence that he split from the Montanists to form his own sect, thus following his own decree that any number of persons should be recognised by the Spirit as a church.[45] The dispute over the Montanist prophecies remained divisive for some time, especially in Asia Minor. Montanist churches and sects survived near the Phyrigian base for a century, before the movement faded away. The 'Tertullianistae' sect lasted until the early fifth century before passing back into the Catholic church. Tertullian declared that the church had betrayed its charismatic origins and become an unspiritual league of bishops – yet his fiery critique was marginalised. It in no way deflected the church from the orthodox position it had painstakingly built.

The church had built a structure to facilitate the propagation of a uniform doctrine, replacing the variety and division characterising the more turbulent ministry of the first century. Alternative approaches such as Montanism carried with them the potential for volatility and confusion, evident even in Tertullian's acceptance then rejection of the heresy. William Le Saint observes that Tertullian's Montanist argument in *De pudicita* imposes a sharp division within the church, between charismatic and non-charismatic members. The bishops, representing the hierarchical church, would be authorised only to teach, while those endowed with charismatic gifts would have the greater spiritual authority to pardon sins. This dichotomy thus 'subverts all effective ecclesiastical government, breeds heresy and schism, and gives over to enthusiasts one of the most important responsibilities of the episcopal order'.[46] It is not surprising, then, that the bishops dismissed Tertullian's charge, and that the Montanist doctrine found expression not in the Catholic church but in smaller and much shorter-lived gatherings.

Montanism represented one front in the conflict between charismatic spiritual power and the authority of the formal church; this particular contest between prophets and bishops was won by the officers of the church. For a sharper insight into the fate of Paul's theology – including his concept of charisma – within the orthodox doctrine, we need to consider the major theological battleground of the second and third centuries: the controversy surrounding Gnosticism.

Spirit versus church: The Gnostic heresies

Gnostics privileged *gnosis* or knowledge – understood as a special spiritual knowledge – above all other considerations. Gnosticism is an ambiguous term, in that it refers both to a diversity of specific Christian sects practising from the second century and to a more general mystical pursuit that includes non-Christian belief systems. Scholarly opinion is divided as to whether Gnosticism existed in any developed form prior to Christianity, although there is no doubt that several of its constitutive elements – Platonism, the mystery religions, astrology and other magical systems, earlier religions such as Zoroastrianism, and Judaism – pre-date the Christian period.[47] The dissident groups confronted by Paul in Corinthians, Galatians and Colossians exhibited Gnostic tendencies, yet most scholars prefer to describe their largely unsystematic spirit-based beliefs as proto-Gnostic.[48]

The Gnostic cult that deeply troubled the Catholic church in the second century comprised a number of Christian Gnostic sects that accepted the outline of the Christian faith, but refigured that faith into a mystical, even occult, system. The Christian Gnostics taught that salvation entailed the special knowledge (*gnosis*) that would deliver 'spiritual' individuals from the material world to a purely spiritual plane. Gnosticism exercised a severe dualism, in which the earthly, bodily world was regarded as degenerate, impure and corrupt. The human soul was considered a divine spark imprisoned in this fallen material world. To its blending of a Platonic otherworldliness and Christian salvationism, Gnosticism added mystical ingredients and a fondness for elaborate mythological apparatus. In many Gnostic systems, the supreme divinity was remote, while a separate creator god or demiurge, often a malevolent deity, oversaw the flawed material world. Intermediate entities such as archons and aeons functioned within a complex structure, inside which select spiritually attuned humans strove to achieve their destiny. Within this structure, Jesus was regarded as a purely spiritual being.

Several leading Gnostic writers explicitly took Paul as their model for a theology based on Spirit: this was a significant factor in the eclipse of Pauline notions such as charisma in the second and third centuries. Paul's theology contained a strong mystical component, expressed in his insistence on the infusing power of Spirit, and in his relative lack of emphasis on church sacrament or structure. This mystical aspect was seized upon by Gnostic advocates of the Spirit, who, like Tertullian in his later years, found no satisfaction for their spiritual yearning in the institution of the church. The abiding principle of the many competing Christian Gnostic sects was that salvation could not be obtained from a simple obedience to church doctrine and sacrament. Rather, ascension to the spiritual plane depended on the revelation of gnosis to those elite spiritual beings capable of detecting it and receiving it. This revelation was attained through mystical instruments such as magic passwords, and through decoding Christian texts so as to disclose their true spiritual meaning. Paul's writings were pre-eminent in this regard for the Christian Gnostics.

The Gnostic writer Valentinus (c.100–160) claimed to have received special wisdom from a follower of Paul named Theudes. This esoteric knowledge was said to have been imparted by Paul to his inner circle, based on his visionary encounters with Jesus as spirit. Paul himself was thereby recruited as the authority for a mystical knowledge available only to spiritually advanced Christians. The Valentinians accepted Paul's tripartite division of the human into spirit, soul and body (1 Corinthians), adapting this structure to an elitist sectoring of humanity: ordinary 'earthly' people with no hope of salvation; members of the Catholic church, who were termed 'psychic', possessing faith but not knowledge; and the Gnostic few, who were preordained as spiritually superior and destined for salvation. In this and similar Gnostic accounts, the Catholic church and the Christian gospels are deemed nothing more than 'preparation for true gnosis'.[49] Valentinus possessed his own Gospel of Truth (uncovered only in 1945 as part of the Nag Hammadi collection) which decreed that the spiritual elect were 'perfect' and destined to return to 'the perfect light'.[50] The Pauline epistles were interpreted by Valentinians as supporting the separation of these spiritual initiates from the rest of humanity, including members of the church. Paul's reference to the firstfruit and lump received by Jesus in Romans 11: 16 was taken to refer to the spiritual elite as first-fruit and 'the members of the psychic church' as 'lump'.[51]

Marcion (c. 110–160) created even greater problems for the church, as his theology was not encumbered by Gnostic mythological machinery, and claimed to reveal the truth of the Gospels through an emphasis on Paul. A former bishop, Marcion developed a following that amounted to an alternative church. He claimed that Paul was the only apostle to have understood the spiritual significance of Jesus, and that Paul had written the only authentic Gospel, mistakenly attributed to Luke. Marcion's corpus of scriptures (the first canon of Christian texts) excluded the Old Testament and the other Gospels; his 'apostolicon' consisted of ten of Paul's letters and an edited Gospel of Luke. Marcion aimed to rescue

Paul's writings from their corruption at the hands of Judaisers, who, he claimed, had falsified Paul's texts to create a spurious connection between the Old Testament and the Gospel. Marcion's challenge to the orthodox church was not via a call to occult knowledge, but through a claim to disclose the 'pure gospel' as it had emanated from Paul.

In its battle with Valentinians, Marcionites and other varieties of Gnosticism, the church had in its favour the internecine bickering of the myriad Gnostic sects, each of which claimed the definitive secret knowledge. In his *Against Heresies*, Ireneaus devotes considerable space to describing various Gnostic doctrines, despite his contention that they propound 'absurd ideas'. (Almost all the Gnostic texts were destroyed: we depend on Ireneaus and other Christian theologians for our knowledge of second-century Gnosticism.) Ireneaus portrays the Gnostics as 'tossed about by every blast of doctrine', wallowing in error, 'thinking differently with regard to the same things at different times' (3.24.2). Against this flux of interpretations, he opposes the 'uniform teaching of the church, which remains so always, and is consistent with itself' (3.29).

The orthodox theologians devoted considerable intellectual energies to saving Paul from Gnostic interpretation. Ireneaus charged the Valentinians with perverting the scriptures in their 'wicked art' of misinterpretation (1.8.1), while Marcion had 'dared openly to mutilate the scriptures' (1.27.4). To refute the Marcionite conviction that Paul possessed special knowledge, Irenaeus quotes Paul himself on the authority of Peter and the other apostles (3.8.1). He also makes the practical observation that if Paul 'had known mysteries unrevealed to the other apostles', this would have been apparent to his constant travelling companion, Luke (3.14.1). Tertullian, in the phase of his career when he defended the church against heresies, contested with Marcion the ownership of Paul. Rejecting Marcion's claim of spiritual gifts in the name of Paul, Tertullian insisted that because the charismatic powers were still alive within the church, 'both Christ and the Spirit and the apostle will belong to my God' (*Against Marcion* 5.8.12).

The church repelled all versions of Gnostic belief, which it condemned as heretical. Rebel practitioners such as Marcion were excommunicated, while the church strengthened its orthodoxy as an unyielding alternative to the mystical strains of Gnosticism. Irenaeus established a canon of Christian scriptures partly in response to Marcion's formulation of his own Paul-centric corpus of writings. The orthodox bishops could reject alternative perspectives as heretical through recourse to an unchanging doctrine and official set of scriptures. Paul could thus be rescued from the grasp of the Gnostics: according to Irenaeus and the orthodox theologians who followed him, it took a perverse misreading of the scriptures to conscript Paul as the source of secret gnosis.

Yet Paul's theology suffered in the wake of this anti-heretical endeavour exercised by the church. The mystical, anti-legalistic aspect of his thought had proven appealing to an array of unorthodox sects. Paul had, after all, decreed that the Christian is saved by divine grace and not by scriptural law; the Gnostics fully exploited this antinomy between spirit and law in Pauline theology. The church responded by strengthening its status as an institutionalised authority, safeguarding the true Christian message within a monolithic doctrine and structure overseen by the bishops. The leading theologians defined Christian doctrine through reasoned argument, based on the official scriptures as an inscription of divine law. To be accepted as orthodox, any theological position had to be consistent with the scriptures and with the basic pattern of doctrine drawn from them. Although the charismata still preserved a place in the writing of theologians such as Irenaeus and Tertullian, that place shrank within church doctrine in the third century.

Cessation

How long did the charismata linger within the margins of the orthodox church? The writings of leading theologians Novitian, Cyprian and Origen provide accounts of the status of spiritual gifts in the middle of the third century, in Rome, Carthage and Greece respectively.

Novitian, an elder in the church at Rome, wrote around 240 of the spiritual gifts infusing the church. After recounting the gifts distributed to the first apostles, he shifts to the present tense, referring to the gifts still evident within the church:

> He ... places prophets in the Church, instructs teachers, directs tongues, gives powers and healings, does wonderful works, offers discrimination of spirits ... and orders and arranges whatever other gifts there are of charismata; and thus makes the Lord's Church everywhere, and in all, perfected and complete.
>
> (*On the Trinity* 29)[52]

Kydd and Forbes both contend that this is firm evidence of the survival of charismata until the 240s, at least as in the Roman church known to Novitian.[53] The list of charismata provided by Novitian corresponds closely with those given by Paul to the Corinthians and Romans.

Around the same time, charismatic activity was associated with Cyprian (died 258), bishop of Carthage and a follower of Tertullian. Letters to and by Cyprian refer to his prophetic abilities and the divine revelation visited to him in dreams and visions. Cyprian even acknowledged in one letter the scepticism within the church concerning such activity: 'And yet, I know that to some men dreams are seen to be ridiculous and visions silly'.[54] Cyprian's correspondence reveals that in mid-third-century North Africa, charismatic powers could still be connected to a leading figure of the church; it also discloses that such powers were doubted, even ridiculed, by elements within the church.

In the Greek East, the theologian Origen (died 255) was a defender of church doctrine who discussed spiritual gifts, comparing their current state with that of the Apostolic age. Since part of his ambition was to justify Christianity on intellectual grounds, Origen privileged 'intellectual gifts' (*logika charismata*) above other charismatic attributes.[55] In his work *Against Celsus*, he refers in four places to 'traces' of the Holy Spirit still evident in his time. In considering the 'demonstration of spirit and power' described by Paul, Origen remarks that 'traces of them still remain among those who live according to the will of the Logos' (*Against Celsus* 1, 2).[56] Origen traces a narrative of decline, stretching from the time of Jesus to his own time, concerning the strength and frequency of the Spirit's manifestation:

> But signs of the Holy Spirit were manifested at the beginning when Jesus was teaching, and after his ascension there were many more, though later they became less numerous. Nevertheless, even to this day there are traces of him in a few people whose souls have been purified by the Logos.
>
> (7, 8)[57]

Origen mentions prophecy, miracles, exorcism, healing and 'wonders' as remaining manifestations of the Spirit. Yet in his time they exist in vestigial form only: they are 'traces' of the original gifts, possessed only by a special 'few people'. The charismatic intensity within the church has dwindled drastically from the communal experience defined by Paul; the gifts may be glimpsed only in certain 'purified' individuals.

Surveying the evidence of Origen, Cyprian and Novitian, Kydd concludes that by the mid-third century, 'the tide of charismatic experience within the Church had ebbed considerably'.[58] While the Roman church as represented by Novitian seemed most familiar with charismata, the 'traces' of charisma discerned in the Greek church are 'sparse and shaky', at least as documented by Origen.[59] After 260, Kydd can find no evidence of charismatic experience within the church, at least up until the end of his survey at 320.[60]

Forbes, however, identifies scattered evidence in the fourth century, specifically concerning prophecy. Even after the repudiation of Montanist prophecy by the church in the late second century, prophecy lingered for some time as a spiritual gift recognised by the church. However, it was increasingly regarded as a gift available only to great saints and other individuals such as martyrs, of 'impeccable orthodoxy'.[61] If Hippolytus could announce at the end of the second century that prophecy was a phenomenon of the past, others disagreed, even into the fourth century. But pronouncements on the continuing experience of Christian prophecy could be met with the charge of heresy if they failed to meet standards of orthodoxy.

The most spectacular – and resounding – example of this concerned Priscillian, bishop of Avila in Spain from 381 to 385. Priscillian claimed that charismatic prophecy was still available to Christians. His faith was harshly ascetic and resolutely spiritual: he and his followers were celibate and vegetarian in order to more readily receive the charismatic gift of prophecy.[62] Following Paul in 1 Corinthians, who 'shuts the way to no one to speak about God',[63] Priscillian insisted that both men and women could receive the prophetic gift of inspired insight into scripture. Priscillian's theology mingled charismatic prophecy with number mysticism, astrology and departures from the orthodox doctrine, allowing his opponents to accuse him of occult practices. He was charged with heresy by the church and executed in 385 on the charge of sorcery, as decreed by Emperor Maximus. This act created a schism in the churches of Spain and Gaul; Priscillianism was outlawed by imperial decree in 407, but lingered as a heresy in the provinces through the fifth and sixth centuries.

There is one firm piece of literary evidence articulating the cessation of charismatic gifts within the church by the late fourth century. In his *Homilies* on 1 Corinthians, written 385–400, John Chrysostom states of 1 Cor 12, concerning the charismata:

> [T]his whole place is very obscure: but the obscurity is produced by our ignorance of the facts referred to and by their cessation, being such as they used to occur, but now no longer take place ... Why did they then happen, and now do so no more?
>
> (No. 29)[64]

At the very least, this passage indicates that the charismatic gifts were no longer practised in the time and place of John Chrysostom: late fourth-century Antioch or Constantinople. In the same passage, John counsels his readers on the means of dealing with their difficult times:

> [L]et us bear up and standing upon the rock, I mean of the divine doctrines and words, let us look down upon the surge of this present life.

Scripture and doctrine now provide the 'rock' for a theologian in the post-charismatic age. Forbes cautions that it is imprudent to generalise from this statement that all charismata had ceased throughout the Christian territory. He acknowledges, however, that there is no clear evidence of glossolalia within the church from the end of the fourth century,[65] while prophecy could always attract the suspicion of heresy.

Suppressed or simply forgotten?

In the middle of the first century, the Christian congregations founded by Paul experienced charisma as an integral part of their religion; every member of those communities was held to possess a charisma. By the middle of the third century, this experience has all but disappeared from the church; there are very few traces left of any charismatic expression at all. In this chapter we have traced the lineaments of this two-century process, identifying the major contributing factors. But the question remains: did the church actively suppress charisma as defined and celebrated by Paul? Or did charisma simply subside, made redundant by developments within the church that were not expressly antagonistic to the charismata themselves?

We can summarise the factors involved in the marginalisation of the charismatic gifts within the church. The concern over false prophets, as exhibited in the *Didache*, implied a recognition that ecstatic utterance could easily be simulated. If prophecy could be suspect, no doubt the other charismata of glossolalia, miracle-working and manifestations of ecstatic possession also came under suspicion: each could be fabricated by charlatans. Even if the divine inspiration were accepted as genuine, ecstatic utterance was often regarded – from Paul onwards – as divisive and problematic. By the early second century, the church had staked its future not on wandering prophets and charismatic individuals but on the office of bishop presiding over a hierarchical structure and a uniform set of rituals.

The transitional process that may be discerned in the late first and second centuries involves the replacement of the unregulated practices of the Apostolic age with a heavily regulated system of procedures ordained by the Church. Prophets are replaced by bishops; the notion of a divine inspiration infusing individuals on a seemingly random basis is replaced by the creed of a divinely sanctioned church, operating for the benefit of all. The transition from oral expression of faith to the veneration of sacred written texts was also highly significant. This process is indeed the master example of the routinisation of charisma, as delineated by Weber in the early twentieth century. Commenting on Ignatius's incorporation of prophetic gifts 'in the service of Episcopal authority', William Schoedel sees 'charisma ... in process of routinization'.[66] Tertullian's diatribe in *De pudicitia* is a last-ditch and passionate protest against the transfer of charisma from spiritual individuals to institutionalised office. Faced with the implacable authority of the church, Tertullian found it necessary to pursue a spiritual path elsewhere.

Several scholars of the period, however, have sounded qualifications concerning a simplistic judgement whereby the charismata are suppressed by an oppressive institutionalised church. Chadwick notes that the sub-Apostolic age was confronted with a wild divergence in practices and interpretations, and with disparate congregations founded according to missionary activity of sometimes dubious authority. The freedom of this period could in practice mean near-anarchy at times. The shift from the unstructured zeal of the missionary period to the formal church authority in place at the end of the second century was not necessarily the triumph of rigidity and 'clerical authoritarianism'. It may be noted that the installation of the three-tiered hierarchy of clergy in the second century was achieved without apparent resistance or controversy.[67]

Forbes resists any simple explanation for the demise of charismatic prophecy within the church. He identifies several pathways within the second century: prophecy in some instances became integrated within the Christian practice of worship, as reflected in the *Didache* and *The Shepherd* of Hermas; it was subsumed within the new church structures, as seen by those bishops who claimed prophetic abilities; it could remain in opposition to the institutionalised church and suffer suppression, as with the case of Montanism; or it could 'simply cease to be a common experience within Christianity'.[68] The overall question of causation is for Forbes elusive, due to insufficient evidence. Kydd similarly cautions about assuming a direct causal relationship between the rise of bishops and the disappearance of prophets. Kydd points out that none of the charismata became 'the exclusive preserve of bishops' and that the vanishing of the spiritual gifts should rather 'be understood as one part of the process of sophistication which the church experienced'.[69] His conclusion is that by the second half of the third century the charismata 'no longer fitted in the highly organized, well-educated, wealthy, socially-powerful Christian communities'.[70]

The charisma of prophecy is the gift with the highest profile in this transitional period, due in part to its central role in the Montanist crisis. If active suppression of the charismata did occur, it was by association with the spiritual pursuits identified as heretical by the church. Aune remarks that following the suppression of Montanism, prophets and their revelations were 'carefully controlled and held in low esteem or even rejected as heretical'.[71] This low esteem, amounting to ridicule, was noted in the mid-third century by Cyprian, from his eminent position of bishop. Apart from Montanism, various Gnostic sects operated a mystical system drawn in part from the anti-institutional component of Paul's thought. This association of Pauline spiritual gifts with heretical movements can only have cast the charismata in a negative light. As church membership became more educated and acquired, in Kydd's word, greater 'sophistication', the charismata could be regarded as an embarrassing relic of an earlier age.

One other contextual factor that should not be underestimated is the need of the early Christians to avoid persecution within the Roman Empire. Persecution, including execution, persisted until the fourth century; imprisonment and martyrdom was common in the first and second centuries. Paul himself was repeatedly imprisoned and physically punished, culminating in his execution ordered by Nero. The Roman authorities could at any time seize upon a civil disturbance involving Christians as a breach of public security.[72] The flavour of Rome's attitude towards the Christians can be gleaned from Roman writers. Seutonius described the Christians as a sect 'which had succumbed to a new superstition that was dangerous to the public'.[73] Tacitus, while recording that Nero fabricated charges against the Christians, nevertheless depicted them as 'notoriously depraved'. Christianity was for him a 'deadly superstition' that had broken out in Rome, one of the 'degraded and shameful practices' flourishing in the decadent capital.[74] Given this level of hostility, the Christian communities needed to avoid public disturbances; a degree of self-regulation – as advocated in the pleas for harmony by Paul, Clement and Ignatius – operated within the congregations. The more spectacular manifestations of charisma were curbed as a result of this voluntary regulation; over time, most of the charismatic functions faded from Christian worship.

Kydd remarks that as the church grew, the spiritual gifts 'just quietly slipped away',[75] as if their impact receded until they were forgotten. Certainly John Chrysostom's frank account at the end of the fourth century conveys such a state of forgetting: John is perplexed by the 'obscure' Pauline charismata. In the second and third centuries, the eclipse of charisma occurred due to a combination of the suppression of heresies and the rationalisation of the church. Ultimately it was a question of authority. Aune pinpoints this factor in the instance of charismatic prophecy. Whereas prophecy in the time of Paul was considered to have 'divine legitimation', the rationalisation of church structures in the second century left prophecy not only redundant but 'dysfunctional'.[76] The authority of prophets was assumed by new church offices: those of teacher, theologian, church leader. This was true not only for prophecy but for all the charismata. Communal authority in the Pauline model – distributed as charismata throughout the congregation – was replaced by the central authority of church institution and doctrine.

Within this church edifice, the more mystical components of Pauline theology – direct revelation, the charismata – could be dismissed as unnecessary. Charisma as an extraordinary spiritual ability was too mystical a concept, too closely aligned with magic, old-fashioned prophecy or dangerous abandon – in short too 'primitive' an idea – to be tolerated by the church. Christianity offered the fundamental spiritual gift – or charisma – of salvation, guaranteed by the mediating organisation of the church itself. According to this doctrine, no other charisma was needed.

5
Where Did Charisma Go?

The cessationist view expressed by John Chrysostom at the end of the fourth century – that the spiritual gifts were no longer evident, and that they were so obscure as to be foreign to contemporary Christianity – became the prevailing line within the church. Yet Paul's charismata had conveyed significant spiritual charge in the first century, which was not entirely dissipated in the second, and lingered into the third and even the fourth. While the church succeeded in curbing the supernatural charismata – along with other mystical tropes – by the fourth century, there remains the issue of that spiritual charge and its residue. Where did the energy and mysticism associated with Pauline charisma go?

One answer is that the spiritual power of charisma was subsumed into church orthodoxy, where it found expression in various officially sanctioned forms. Another is that the idea of charismatic abilities bestowed directly from the Holy Spirit – without mediation through the church – lived on, in an often subterranean existence. Over the centuries it broke out periodically inside and outside the institutionalised frame-work, associated with individual mystics or heretical pursuits. Holy men, healers, monks and prophets of varying description practised an unorthodox spirituality outside the domain of orthodoxy; at times their mystical orientation was exerted within the church, often prompting repression or expulsion.

In all these activities and beliefs, the word 'charisma' was rarely used in the Latin west, although it maintained some presence in the Greek east. If the extravagant spiritual gifts were sealed off as entities peculiar to the very early, 'primitive' church, then the word originally used to designate them – charisma – became largely inactive as well. If we are to trace from the fourth century the intermittent passage of the belief in spiritual gifts, it will in many instances – particularly in the west – be a mapping via equivalence. Terms equivalent to charisma, and to the related idea of direct infusion by the Spirit, emerged over the centuries. Because the religious idea associated with first-century charisma was most often regarded as a vestige of primitive Christianity, that idea was for long stretches of time hidden from view. Yet it is possible to glimpse it – bubbling up to the surface before receding – over a protracted time span. It was known by many names and, depending on the circumstance, greeted with suspicion or repression – but it was never fully or finally submerged.

The church in power

The authority of the church was enhanced by several developments in the fourth century. The most significant of these was the conversion of Constantine Augustus to Christianity in 312, allowing Christians freedom from persecution. After Constantine became sole emperor in 324, he favoured Christianity over the pagan religions: churches were built, several funded by the emperor himself; the wealth and resources of pagan temples were appropriated for Christianity. Constantine also oversaw doctrinal matters, convening a council of over 200 bishops at Nicaea in 325 to subdue theological controversies and achieve a uniform creed. Christian territory was sectored at the Council of Nicaea into the three dioceses of Rome, Alexandria and Antioch; this was expanded in the fifth century to a division of five sees: Rome, Constantinople, Alexandria, Antioch and Jerusalem. Rome was implicitly understood as being the 'first among equals', yet it is also significant that all the major Ecumenical Councils – which determined doctrinal policy for the whole church – were held in the east, close to the centre of imperial power. Differences of emphasis became apparent between the Greek east and Latin west churches many centuries before their official schism in 1054.

The church entered a new relationship with political power from the fourth century, entrenched when Christianity was declared the official religion of the Roman Empire by Emperor Theodosius in 380. Bishops assumed even greater authority, recognised by the state as religious leaders with civil status similar to that of a magistrate. They adopted insignia and ceremonial costume, were addressed as 'your Holiness' and enjoyed a new level of pomp in the major cities. In the Greek east, church ritual became a dramatic and spectacular ceremony, engendering a sense of holy awe. In the Latin west, spiritual reverence came to be invested in the Roman bishop, who was known as the pre-eminent Pope from the sixth century. By the fifth century, the church had become a significant landowner with both secular and spiritual authority; its bureaucracy offered prestigious careers; it boasted grand churches and lavish ceremony; its huge financial resources and political influence made it an integral part of society.

This scenario was far removed from the reality of Paul's time, when Christianity had no churches, scant resources, few followers, and was liable to persecution by the state. The communal sensibility applied by Paul to the charismata was to a large extent generated by the exigencies of his situation. It can be no surprise that this Pauline notion was eclipsed once the church had developed more stable and more sophisticated modes of religious authority. As we have seen in the previous chapter, from the second century some charismatic powers were transferred from prophets and other inspired individuals to church officeholders such as bishops. From the fourth century, bishops derived their authority from both church and state, yet some exceptional individuals were believed to combine supernatural powers with their worldly administrative skills. Bishop Ambrose of Milan, whose authority was such that he could successfully order Emperor Theodosius to perform public penance in 390, was thought to possess spiritual powers, including visions (attested to by his protégé, Augustine[1]). Ambrose wrote in *On the Holy Spirit* (c. 380) that

> just as the Father gives the grace of healings, so the Son also gives it, just as the Father gives the gift of tongues, so the Son also has bestowed it.
>
> (2. 150–2)[2]

Christopher Forbes notes that while it is possible to interpret this text as dealing with the 'extended present', it is more likely that Ambrose is attesting to the survival of miraculous healings and glossolalia into the late fourth century.[3]

In such instances, the tradition of the charismatic holy man was seen to survive in the person of a bishop. There could be no suspicion of heresy or misguided mysticism when the figure in question was as eminent and venerable as Ambrose. But these cases became increasingly infrequent, as many bishops were noted more for their earthly concerns and ambitions than for their spiritual prowess. Only rare individuals, later canonised as saints, were deemed by the church capable of exercising miraculous powers from within the institutionalised faith. Spiritual awe was more likely to be experienced in liturgy and ritual, particularly in the east, where the power of the Spirit was thought to manifest itself through sacrament with such intensity that the 'Lord's table' was perceived as a site of 'terror and shuddering'.[4] The Orthodox patriarch and the Catholic pope increasingly became the focus of spiritual power for the churches they represented.

Grace but not charisma: Augustine's interpretation of Paul

The legacy of Paul's theology can be gleaned in the fifth-century Christian philosophy of Augustine (354–430), bishop of Hippo, a major shaping influence on Christian thought. Paul is a powerful presence in Augustine's writings; but Paul's emphases are realigned in Augustine's theology of the fifth century. Augustine upheld the Pauline notion of grace, which comes as a free gift from God to deliver humanity from its fallen state (the result of original sin). Yet while divine grace as the gift of salvation is pre-eminent in Augustine's religious thought, the other gifts of grace, or charismata, are not prominent.

In his *Confessions*, written around 400, Augustine recounts the central role of Pauline notions in his acceptance of Christianity following a tortuous internal struggle. A turning point was the preaching of Ambrose, whose refrain 'The letter kills, but the spirit gives life' was from Paul's second letter to the Corinthians. Augustine then found in Paul's writings a 'pure eloquence' and spiritual charge surpassing that of the Platonist philosophers he had previously espoused (7: 20).[5] The epiphany prompting his famous conversion comes after a chance reading of one passage from Romans. When advocating Paul's epistles as a guide, Augustine refers to the spiritual gifts of Corinthians:

> Now let whoever is able in his understanding follow your apostle when he says that your love 'is shed abroad in our hearts by the Holy Spirit, which is given to us'; also when he teaches 'concerning spiritual gifts' and shows unto us a more excellent way of charity.
>
> (13: 7)

Augustine's emphasis, however, is not on the supernatural aspects of the charismata, which he does not mention, but on the uplifting power of Spirit and the charity which emerges in its wake. The gift of God's grace is universalised in Augustine: the emphasis is on the gift of light, which 'moves upon every mutable thing' (13: 10), while Christians are made spiritual through the grace accorded to the Church (13: 23).

Augustine elsewhere appears to espouse the cessationist perspective concerning the charismata, although he is inconsistent on this matter. Commenting on Acts 2: 4, he remarks that at 'the Church's beginning' the Holy Spirit 'fell upon the believers, and they spoke with tongues unlearnt'. He adds that this form of utterance was a sign of the Holy Spirit, 'fitted to the time', which had then 'passed away'. He contrasts the contemporary condition of faith with that recorded in Acts, when the laying on of hands could bestow miraculous powers: 'we no longer expect' such activity, he observes. This leads Augustine to question how the presence of the Spirit may now be discerned, if glossolalia and other spiritual manifestations no longer occur:

> If then the Holy Spirit's presence is no longer testified by such marvels, on what is anyone to ground assurance that he has received the Holy Spirit?
>
> (Homily 6 on the First Epistle of John, Ch 10)[6]

Augustine's answer is that evidence of the Spirit must now be detected within, rather than in external displays: 'Let him enquire of his own heart: if he loves his brother, the Spirit of God abides in him'. Augustine presents a similarly cessationist view on the charismata in his *On the True Religion*:

> These miracles were not allowed to last until our times lest the soul ever seek visible things and the human race grow cold because of familiarity with those things.
>
> (25. 47)[7]

However, Augustine shifted his position on miracles later in his life. One passage in his *City of God*, written towards the end of his career in the period 412–27, appears to accommodate contemporary belief in spiritual gifts of the supernatural order. Book 22 Chapter 8 begins with Augustine concerned once again with the difference between the miraculous past and the present: how is it, he asks, 'that you have no such miracles nowadays, as you say were done of yore?' Augustine provides an answer that articulates the cessationist argument:

> [T]hey [miracles] were necessary, before the world believed, to induce it to believe; and that he that seeks to be confirmed by wonders now is to be wondered at most of all himself, in refusing to believe what all the world believes besides him.[8]

That is, miraculous manifestations were required in the earliest stages of the faith to inspire belief, but are no longer needed four centuries later, when faith is assured.

Augustine then seeks to counter opponents who refuse to believe that any miracles were ever performed in the name of Christianity. He points to their documentation in the scriptures, but also states that there are some miracles 'wrought even now in His name, partly by the sacraments, partly by the commemorations and prayers of the saints'. He acknowledges that these feats are not as 'glorious' or 'famous' as those of earlier times, because they have not been given 'lustre' and international renown by the scriptures. They may be known only locally, in the city or region where they were performed. Augustine proceeds to recount a list of 18 recent miracles that he has personally witnessed, or that have been described to him, adding the comment that he knows of too many more to list them all in the brief space he has allocated. The feats are miracles of healing: palsy and cancer cured, sight returned, revival from severe accident and – in four cases – revival from death. Exorcism of devils is involved in two instances of healing.

In his *Retractions*, written near the end of his life in 427–8, and intended as a revision of his earlier works, Augustine revisits his statements on the cessation of miracles. He supports his previous claim in *On the True Religion* that miracles 'were not allowed' to last into the present. In the contemporary world, the Spirit does not visit tongues on the baptised, 'nor are the sick now healed by the passing shadow of the preachers of Christ', as documented in Acts. 'Even though such things happened at that time', Augustine declares, 'manifestly these ceased later'. He then qualifies his earlier assertions, which are not to be interpreted to mean that 'no miracles are believed to be performed in the name of Christ at the present time'.[9] Augustine supports this position with reference to the healing miracles he detailed in *City of God*.

There are two observations to be made regarding this remarkable passage in *City of God*, which contradicts Augustine's earlier cessationist position. First, Augustine is not declaring that all the Pauline charismata are functioning in the fifth century as they did in the first: there is no mention of prophecy, glossolalia or many of the other gifts. The miracles are almost all connected to healing, upholding Christian faith over the skills of surgeons, who had professed helplessness in the face of these ailments and afflictions. Contact with holy relics is in some instances shown to be more effective than the methods of medical practice. The narrow range of the miracles, then, needs to be taken into account, as does the function these feats serve in Augustine's broader goal in *City of God*. The healing miracles reveal cure by faith – reflecting the City of God – in cases where cures attempted by the earthly city of man have failed. Secondly, Augustine's inconsistency on the matter of miracles perhaps reflects a tension in mainstream theology of the early fifth century: a recognition of the distance between the present and the early pneumatic church jostles with an unwillingness to cede the spiritual gifts altogether.

The mystic fringe

Another means of discerning the fate of charismatic energy after its eclipse is to follow the trail of mysticism. In the third and fourth centuries, this was embodied in the hermit, or holy man in the desert. Hermits continued the ascetic tradition and self-deprivation pursued by earlier mystics and prophets. In the early fourth century, Antony's well-publicised spiritual quest in the Egyptian desert was an inspiration for other individuals seeking a spiritual alternative to the increasingly mainstream Christian faith. Rural areas removed from the central base of Rome were more likely than cities to accommodate unorthodox practices, including extreme asceticism and inspired prophecy. Montanism and other heretical sects survived longest in Africa and the Near East, while individual mystics could draw on long traditions of the wise man or mystical recluse. Manichaeism, a form of Gnosticism founded by the Persian prophet Mani in the third century, also exerted an influence for centuries. At one point it included in its devotees Augustine, prior to his conversion to Christianity; it continued to fertilise many dualist sects on the fringes of the church from the fourth century.

There is some suggestion that charismatic powers, specifically glossolalia, were thought to occur within the early Monastic movement. Forbes cites the story told of the fourth-century-monk Pachomius, a founder of monasteries in Egypt, who was said to receive from heaven the gift of languages he had never learnt. Forbes admits that the story is clearly folklore, yet it indicates that its author believed in the possibility of such a divine gift, even if bestowed only on a great saint.[10]

The church's response to the hermetic tendency was to organise the desert dwellers into heavily regulated communal orders. In eastern Asia Minor, Basil of Caesarea sought to qualify the solitary life pursued by the Egyptian hermits: such a pursuit, he wrote, served only 'the needs of the individual … in conflict with the law of love'.[11] Basil composed the first rule for Christian monasteries in the mid-fourth century, elevating group discipline and restraint over the individual mystical quest. In the early fifth century, the Scythian monk John Cassian organised monasteries in the west based on the eastern model, emphasising the virtues of prayer and ascetic order. Cassian regarded the 'miracle-mongering' attributed to hermits and ascetics in the popular imagination with extreme distaste,[12] emphasising instead orthodoxy and rigour within the monastery. The Benedictine Rule of the sixth century followed these principles, encouraging not individual mystics but dutiful and disciplined students with a strong communal sensibility.

Away from the monasteries, there were some instances of Christian holy men, generally in isolated areas, who were purported to have supernatural powers. They lived as recluses, following hermetic tradition involving purification and self-deprivation. One example was Theodore of Sykeon in Anatolia (died around 612), a holy man described as a Christian shaman by John Ashton.[13] Theodore, who was credited with miracle-working and exorcisms, was later made a saint. In some regions, a divide between monastery and church emerged in the minds of Christians. Monks were thought to have higher spiritual credentials than priests and bishops, in a manner reminiscent of Tertullian's bifurcation of the church into unspiritual bishops and those individuals directly infused by Spirit. The belief persisted for many centuries in the churches of Asia Minor that the power to forgive sins was the prerogative of monks, because only they possessed sufficient holiness to confer the Holy Spirit in the act of penance.[14]

Charisma in the eastern church

Christian theology in the eastern, Greek and Syriac-speaking churches developed some fundamental points of difference from the Catholic church of the Latin west. Augustine's notion of original sin, from which the gift of divine grace must free humanity, was not accepted in the eastern church. This basic difference points to distinctive qualities evident in the theological discourse of the east, and also in the liturgy of eastern churches. Baptism was understood in the east not as the washing away of inherited guilt and original sin, but as *photismos* or spiritual illumination, a welcome to the Holy Spirit and the church. Paul Meyendorff characterises eastern Christianity as 'an eminently positive theology', whose goal is the eventual deification of the baptised individual.[15]

As the means of entry to this participation in the divine, baptism was venerated as a charisma in eastern liturgy: it is a free gift from God with a promise of new life. Two of the leading theologians of the fourth-century eastern church, Gregory of Nazianzus and Gregory of Nyssa, refer to baptism itself as a charisma, translated as 'Baptismal Grace'.[16] The rituals and wording comprising liturgy were considered the perfect expression of the divinisation sought by worshippers, hence the heightened significance accorded to sacrament in the eastern church. Tradition, understood as the body of wisdom accumulated in the scriptures and the writings of the church fathers, also held an elevated place in the eastern church. Exegesis of the canonical scriptures was thought to add to their worth, so that accumulated insights were passed on through the generations, forming a 'golden chain' of accrued theological wisdom.[17] Such a depth of consensual biblical interpretation and doctrine also formed the base for the refutation of heresies, in the manner pioneered by Irenaeus in the second century. The leading eastern theologians – known as the 'patristic' authors – of the fourth and fifth centuries maintained this exegetical tradition; references to charisma are found in some of their works.

Gregory of Nazianzus (c. 330–90) commented exegetically on the diversity of gifts outlined in the scriptures, while referring to the charisma of *diakrisis* – or discerning of spirits – within the church. He also wrote that it was not the practice of saints to glory in the charismata.[18] Athanasius of Alexandria (c. 300–73), who published the widely popular *Life of Antony*, wrote of the gift of tears as a charisma.[19] This practice, emerging from a monastic context, was understood as a spiritual gift bringing joy through tears of contrition. Basil of Caesarea (330–79) had a practical conception of charismata: for him they were divine gifts bestowed on all those performing a function for the church. Befitting the tenor of his *Rules* for monastic life, Basil focused on the pragmatic services pursued as charismata: guiding, consoling or admonishing others, expounding the scriptures and deriving spiritual benefit from them.[20] John Chrysostom of Antioch (c. 350–407) wrote extensive exegetical works, commenting in his Homilies on those passages referring to charismata. Having spent at least four years in solitude in the desert, John abandoned that direction, writing critically of the contemporary belief in the gifts, particularly in the monastic setting. For John, pursuit of charismata should not become a pretext for loosening ascetic discipline. The charismata belonged to the earliest church, when the apostles had the power to raise the dead – and that is where, according to John, the charismata should remain.[21] Theodoret of Cyrus (c. 393–466) described the charismatic gifts as 'visible signs' of grace given 'in former times', as recorded in 1 Corinthians; he observed that grace is still imparted 'in our time', but 'it may not take the same form as it did in those days'.[22]

Offsetting the conservatism and suspicion of innovation deriving from the eastern love of tradition was the conviction that this tradition must be enlivened by the Holy Spirit. Monastic spirituality, with its mystical undertow, coloured eastern Christianity to a significant degree: the city of Constantinople alone housed over 300 monasteries by the sixth century.[23] The Byzantine church in particular emphasised the mysterious elements of faith, along with the need for worshippers to reach a heightened sense of being spirit-filled.[24] This presiding tendency made possible the periodical outburst of charismatic worship and theology. Such activity often emerged from the monastic environment which contained, in the east, loose confederations of monks not always bound by the strict orders and rules followed in the west. The monastic setting meant that mystical pursuits could at times evade charges of heresy – although official censure and punishment were in some instances invoked by the church.

The most striking figure in this regard is Symeon the New Theologian (949–1022). A monk based in Constantinople, Symeon became associated with the idea that charismatic monks constituted a third form of authority in the Byzantine world, alongside the church patriarch and the emperor.[25] In works such as *Hymns of Divine Love*, Symeon advocated the direct experience of the Spirit, insisting that such divine contact is available to all:

> Do not say that it is impossible to receive the Divine Spirit …
> Do not say that men do not see the divine light
> or that this is impossible in these present times!
> This is a thing never impossible, friends.
>
> (Hymn 27, 121–32)[26]

Such a call for unmediated spiritual experience recalled earlier challenges to the institutional church dating back to the Montanists and Tertullian. Symeon believed that spiritually enlightened monks performed a pneumatic ministry beside the hierarchical church offices.[27]

Symeon at one stage received the support of the patriarch, but was ultimately exiled following clashes with church authorities. Nevertheless his writings provided an inspiration for later forms of mysticism within the Orthodox faith. The strength of monastic spirituality within the eastern church is one of the reasons that an alternative viewpoint to the cessationist perspective could persist – and occasionally flourish – as in the theology of Symeon and his followers. However, official church reproval, in the form of expulsion or the charge of heresy, was always a possibility if religious practice strayed too far from the institutional path.

Implicit charisma: Equivalence

In the west, the Greek 'charisma' was transliterated into Latin and appeared in the writings of Tertullian and other early theological works composed in Latin. The term receded in use in the west as the idea of charisma lost ground in mainstream theology. As noted in the previous chapter, Tertullian, a passionate advocate for the role of charismata in Christian life, considered the Latin *donum* (gift) too weak to serve as a synonym for charisma. Writing around the year 200, he preferred the stronger *donativum*, referring to those gifts bestowed by the emperor at special moments of munificence. Only such elevated gifts could serve as a Roman parallel, expressed in Latin, for the spiritual gifts known to Christians as charismata. Yet 'donum' became, along with *gratia* (grace), the normal term in Latin theological texts to refer to the spiritual gifts. This in itself devalued the charge of the charismata: they were 'gifts' bestowed at the earliest stage of the church, usurped in importance by later gifts such as sacrament and canonical scripture.

But if the word charisma faded into disuse, it would be imprudent to conclude that the idea of charisma lay dormant, even in the western church. The spiritual energy associated with charisma in the first century found other outlets. Dissatisfaction with the institutionalised church did not die with Tertullian. Anti-clerical sentiment fostered alternative versions of creed and worship, many of which were condemned as heretical. The challengers to the orthodox faith generally looked back to the church's earliest stage for inspiration: they craved more spirit, less law – and could thus claim Paul as their source. The mystical hue of these alternative creeds enveloped the Pauline charismata, even if not by name. Prophecy, direct infusion by the Spirit, ecstatic utterance, speaking in tongues: these and other faculties were invoked by many revivalist practices within the church.

The rest of this chapter is, then, an attempt to trace the course of the idea of charisma – as spiritual gift, including supernatural aspects – even while the word charisma lay largely unused. When 'charisma' returns to vigorous usage in theological circles in the nineteenth century, and when it erupts into common usage in the twentieth, it re-emerges into an environment not unfamiliar with the charismatic – even if known by other names.

An equivalence: 'Enthusiasm'

This path has already been traced, in an inimitable manner, by R. A. Knox in his book *Enthusiasm*, published in 1950. Knox uses 'enthusiasm' as a term fit to embrace the charismatic and mystical elements within Christian history, from the first century to the nineteenth. Knox is unusual in his approach to the topic. Whereas most studies of charisma, ecstatic utterance or spiritual giftedness adopt a neutral tone, or exhibit a post-Weberian sympathy for the charismatic before it is routinised, Knox is openly disdainful of the impulse. If it constitutes a 'chapter in the history of religion', for Knox it is a regrettable chapter. 'Enthusiasm' is Knox's pejorative term to convey 'the elusive thing' that runs through the history of the church, arising periodically 'by a kind of fatality',[28] generating disruption and disunity.

In Knox's view, the 'fugal melody that runs through the centuries' is inspired every time by an elite within the community, who consider themselves more attuned to the Spirit than their fellows. The recurrent situation charted by Knox involves schism and mainstream opposition, followed by internecine schisms within the schism, and the inevitable evaporation of the initial fervour: 'prophecy dies out, and the charismatic is merged into the institutional'.[29] Knox here embraces Weber's theory of the routinisation of charisma as a recurrent motif in the history of Christianity; in doing so, he uses 'charisma' as an equivalent term for enthusiasm. His preferred term, one too cumbersome to repeat often, is 'ultrasupernaturalism', which encompasses the goal of the spiritual enthusiast through the ages, for such a person 'expects more evident results from the grace of God than we others'.[30] This goal is inspired by a vision of the early church as a golden age, one 'visibly penetrated with supernatural influences',[31] as recounted in Acts and the letters of Paul.

Knox situates himself in the rational Christian mainstream: the enthusiasts quote a hundred texts, he notes, before adding: 'we also use them, but with more of embarrassment'.[32] He identifies the anti-institutional and anti-intellectual characteristics of enthusiasm, flowing from its 'different theology of grace'. All of these observations could be made of Paul's theology; yet Knox is critical not of the apostle but of his followers, who, according to Knox, repeatedly misunderstood Paul's teaching. This error was first committed by the Corinthians; for Knox the error recurred in every revivalism through many centuries: 'there is no aberration of Christianity which does not point to him [Paul] as the source of its inspiration'.[33] Each revival of enthusiasm contains the 'symptom' of ecstatic behaviour, manifest in inspired prophecy or in trances in which people are 'destitute of their senses' or in 'the convulsive movements from head to foot' that consume their hosts for hours on end.[34]

The first expression of these 'symptoms', and the first manifestation of enthusiasm, was at Corinth where, Knox notes, spiritual gifts were 'lavished in a profusion scarcely credible to the modern reader'.[35] Because Paul acknowledged the charismatic powers, Knox has no choice but to admit their existence; he cannot resist, however, conveying his disdain for a faith displaying supernatural attributes. Christian worship at first-century Corinth, he remarks condescendingly, resembled 'what we should expect ... from some country-side Bethel at the height of a Welsh revival'.[36] Knox's interpretation of 1 Corinthians has Paul determined to regulate and limit the scope of the supernatural faculties. Paul's aim is to check 'the unwholesome preoccupation with the *charismata* in their more startling forms';[37] Knox's Paul is on the side of discipline against the excesses of enthusiasm. Paul is thus, in Knox's reading, the first to administer the necessary curb against enthusiasm within the church; this contest between the institutional and the charismatic reappears 'in varying forms under other skies' throughout church history.

Knox's version of Paul's relationship with the Corinthians is as partial – from the opposite perspective – as the enthusiasts' interpretation, which he so evidently deplores. Nevertheless his historical study of enthusiasm is useful for a history of charisma covering the many centuries when the term itself was seldom used. Commencing from Corinth as a starting point, Knox surveys the revivals of enthusiasm, a term closely aligned with the Christian idea of charisma. Second-century Montanism is the first major recurrence of enthusiast symptoms, 'in an acute form': the Montanists strove for a 'pneumatic' or intensely spiritual church,[38] with ecstatic manifestations in prophecy. After the repression of Montanism and other heresies by the church, Knox observes sporadic outbreaks of enthusiasm through the Middle Ages, largely inspired by eastern spiritual pursuits. The Reformation is the trigger for latter-day enthusiasm, first expressed by the Quakers and the Pietists, then more fully in Methodism, with all manner of splinter groups and outbreaks.

The age of heresy

Knox sketches (admittedly inexact) trajectories leading from early movements such as Montanism and Manichaeism to the mystical pursuits often outlawed by the church in the Middle Ages. A seventh-century sect known as the Paulicians emerged in Armenia, holding the dualist view characteristic of Manichaeism. Another sect, the Messalians, had a similarly Gnostic faith, but one more compatible with a revivalist version of Christianity: they possibly inherited aspects of Montanism, and were known as 'The Enthusiasts'.[39] A later heretical sect active in the Balkan region, known as the Bogomils, absorbed the outlines of both Paulician and Messalian worship. The Catharists – much better known to posterity than their predecessors – came into contact with the Bogomils in Bulgaria, before flourishing in Western Europe in the twelfth century.

Taking their name from the Greek *katharos* (pure), the Catharists upheld a Gnostic-type dualism which impelled them to lead a purified life. The Cathar sect held, like many Gnostics before them, that the material world was intrinsically evil, and that it was not created by God but by a malevolent spirit. They rejected Christian sacraments, replacing them with their own rites, and ordained their own bishops and deacons to replace Catholic offices. Outlawed as a heresy, the Cathars suffered violent repression, especially in southern France.

The Cathars were only one of many sects deemed heretical by the Catholic church. Pope Lucius III listed several more in a decree of 1183, including Passagins, Josephins, Poor Men of Lyons, Patarins and Arnaldists.[40] The church responded to the problem of the Cathars (known as Albigensians in France), and the proliferation of other heresies by establishing the Inquisition or Holy Office around 1232. The Inquisition was a court of the church charged with the detection and punishment of heretics, approved by Pope Gregory IX. Torture and death were regular punishments, made notorious by the Spanish Inquisition, founded in 1479. The Inquisition compiled an Index of proscribed books in 1557, containing works condemned as heretical.

In this age of suspicion and persecution, there was often a very fine line between acceptable thought or practice and heretical positions. Christopher Brooke observes that the 'stern asceticism' upheld by many monastic leaders was supported by the view that the world was almost entirely evil, even if created as good. This perspective was separated by only 'the narrowest of margins' from the Cathars' heretical position that the world was evil in its making.[41] A strain of mystical Christianity survived within the church, so long as it abided by the approved regulations of worship. The proscribed heretical sects were found guilty of holding false views on the sacraments; yet within the orthodox framework, the idea of divine inspiration – often manifest in visions – could be permitted. The Messalian sect, for example, believed that 'pure prayer' was the only true means of finding communion with God: they were condemned as heretical because they rejected the need for baptism and other sacraments. Yet the mystical pursuit known in the east as Hesychasm managed to survive charges of heresy similar to those brought against Messalianism. Gregory Palamas (1296–1359), Archbishop of Thessalonica, took inspiration from Symeon the Theologian and other monastic spiritualists, promoting Hesychasm in the fourteenth century. Derived from the Greek word for silence, Hesychasm built on the monastic searching for a form of ecstasy in contemplation; it resisted charges of heresy to remain an officially sanctioned religious practice in the late Byzantine world.[42]

In the west, three famous female visionaries, spanning the eleventh century to the sixteenth, were canonised by the church. Hildegard von Bingen (1098–1179), abbess of her own convent, was renowned for her visions and prophecies, earning her the respect of rulers who consulted her. Her visions were expressed in her enduring song compositions. Joan of Arc (c. 1412–31) at the age of 13 claimed to hear the voices of saints exhorting her to lead France against the English; captured by the English and burned as a heretic and sorcerer, she was eventually made a saint in 1920. Teresa of Avila (1515–82), who revived the Carmelite rule in convents, was well known for her asceticism and mystical writings.

These and many other canonised individuals maintained a mystical orientation – professing visions and other miraculous faculties – within the orthodox tradition. Individual charismata such as prophecy, direct inspiration and miracle-working survived in the feats of these revered figures. There was a major distinction, however, between the achievements of these famous saints and the charismata described by Paul. The communal aspect of Paul's vision does not survive: the spiritual gifts are available only to the remarkable few, unimpeachable figures (often, like Hildegard and Teresa, ensconced in convents or monasteries) who performed their wonders within the safeguards of the church apparatus. Those movements propounding the view that direct contact with the Spirit was available to all within the community, offering spiritual empowerment to the many, were among the sects repressed as heretical. They suffered the same fate as the Montanists and Priscillianists of earlier centuries; the Inquisition merely exacted a more thorough, and often more violent, repression.

Doctrinal charisma

The official position of the medieval Catholic church regarding charismatic phenomena was articulated by the philosopher and theologian Thomas Aquinas (c. 1225–74). Aquinas's fusion of Aristotelian method and Christian theology – evident in his massive *Summa Theologica* – was the foremost work in the scholastic tradition, and exerted great influence on succeeding Christian thought in the west. Aquinas argued that reason could detect the work of God in nature, and that truth could be known through both natural revelation and the supernatural revelation associated with faith. Revelation by supernatural means was for Aquinas largely represented in the scriptures, the ancient prophets and the tradition encompassed by the church. Yet he also allowed for the occasional glimpse of divine revelation; he himself claimed to have experienced a mystical experience near the end of his life. Aquinas believed that through reason and faith, the Christian achieved sanctification at death, when the essence of God is finally comprehended.

Within the vast systematic apparatus of *Summa Theologica*, there is a role for charisma as one form of grace. In Aquinas's terminology, the spiritual gift is *gratia gratis data*, generally translated as 'gratuitously given grace' or 'gratuitous grace'. Aquinas states that the gratuitous graces are 'ordained for the manifestation of faith and spiritual doctrine' (IIIa 7.7).[43] He follows 1 Corinthians in identifying 'the grace of healing', working of miracles, prophecy, discerning of spirits, 'kinds of tongues' and their interpretation: these are 'enumerated here under the gratuitous graces'. For Aquinas these powers imply a 'super-eminent certitude of faith, whereby a man is fitted for instructing others' (III. 4). These graces have the function of allowing an individual to 'help another to be led to God'; a gratuitous grace 'embraces whatever a man needs in order to instruct another in Divine things which are above reason' (III. 4). As well as the graces of supernatural character, Aquinas lists among the gratuitous graces 'understanding, piety, fortitude and fear'.

The charismata – renamed here gratuitous graces – have in the Thomist system an instrumental function. Their role is to empower one Christian to lead others to the place where they may be saved. The gratuitous graces are subordinate and inferior to the sanctifying graces, which render individuals holy and lead them to the divine. Aquinas again cites Paul as support for this relegation of the charismata: in 1 Corinthians Paul advises his listeners that charity (which for Aquinas pertains to sanctifying grace) is the more excellent way. Sanctifying grace is nobler as it 'ordains a man immediately to union with his last end'; gratuitous grace is only preparatory to that end. The manifestations formerly known as charismata merely lead individuals to that point where the sanctifying graces impart holiness and final perfection (III. 5).

Aquinas's exhaustive taxonomy preserves a role for the spiritual gifts, but it is a restricted one. It is primarily a support function to the power of the sanctifying graces. Spiritual gifts are considered transitory, resulting from the 'special intervention of God in man's faculties and operations'.[44] They arise when there is a temporary need to elevate human abilities beyond their natural capacity, imparting a 'supereminent certitude of faith'. The goal of the gifts is to bring others to faith, through instruction, teaching or other means. The extraordinary gifts such as prophecy may operate in this capacity, yet Aquinas also allows for institutional functions to be imbued with grace. The exercise of sacred orders, ecclesiastical jurisdiction and papal infallibility are all considered to have supernatural origin: they constitute a more permanent embodiment of gratuitous grace.[45]

Royal charisma

If the Thomist system installed the miraculous and revelatory within a tightly structured doctrinal machinery, medieval life outside this theoretical apparatus was awash with mysticism. Accepted church practice in the medieval period often veered very close to the magical rites otherwise condemned as pagan sorcery. Keith Thomas, noting the medieval church's condoning of prayers and rituals used as charms, and the association of objects of ecclesiastical ritual with aura in the eyes of worshippers, states that the church 'appeared as a vast reservoir of magical power'.[46] The ultimate magical power, however, was thought to reside in the monarch. The healing power of the royal touch was publicly administered in France and England from the eleventh century; the rite continued until the reign of Queen Anne in the early eighteenth century. A range of skin complaints and infections such as scrofula was collectively known as the King's Evil; it was widely believed that the laying on of the monarch's hands could dispel the condition. Many thousands of sufferers received the touch of the royal hand in the belief that the monarch possessed sacred healing power.

A book by John Browne, published in 1684, purports to be a treatise on *charisma basilicon*: royal charisma or the royal gift of healing. The book combines anatomical study of 'glandules & strumaes, or Kings-evil swellings' with the conviction that these ailments may be cured by the 'imposition of hands' of the monarch. Browne notes in the extended title of his work that this rite has been 'performed for above 640 years by our kings of England', generating 'admirable effects, and miraculous events'.[47]

An earlier book by William Tooker, published in 1597, refers to the charisma of the monarch as the gift of healing (*donum sanationis*), with specific reference to Queen Elizabeth, who has the 'grace of miraculous healings' bestowed on her. Elizabeth possesses this power to heal by the laying on of hands because the kings of England had been inaugurated into this charisma, 'given the healing power by God'. Tooker adds that this 'heavenly grace' is supported by religious ceremonies and prayers, with the admirable outcome that the Queen heals daily by the application of her hands.[48]

The miraculous gift of healing vested in Charles I in the seventeenth century was described by a follower as a 'supernatural means of cure which is inherent in your sacred majesty'.[49] The church supported this administration of royal magic, even after the Reformation. The ritual of royal healing was part of the Book of Common Prayer from 1634; in England Anglican chaplains read from St Mark – 'They shall lay hands on the sick and they shall recover' – while the monarch laid hands on the queue of sufferers.[50]

This dispensation of the gift of healing by the monarch, as sanctioned by the church, is a long way from the communal charismata celebrated by Paul. The medieval belief in the aura and divine touch of monarchs (persisting, remarkably, into the eighteenth century) was a mystical notion; it partook of the supernatural aspect of charismata, one of which was the gift of healing. But this gift is now believed to be invested by God in the elite figure of the monarch: the guiding principle is heredity, not community. The charisma is vested in the institution: any king or queen holding the position will receive the faculty of healing. The earliest spirit of charisma, by which the divine gift could land on any individual, irrespective of birth or rank, is in this practice completely institutionalised.

The Protestant paradox

The Protestant Reformation of the sixteenth century was impelled, in large part, by a rationalist impulse. Martin Luther and the other leading figures demanded reform of the church which in their judgement had become contaminated by corruption, reprehensible practices (the sale of indulgences and church positions) and excessive emphasis on

hierarchy and sacrament. Protestantism emerged as a Christian alternative in which salvation is attained by faith unmediated by the church
and its symbolic practices, such as the intermediary role of saints.
Luther asserted that the Bible should be the sole source of authority,
thereby rejecting the authority of the Pope.

Renaissance humanism, individualism and the impact of the printing
press were all integral to the rise of Protestantism. Yet the Reformation
also spawned a myriad of denominations, sects and movements with a
mystical or ecstatic bent, including the Pentecostal movement of the
twentieth century. A religious doctrine (or, more accurately, range of
doctrines) born in the Renaissance and shaped in the Enlightenment,
Protestantism nevertheless generated revival after revival of 'primitive'
expressions of faith, featuring direct visitation of the Spirit, physical
manifestations such as quaking and shaking, belief in prophecy, miracle-
working and healing and even messianic cults.

There are a number of ways to explain this paradox. In dismissing
much of the institutionalised and hierarchical Catholic church, Luther
and the other reformers such as Calvin and Zwingli emphasised instead
a direct, personal relationship with God. Luther's inspiration largely
derived from Augustine and Paul, particularly Paul's insistence in
Romans that faith in the gospel brings salvation. Luther not only reopened a theological direct route to Paul, justifying a disregard for empty
ceremony and stifling hierarchy, but also allowed succeeding generations to rediscover the Pauline emphases on community and spiritual
gifts. The Catholic and Orthodox theologies emphasised tradition, the
guiding exegesis of the scriptures by generations of theologians stretching back to the early fathers and the 'great fathers' of the fourth and
fifth centuries such as Augustine and Chrysostom. This was replaced in
Protestantism by a direct engagement with the Bible. Post-Reformation
revivalists often based their creeds on their own interpretation of Paul;
in many instances those interpretations were made by individuals who
favoured inspiration over education in theology.

Knox makes the further observation that the Reformation 'created a demand for simplicity' that it did not fully satisfy. As a result,
'[e]nthusiasm had but to lift its voice, and it was certain of a hearing'.[51]
Another important factor is the role of mysticism in fostering the
Reformation, establishing an undercurrent within Protestantism that
the rationalist imperative was never fully able to dispel.

The prehistory of the Reformation contains mystical as well as rationalist elements. Francis of Assisi (1181–1226) personified the 'holy fool'
tradition and was believed to have received divine visions and the

stigmata; his anti-hierarchical humanism fed into the early Renaissance. The Waldenses sect, founded in France in the twelfth century, and able to survive persecution by the church as heretical, was one of several movements advocating values similar to those of Francis, devaluing institutional authority while elevating lay opinion. The Dominican monks Meister Eckhardt (1260–1327) and Johannes Tauler (c. 1300–61) advocated a direct spiritual path to God, their mysticism incorporating a pre-Reformation dismissal of ceremony and official ritual. The Anabaptists proclaimed a 'spiritual church' with similarities to earlier sects such as the Albingenses.

Only a few years after Luther's nailing of the theses, Protestant leaders were forced to deal with a collection of groups later termed the 'Radical Reformation'. This assortment of Anabaptists, spiritualists and prophets had in common a quest for divine immediacy.[52] Their emphasis on inner spiritual experience carried with it rejection not only of the institutionalised Catholic church but also in some cases relegation of the importance of scriptures. The radicals could profess the gift of prophecy, as in the case of the Zwickau prophets in Germany, or claim for themselves mystical union with the divine, in the case of the Anabaptists or numerous individual spiritualists. Even though Luther had served as their initial inspiration with his accentuation of the interior relationship with God, he could not accept their mystical orientation, dismissing the radicals as 'Schwärmer', or uncontrollably buzzing bees. Calvin was sharper in his displeasure, deriding the radicals as 'fanatics', 'scatterbrains', 'scoundrels' and 'mad dogs'.[53] In 1520, Luther rejected claims to direct revelation, asserting instead the 'dogma of the absolute authority of Scripture'.[54] As a result, a 'distrust of mysticism' fell early on the Protestant movement, with the effect that all subsequent urges to revelation faced an 'attitude of suspicion'.[55]

Despite this condemnation of the mystical tendency (the Anabaptists were persecuted by Protestants and Catholics alike) and despite the ascetic tenor of much early Protestantism, movements claiming direct revelation have been numerous, continuing from the earliest period of the Reformation. Evangelical preachers – propounding the basic Protestant creed of allegiance to the Bible and salvation by faith – have been free to establish their own denominations or churches. The Quakers, founded in England in the mid-seventeenth century, proclaimed revelation available to all worshippers, without the need of mediation through clergy or sacrament. Quakers made themselves available for the entry of the Spirit into their person, a process described in many forms, including that of an 'inner light'. Their open disrespect for social privilege and elites shocked seventeenth-century society, as did the convulsions that could overtake worshippers. An observer described these manifestations as 'dreadful Tremblings in their Bodies and Joints, with Risings and Swellings in their Bowels: Shriekings, Yellings, Howlings and Roarings'.[56] The French prophets of Cévennes, who fled to England to escape persecution in 1706, inspired other forms of ecstatic worship. These prophets asserted that outpourings of the Spirit were manifest in the forms of child prophecy, and convulsions afflicting preachers, leading to divine revelation.

Methodism emerged in the 1730s as an evangelical movement within the Anglican church. Its co-founder John Wesley professed a horror of mysticism; yet charges were brought against early Methodism as a form of enthusiasm. The Methodists were challenged by the Bishop of London to justify why 'they profess to think and act under the immediate guidance of a divine inspiration ... when they claim the spirit of prophecy'.[57] Paroxysms experienced by worshippers at Methodist services were dismissed by detractors as either lunacy or hysteria. Similar manifestations were reported in the United States as part of its 'Great Awakening' in the 1730s. The Calvinist Jonathan Edwards wrote of 'persons waxing cold and benumbed, with their hands clenched, yea, and their bodies in convulsions'.[58] Edwards wrote profusely on the subject of revival, understood as an intensification of the normal activity of the Holy Spirit:[59] for him, revival sat within the great tradition of orthodox Christianity, including the Puritan version of the faith. He was critical of the emphasis on extraordinary spiritual gifts, condemning the desire for these gifts as 'childish';[60] the ordinary work of the Spirit, in effecting salvation, was for Edwards more glorious and more pertinent. Other preachers of an evangelical bent such as George Whitefield taught that the 'New Birth' experienced in revival generated such phenomena as evidence of the Spirit. W. R. Ward remarks that this approach drew on a long history in the 'Protestant underworld', exciting initial enthusiasm; but it also attracted reproach from the Protestant authorities.[61] The American Great Awakening had subsided by 1744, while the convulsions at Methodist services had also receded by the early 1740s.

The Shakers, mockingly named as 'Shaking Quakers', took inspiration from the spirit of the French prophets and Quakers, emerging as a separate movement in 1747. Under the guidance of Ann Lee, who claimed to receive visions, the Shakers established a colony in the United Sates in 1774. This community was part of a new wave of revivalism in America in the early nineteenth century: worshippers in several denominations were known to experience convulsions or otherwise to be 'particularly gifted in prophecies, trances, dreams, rhapsodies'.[62] When the Presbyterian synod disapproved of this orientation, many worshippers responded by joining the Shakers, who numbered 6000 members in the 1820s.

Later revivals included the Irvingites in Britain, based around a Presbyterian preacher named Edward Irving. In 1830 Irving prayed openly for the return of Pentecostal gifts; his followers considered his prayer answered when glossolalia and prophecies broke out within his congregation. Ejected from the Presbyterian church, Irving formed his own 'Catholic Apostolic Church', in which services were interrupted by members prophesying in tongues, to be interpreted by others in the congregation if they were 'Gifted Persons' functioning 'in the Spirit'.[63] Knox points out that for Paul prophecy and the gift of tongues were different charismata; for revivalists such as the Irvingites, the two gifts could merge into one spiritual manifestation. The resultant prophecies, often conveyed in a mishmash of languages, could be largely unintelligible, prompting a scepticism in some observers concerning the provenance of such prophecies.

This sceptical approach also emanated from within mainstream Protestant theology which, in the nineteenth century, exhibited a pronounced disdain for mysticism. John Ashton detects the continuation of this disdain in the major twentieth-century theologians Dibelius, Barth and Bultmann, who evinced 'a distaste (even a horror)' towards the mystical 'that goes right back to Luther'.[64] Such reproach, however, did little to prevent the outbreak of fresh revivalisms, each seeking experience of the Spirit, each revelling in ecstatic manifestations. Revival continued in the second half of the nineteenth century, culminating in the Pentecostal movement of the early twentieth. In the 1960s, the intense experience of the Spirit was given the name Charismatic Renewal. This trail will be taken up in Chapter 7.

6
Weber Reinvents Charisma

Charisma as theorised and defined by Max Weber (1864–1920) is one those terms, like Thomas Kuhn's 'paradigm shift', that has exerted an influence far beyond the discipline in which it was first encased. Weber articulated 'charisma' as one of three forms of authority within his massive work *Wirtschaft und Gesellschaft*, published posthumously in German in 1922, translated to English first in 1947 and later in 1968 as *Economy and Society*.[1] Unfinished and spanning almost 1500 pages, *Economy and Society* was a summation of Weber's sociological purview of social structure and world history. His definition and detailing of his theory of charisma, scattered throughout *Economy and Society*, and in several other minor works, installs charisma as a central concept within Weber's theory of legitimate domination, which in turn constituted one element in the vast Weberian sociological apparatus.

Yet 'charisma' quickly escaped the boundaries of this theoretical system. Already in 1959, only 12 years after the publication of *Economy and Society*'s first English translation, the *Times Literary Supplement* could declare:

> Max Weber would doubtless have been horrified, had he lived, to see the uses to which his doctrine of the 'charisma' which descends upon the born leader was to be put.[2]

By the 1960s, 'charisma' was widely used in the press to refer to certain politicians with exceptional appeal, notably the Kennedys; the word was later applied to other public figures: actors, pop stars and other celebrities. The popularisation of Weber's concept entailed a broadening of its definition, and certainly a broadening of its application: Weber was concerned with authority and leadership, not with celebrities. However, whenever charisma was invoked, from the 1950s onwards, to describe an individual's galvanising appeal, magnetic charm or ability to command a following, the invocation was of Weber's notion of charisma, with slight modifications.

Certainly this was a secular version of charisma, as defined by Weber, removed from the ancient Christian concept of charisma as gift of God's grace. While Weber himself acknowledged the Christian discourse from which he borrowed the word 'charisma', later social theorists and commentators possessed only a weak grasp of the term's original religious significance. Wolfgang Mommsen, author of several works on Weber and his thought, wrote in 1974 that

> Weber had derived this concept from the usage of the early Christian communities, where charisma was considered a divine gift, by which God himself had designated certain persons as leaders.[3]

Even a cursory reading of the Christian source – the epistles of Paul – would have revealed to Mommsen and other scholars that leadership is nowhere mentioned there as a charisma. But the Weberian definition had by then become so thoroughly entrenched in both social thought and popular discourse that even religious historians could fall under its spell. Martin Hengel's *The Charismatic Leader and His Followers*, published in 1968, applied Weber's theory of charisma to religious – including Christian – history, while John Howard Schütz in 1974 interpreted the bestowal of charisma in the first-century Christian communities as the ascription of (Weberian) authority.[4] The Weberian model of charisma was imposed, in these instances, on the early Christian setting, in which charisma had been understood not as the power of an individual leader, but as a communal blessing.

One of the reasons that Weber's secular concept could supplant the religious idea, befuddling even some religious scholars, was that the Christian notion of charisma had very little presence in the broad community at the beginning of the twentieth century. Although 'charisma' had retained, at the time of Weber's work on *Economy and Society*, a place within Christian theological discourse, this constituted no more than a marginal status within that specific field. Until the Christian Charismatic renewal of the 1960s, the religious sense of 'charisma' lay largely dormant. The status and meaning of the idea of charisma in the twentieth century, and into the twenty-first, may be attributed to its reinvention by Weber.

This is a basic assumption in the scholarship on charisma and celebrity. In his study of charisma published in 1990, Charles Lindholm declares that the word 'charisma', although '[v]irtually unknown a generation ago', is now 'a part of the vocabulary of the general public'; he acknowledges that Weber 'was the first to introduce the term "charisma" into sociology'.[5] P. David Marshall, in *Celebrity and Power* (1997), remarks that as a result of Weber's 'reinvestment in the term, *charisma* in its modern usage is roughly synonymous with how Weber describes it'.[6] Lewis Coser, writing in 1969, simply states that the Weberian term charisma has 'become part of everyday language'.[7] Irvine Schiffer, in his psychological study of charisma published in 1973, also credits Weber with the 'first conceptualization of the term charisma',[8] but as Schiffer points out, Weber did not conjure this concept from thin air.

'Charisma' before Weber

Although the word 'charisma' was rarely used for many centuries, it survived within Christian discourse in its ecclesiastical Latin form through to the seventeenth century, maintaining its Pauline meaning of spiritual gift granted by God.[9] William Tooker's book, published in Latin in 1597, concerned 'Charisma siue Donum sanationis' (charisma or the gift of healing), detailing this charisma as a divine gift in possession of the monarch. In the seventeenth century, Christian theologians reverted to the Greek form of the word: in 1644 John Bulwer wrote in his *Chirologia, or the naturall language of the hand* ... of 'that Charisme or miraculous gift of healing'. In 1642 Bishop Montagu referred to 'the Charismata of grace' in his *Acts and Monuments of the Church before Christ Incarnate*. 'Charisme', a transliteration of the Greek χάρισμα, in these works retained the strictly Christian meaning of 'free gift or favour specially vouchsafed by God'.[10] The Greek could be used, however, with the more general meaning of 'gift', as in R. Mayhew's book, published in London in 1676, *Charisma Patrikon, a Paternal Gift, or, The Legacie of a Dying Father, to His Living Children* ... .[11]

By the nineteenth century the Anglicised 'charism' had replaced the Latin 'charisma' or Greek 'charisme' in theological studies of the early church published in English. *The Life and Epistles of St Paul* by John Conybeare and J. S. Howson, published in 1852, defined the 'gift' of prophecy as 'that charism which enabled its possessors to utter, with the authority of inspiration, divine strains of warning'. John Colenso, writing in *Evangelical Christendom* (1862), stated that Paul spoke 'of various charisms or graces'. The English usage of 'charisma', replacing 'charism', appeared in an *Encyclopedia Britannica* entry in 1875, in which it was recorded that the German theologian Friedrich Schleiermacher (1768–1834) said of another scholar that he possessed a 'special *charisma* for the science of "Introduction"'.[12] Schleiermacher, who developed the discipline of hermeneutics from its theological origins, was read by Weber as a university student.[13] Schleiermacher's usage of 'special *charisma*' suggests a broader meaning of gift or talent, and anticipates to some extent the word's secular connotation in the twentieth century.

However, the most common definition of 'charisma' (drawn from the German via its Latin base) and 'charism' (which persisted as an Anglicised version of 'charisma') remained 'grace, talent bestowed by God'[14] and existed almost exclusively within Christian scholarship. The *Religious Encyclopedia*, edited by Philip Schaff and published in 1883, noted that church offices were 'impossible without charismatic endowment'. Pfleiderer's *The Influence of the Apostle Paul*, translated into English and published in 1885, discussed the 'Pauline spirit of evangelical freedom and individual charismatic enlightenment'.[15] Usage of 'charisma' and 'charismatic' until the early twentieth century was largely restricted to biblical commentary, theological scholarship or liturgy. The debates within German theological scholarship of the late nineteenth century concerning charisma provided the inspiration for Weber's refiguring of the term.

Within the broader discourse of general usage, 'charisma' at the beginning of the twentieth century had little or no profile: the word was barely known. It has been observed that the 'same general sentiment was expressed by the term *prestige*'.[16] 'Prestige' in the nineteenth century had the connotation of 'impressive or overawing influence, glamour'. John Stuart Mill wrote in 1838 of the prestige with which Napoleon 'overawed the world'; Joseph Conrad wrote in 1900 of a friend's 'extraordinary prestige', the 'prestige of a quiescent bomb'.[17] Only later in the twentieth century did 'prestige' acquire the meaning of 'status': by the late 1930s it was connected with social status, and by the 1950s it was heavily used in compounds such as 'prestige-conscious'.[18] Theodore Abel's 1938 account of Hitler's rise to power, employing Weber's theory of charismatic leadership as an explanatory device, uses 'prestige' in its old sense at the same time as introducing Weberian charisma. Hitler, wrote Abel, was endowed by his followers 'with that highest degree of prestige' emanating from their belief in his 'superhuman power', which Abel describes as 'the basis of what Max Weber has called charismatic leadership'.[19] Before long, this meaning of 'out-of-the-ordinary' powers or qualities would pass from 'prestige' to 'charisma'. The semantic shift undergone by 'prestige' in the twentieth century was at least in part associated with the popular acceptance of 'charisma' as defined by Weber. By the mid-twentieth century, one would have referred to Napoleon's charisma, or to a friend's extraordinary charisma: Weber's term had by then usurped a semantic function previously performed by 'prestige'.

At the beginning of the twentieth century, when Weber was formulating his theory of charisma, 'prestige' was the closest available term to convey the innate authority he wished to describe. Rather than deploy a current word such as prestige, however, Weber chose to appropriate an ancient word, resonant for him with religious connotations, reinventing the word as a key term within his sociology of authority. His remarkable success in this ambition, the subsequent general acceptance of 'charisma' and semantic shift of 'prestige', all indicate that 'prestige' was inadequate to convey the force of intrinsic authority intended by Weber (the primary meaning of 'prestige', after all, had been illusion or conjuring trick). 'Charisma', with its religious roots of 'spiritual gift', proved to be much better suited as a vehicle for Weber's ambition.

Weber's disenchanted world

Charisma assumed such importance for Weber in the last decade of his life that it has been described as 'the archetype of Weber's political sociology'; for him it came to represent 'the only creative force in history'.[20] To appreciate the significance of charisma in Weber's thought, we need to situate Weber within the political and intellectual environment of his time. Weber's intellectual formation occurred in the last three decades of the nineteenth century, while his published writing career spanned the first two decades of the twentieth. Weber witnessed the height of European nationalism, and its political expression in imperialism; he observed the international development of urbanism, mass-industrial processes, and large-scale bureaucracies in both the public and private sectors. He was in many ways a citizen of modernity.

It has been asserted by several commentators that Weber occupied a crucial juncture not only in German or European history but 'in the development of Western civilisation'.[21] The decline of the aristocratic ruling class and its replacement by a managerial industrial class; political upheaval and the challenge of Marxism; the waning of religion as a binding social force; the triumph of science, accompanied by the doctrine of progress; and a rationalising overhaul of all cultural endeavours, from mass production and design to intellectual disciplines, including history and the 'social sciences': Weber lived through all these processes, and engaged with them in his work.

Weber's father was a politician, a member of the Reichstag for the National Liberal Party; his mother was a devout Protestant with humanitarian concerns. The growing estrangement between his patriarchal, bourgeois father and his compassionate religious mother has been posited as a significant factor in Weber's intellectual development; it is sufficient to note that from his father he absorbed a liberal scepticism and political emphasis on the individual, while from his mother he was exposed to the social consequences of religious belief.[22] The family home in Berlin was frequented by many of the liberal intellectuals and politicians of the day, fostering a connection between political thought and action that remained important for Weber. His studies at university in Heidelberg included law, political economy, medieval history and the history of philosophy, while he read widely in theology and philosophy. The scope of his research interests was reflected in his doctoral dissertations: on medieval trading companies and the history of ancient agrarian institutions. He accepted a chair at Heidelberg in 1896, but suffered a nervous breakdown in 1897, following the death of his father; Weber's psychological and physical health remained so poor that he was debilitated until 1903, when he became a co-editor of the social science journal *Archiv für Sozialwissenschaft.*

Weber's enormous range of intellectual interests in part resulted from the tradition of German scholarship, which, at the end of the nineteenth century, was still able to generate 'universal scholars'.[23] Intellectuals were expected to be multilingual (Weber learnt Spanish, Italian, Russian and Hebrew in pursuit of his studies) and to specialise in several disciplines. A command of history, philosophy, theology, psychology, philology, literature and the classics fostered German intellectuals of the calibre of Nietzsche and Weber, to name just two of the most influential universal scholars; such figures became much rarer in the twentieth century, as academic research came to favour specialisation over generalisation.

Weber considered that the intellectual world of his time bore the imprint of Marx and Nietzsche, and that any theoretical project must confront those two definers of modernity.[24] His relationship to both was ambivalent; his own theories of economy, history and society managed to steer a path between them. Weber shared with Marx the goal of analysing the interrelated constituent elements – economic and political – of social structures on a historical basis,[25] but he rejected as illusory any Marxist 'laws' of history. Weber's *The Protestant Ethic and the Spirit of Capitalism* contested the Marxist conviction that the cultural superstructure was determined by the economic base; for Weber capitalism itself could be shown to have emerged due to a number of causal factors, among them the force of religious doctrine. Whereas Marx regarded control of the means of production as the crucial factor in political developments, for Weber the means of administration – of the state, of corporations, of bureaucracies – was paramount. Weber saw all political and social systems as subject to 'inescapable universal bureaucracy';[26] consequently he had no faith in Marxist revolution, foreseeing that a Marxist state would constitute not a dictatorship of the proletariat but a 'dictatorship of the official'.[27]

Nietzsche's elevation of the extraordinary individual – the *Übermensch*, 'overman' or superman – above the mass of humanity was a significant influence on Weber's formulation of the charismatic leader. Nietzsche's overman was not so much a leader as a pointer to the 'overcoming' of flawed humanity: this overman was a maverick outsider, a smasher of conventions, abiding by his own code of values and entirely dismissive of accepted norms and morality: 'beyond good and evil'. The veneration of the creative individual personified in the overman offered far more appeal to Weber than did Marx's class-based collective agent, the proletariat. Nietzsche's heroic figure was also transhistorical, performing a dramatic role within Nietzsche's idiosyncratic philosophy of history. Weber constructed transhistorical personae within his own far more systematic world history, in the form of 'ideal types', figures such as the charismatic leader who recurred across history. In addition, Weber shared Nietzsche's declinist narrative of the history of civilization: neither embraced the promise of modernity; both rejected the doctrine of progress, which was for Nietzsche 'merely a modern idea, that is to say a false idea'.[28] Finally, both writers had a fondness for prophetic declamation, expressed by Nietzsche within his invented pseudoreligious Zarathustra framework: 'Behold, I am a herald of the lightning and a heavy drop from the cloud; but this lightning is called *overman*'.[29] Weber's prophetic mode was much more restrained, but in his later years he took inspiration from reading the Hebrew prophets, who represented for him early incarnations of the charismatic leader; some of Weber's late writings and speeches contain a prophetic overtone.

Despite Weber's affinities with Nietzsche, there were also important points of difference. Weber could not embrace Nietzsche's aristocratic disdain for the human herd, above which the 'overman' was raised. Nietzsche's hero was removed and alienated from society (like Nietzsche himself); Weber by contrast theorised the extraordinary individual 'as a social creature' functioning within a community.[30] For the 'wilful genius' or charismatic leader to obtain a following, he would need to empathise with his peers, rather than exult in his superiority from a lofty position. Weber also had no interest in the vociferous atheism of Nietzsche, regarding such excess as a 'painful residue of the bourgeois Philistine'.[31] Whereas Nietzsche waged an intellectual war on Christianity, condemning it as a form of moral sickness, Weber – who described himself as 'unmusical' in religion – devoted much of his intellectual output to a measured analysis, without value judgement, of the social and political consequences of religion, including Christianity.

Weber's politics were Liberal, explicitly bourgeois, laying acute emphasis on the role, rights and freedom of the individual. He extended the idea of the individual as political agent to that of the nation, publicly advocating from 1895 a policy of imperialist expansion. This ideology of 'liberal imperialism' became socially acceptable in Germany partly through Weber's speeches and writings:[32] military expansion was regarded as a legitimate means of ensuring national vitality. While espousing nationalist and imperialist views, Weber also wrote critically of the German political system, advocating constitutional reform and a parliamentary form of democracy; after the war he was involved in the deliberations that led to the parliamentary system of government. Weber remained committed to both democracy and capitalism as the systems most compatible with individual freedom and an open society, but in the last two decades of his life he became increasingly pessimistic regarding their future. He feared that capitalism would inevitably stagnate as markets and territory reached their limits, and that democracy would be overwhelmed by the escalating machinery of bureaucratisation. Weber dreaded the prospect of a world 'filled with nothing but those clogs who cling to a little post and strive for a somewhat greater one'. For him the 'passion for bureaucratisation' was 'enough to drive one to despair'. Weber strongly believed that advocates for a free society must set themselves against the bureaucratic machinery, 'in order to preserve a remnant of humanity from this parcelling-out of the soul, from this exclusive rule of bureaucratic life ideals'.[33]

Weber connected the insidious and overpowering trend to ever-larger bureaucracies with the principle he identified as rationalisation. Throughout history, Weber observed, civilisations sought to refine their methods and systems of production by rationalising their efficiency. But more efficient methods were also more predictable, hence less spontaneous and inevitably more bureaucratic. Rationalisation for

Weber meant 'routinisation', depersonalisation, the growth of rigid social structures and the loss of personal freedoms. Weber lamented the decline of the inspirational, the irrational, the charismatic, within this 'iron cage' of rationalisation. Yet he believed that the older irrational force persisted, if only in diminished form, as he publicly remarked in a speech, 'Science as a Vocation' made at Munich University in 1918:

> The fate of our times is characterised by rationalization and intellectualisation and, above all, by the 'disenchantment of the world'. Precisely the ultimate and most sublime values have retreated from public life ... nor is it accidental that today only within the smallest and intimate circles, in personal human situations, in *pianissmo*, that something is pulsating that corresponds to the prophetic *pneuma*, which in former times swept through the great communities like a firebrand, welding them together.[34]

This well-known passage contains the essence of Weber's world view near the end of his life: a tone of lament at the modern 'disenchanted' world, coupled with the sustaining hope in a revival of spirit, here connected by Weber, in his prophetic mode, to early religious communities. Although the contemporary reference here is somewhat obscure, in another speech made that same year, 'Politics as a Vocation', Weber associated spirit with 'personal *gift of grace* (charisma)' which operates still in the political sphere, including parliamentary democracy.[35]

In general terms, Weber's thought bore the influence of two intellectual currents of late nineteenth-century Europe. The first was the late Romanticism that overlapped with early modernity. Many of the themes of Weber's work are evident in the late Romantic impulse: an adverse attitude to modernity and the mechanisation of life, resistance to the idea of progress, nostalgia for an unsullied past. The Romantic cult of the genius – the rare, inspired, creative individual – was also a constituent factor in Weber's construction of the charismatic leader. The historian W. E. H. Lecky, writing in 1867, had extended the notion of genius as hero from the artistic realm to the political:

> There arise from time to time men who bear to the moral condition of their age much the same relations as men of genius bear to its intellectual condition ... the magnetism of their perfections tells powerfully upon their contemporaries. An enthusiasm is kindled, a group of adherents is formed, and many are emancipated from the moral condition of their age.[36]

Weber's charismatic leader is a heroic figure in this mould: a rare, inspired individual blessed with the power to emancipate his peers. As several commentators have noted, the dichotomy evident in the world view of the late Weber pitted charisma against rationalisation as 'eternal rivals';[37] and because charisma for Weber functioned through special individual leaders, the contest was 'hero vs. bureaucrat',[38] or, more accurately, charismatic hero vs. bureaucracy.

The other important intellectual current was the secularisation of theological traditions and concepts. Nineteenth-century German intellectual effort established the foundations for disciplines such as history on a rational basis, as evident in the historical works and method of Ranke; on the other hand, the idealism of Hegel drew much of its propulsion in its philosophy of history from a 'demythologised' Christianity. Empiricism and idealism could fuse in the one endeavour: Ranke himself drew on idealism and wrote universal history late in his career. In the later nineteenth century, the philosophers Dilthey and Rickert aimed to lay a philosophical foundation for German historicism, which for Dilthey had achieved 'the definitive constitution of history as a science ... and of the human sciences in general'.[39] Weber was influenced by the philosophy of history of Rickert in particular, as well as by the writings of his friend Georg Simmel, author of *Philosophy of Money* and proponent of a tragic view of the history of culture. Weber was also familiar, through his studies of religion, with the secular appropriation of methods formerly associated with religious tradition. Exegesis and hermeneutics were techniques of religious scholarship that had been adapted as methods of secular intellectual work. The religious origins of secular political thought also exercised German historians in the late nineteenth century: Georg Jellinek, a friend of Weber's, published a study in 1895 demonstrating the religious roots of the Rights of Man.[40] Weber's studies in theology and Christian history left him ideally placed to develop this confluence. His refiguring of the Christian concept of 'charisma' was his enduring exercise in the secularisation – and transformation – of religious thought.

Finally, two specific characteristics of Weber as intellectual are pertinent to a discussion of his work. The first is his paradoxical relationship to rationalisation. While he deplored the social and cultural effects of rationalisation, he also acknowledged its effectiveness. His own intellectual work in sociology situated him within the rationalised social sciences celebrated by Dilthey as the definitive scientific constitution of these disciplines. Weber's method was dry, explicitly value-neutral; for him, science, including the social sciences, should coolly describe sociocultural forms, including values, so that readers may decide rationally on a course of action.[41] Weber did not deny that rationalisation generated improved productivity, especially on a large scale. Because he accepted its inevitability – and, in its wake, inevitable bureaucracies – Weber succumbed to a pessimism in his later years. He also felt compelled to propose, in the form of charisma, a countervailing force to rationalisation, even if the insurmountable force of modern bureaucracy relegated charisma to a function within its apparatus.

Weber was a brilliant synthesiser of ideas and bodies of knowledge, rather than a startling intellectual innovator. The ideas for which he is most well known – the 'disenchantment of the world' and 'charisma' – were borrowed from other authors: the former from Friedrich Schiller,[42] the latter from Rudolf Sohm. His prodigious reading and mastery of a wide range of disciplines equipped him with the means to forge concepts from divergent components. His analysis of contemporary politics and society drew on world economic and religious history, so that, as Lewis Coser remarks, his work was 'a highly creative response to social and psychological pressures'[43] experienced in his time. The creativity and depth of Weber's intellectual powers are evident in his reinvention of charisma: he reached back to ancient religion in order to devise a counter to the modern world he inhabited.

Weber on charisma

Weber's first fleeting mention of charisma comes not in *Economy and Society*, but in *The Protestant Ethic and the Spirit of Capitalism*, originally published in two issues of the *Archiv* journal in 1904–5. Weber reworked this material as a volume in his series on the sociology of religion, published in 1920; an English translation by Talcott Parsons was published in 1930. Weber refers to charisma near the end of his famous account of the Protestant – largely Calvinist and Puritan – foundations of the spirit of capitalism. Weber notes that one strand of asceticism, within the Zinzendorf branch of Pietism,

> glorified the loyal worker who did not seek acquisition, but lived according to the apostolic model, and was thus endowed with the *charisma* of the disciples.[44]

A translator's note by Parsons states, mistakenly, that '*Charisma* is a sociological term coined by Weber himself'. Parsons's ignorance of the word's history prior to Weber's appropriation of it is an indication of the obscurity of 'charisma' before its refiguring in Weber's writings. Parsons provides a perfunctory definition of charisma drawn from his reading of *Wirtschaft und Gesellschaft*: 'It refers to the quality of leadership which appeals to non-rational motives'.[45]

The concluding pages of *The Protestant Ethic* step forward into the modern world, in which Puritan asceticism and faith have given way to 'the tremendous cosmos of the modern economic order'.[46] Weber's pessimism is already apparent in his reference to the 'iron cage' of the society made possible by machine production. He leaves the future of such a society open, perhaps to be explored in his later works:

> No one knows who will live in this cage in the future, or whether at the end of this tremendous development entirely new prophets will arise, or ... mechanised petrifaction.[47]

One of the aims of Weber's *Economy and Society* was the tracing of the historical development of rationalisation;[48] yet this huge work encompasses much more. Weber wrote *Economy and Society* over two periods: what became Part Two was written from 1910 to 1914; Part One was begun in 1918 and remained unfinished at his death in 1920. Part One contains 'conceptual exposition' of sociological terms and categories; it introduces Weber's three types of legitimate domination, including charismatic authority. The much longer Part Two surveys social formations, law, economics and religion within a world history perspective; charisma is analysed here with regard to its 'transformations' and with specific reference to the history of religion. Because Weber never had the chance to refine and complete *Economy and Society*, it remains an uneven, inconsistent work. The two sections, written either side of World War I, pursue different emphases: the earlier Part Two has a historical framework, the later Part One is a more static, schematic overview. The treatment of charisma varies slightly in accordance with these differing emphases, which has prompted some commentators to claim that Weber 'sometimes contradicted himself' in *Economy and Society* concerning charisma.[49]

Part One has the advantage, however, of containing Weber's definition of charisma:

> The term 'charisma' will be applied to a certain quality of an individual personality by virtue of which he is considered extraordinary and treated as endowed with supernatural, superhuman, or at least specifically exceptional powers or qualities.[50]

For Weber, this universal phenomenon constituted one of the three 'types of legitimate domination' or three 'pure types of authority'.[51] Weber provides a simple definition of domination as 'the probability that certain specific commands (or all commands) will be obeyed by a given group of persons'.[52] The three types of legitimate domination formulated by Weber are the rational-legal, in which 'obedience is owed to the legally established impersonal order'; the traditional, resting on 'an established belief in the sanctity of immemorial traditions and on the legitimacy of those exercising authority under them'; and the charismatic, based on 'devotion to the exceptional sanctity, heroism or exemplary character of an individual person, and of the normative patterns or order revealed or ordained by him'.[53]

For all the emphasis made by commentators of the charisma-vs.-bureaucracy bifurcation in Weber, it should not be forgotten that charisma takes its place, in Weber's sociology of domination, within this tripartite structure. Weber contrasts charismatic authority with the other two types of domination by accentuating the crucial role of the 'charismatically qualified leader'. Whereas the rational-legal grounds of authority are derived from the legality of 'enacted rules', charismatic authority is based on 'personal trust' in an exceptional leader by his followers. And although traditional authority may reside in the person of an individual leader, obedience in such a social formation is owed to the position – bound by tradition – occupied by that person. Charismatic domination differs from both scenarios in that the charismatic leader 'as such' is obeyed, as a result of his heroism or 'exemplary qualities'. Charismatic authority will continue for as long as that leader can repeatedly demonstrate charismatic powers, so that his followers maintain their belief in his charisma.[54]

Having introduced the concept of charismatic authority, Weber acknowledges his intellectual debt concerning the term 'charisma': the 'concept of "charisma" ("the gift of grace") is taken from the vocabulary of early Christianity'. Weber notes that the church historian Rudolf Sohm was 'the first to clarify the substance of the concept, even though he did not use the same terminology'.[55] In Part Two of *Economy and Society*, Weber elaborates on Sohm's contribution: it is 'to Rudolf Sohm's credit that he worked out the sociological character of this kind of domination' – that is, charismatic. Sohm, however, had restricted his study to the early Christian church; Weber's innovation was to propose the universality of charismatic authority: in principle, he states, 'these phenomena are universal, even though they are often most evident in the religious realm'.[56]

Weber mentions that other historians of religion, including Holl in *Enthusiasmus*, had clarified 'important consequences' of charisma; it is, he notes, 'thus nothing new'.[57] Sohm's work was part of a debate on early – or 'primitive' – Christianity among German theologians in the second half of the nineteenth century. F. C. Bauer, for example, had proposed a naturalistic interpretation of the Pauline charismata, asserting that 'the charisms are originally nothing but the gifts and qualities which each man brings with him to Christianity'.[58] The significant contribution of Sohm, in his *Kirchenrecht I* (published 1892) and *Outlines of Church History* (published 1887, English translation 1895) was his study of the transition within the early church in terms of government and authority. Sohm notes that in the very early church, members were bound together 'solely through the gifts of grace (χάρισμα)'; apostles, teachers and prophets constituted a 'purely spiritual' government: 'they ruled, but without legal authority'.[59] Sohm traces the 'astonishing transformation' by which the church, largely through its investment in the hierarchical position of bishop, developed a 'definite, legal constitution': the church was no longer a spiritual entity founded on the communion of believers and their charismata, but was instead founded 'upon the *office*'.[60] This transformation identified by Sohm was an instance of the historical process theorised by Weber, in *Economy and Society*, as the 'routinisation of charisma'.

In expanding on his definition of charismatic authority, Weber states that the charismatic individual's exceptional powers are 'regarded as of divine origin or as exemplary, and on the basis of them the individual concerned is treated as a "leader"'.[61] Weber's reinvention of the term 'charisma' is distilled in this sentence. He has appropriated the word – and its spiritual, supernatural associations – from early Christianity, but he has replaced the communal sensibility emphasised in the Pauline charismata with a focus on the individual leader. By ignoring Paul's conception of charisma as a communal blessing spread across group members, Weber has redefined the term as a specific form of domination, an individual endowment used by remarkable leaders to command authority over their followers. Furthermore, while Paul's use of the word related strictly to the close and small Christian communities of his time, Weber generalised charisma to express an 'extraordinary' quality manifest across cultures and throughout history.

Weber provides an initial sketch in Part One of the origins of charismatic authority. In 'primitive circumstances', he writes, charisma is thought to rest on the magical powers of prophets, leaders in the hunt, war heroes, or 'persons with a reputation for therapeutic or legal wisdom'.[62] Other historical examples offered by Weber are the berserk, the shaman, the frenzied fighters of Byzantium, and – in more recent times – Joseph Smith, founder of Mormonism, and the *littératueur* Kurt Eisner. The decisive factor in charismatic domination is the recognition of the leader by the followers, which is freely given, initially guaranteed by a proof, 'originally always a miracle', resulting in 'absolute trust' in the leader.[63] Once the leader has proven his charismatic credentials, it is the duty of the community to become his followers, to accept the sacred authority of his position. Weber calls this moment 'pure charisma', announced as a 'call' (such as that experienced by a prophet), a mission or spiritual duty. The rise of a charismatic leader is revolutionary in that it sweeps aside existing authority and tradition: charismatic authority 'repudiates the past'. The charismatic leader installs no hierarchy or system of rules; charismatic leadership is opposed to bureaucracy and all rational forms of domination: it is 'specifically irrational in the sense of being foreign to all rules'.[64] Weber's general description of the charismatic type of domination includes the declaration that in traditionalist periods, 'charisma is *the* great revolutionary force'.[65] Since it is based on an emotional relationship between leader and followers, it is also unstable and impossible to sustain.

Weber acknowledges, in Part One, the limitations of his typology of the 'pure' forms of domination, which are 'not usually' to be found in historical cases: they are, rather, ideal types. The types become more relevant to 'empirical systems of authority' through their transformation, by routinisation or combination with other forms of authority, resulting in such constructions as 'the charisma of office'.[66] While charismatic authority 'in its pure form' may be 'foreign' to everyday routine structures, some form of compromise is inevitable if such an authority is to attain permanence. Weber outlines the routinisation of charisma as the inevitable process awaiting a successful charismatic leadership. Because this leadership cannot achieve stability, it must become 'either traditionalized or rationalized, or a combination of both'.[67]

Many instances of charismatic authority will terminate, on the death or dislodgement of the charismatic leader, or if that leader can no longer demonstrate extraordinary abilities and therefore loses his following. But if the charismatic authority is secure, and a charismatic community continues after the disappearance of the 'personal charismatic leader', then the problem of succession becomes crucial. Succession may be implemented in various ways: the search for a replacement charismatic leader (the Dalai Lama), revelation according to oracles or other techniques (amounting to a form of legalisation), designation by a charismatic leader of his own successor, the designation of the successor by an administrative staff (the election of the Pope), hereditary charisma (the divine right of kings, royal families), the transfer of charisma to an office of government. Hereditary charisma is the routinsation of a personal charisma into a traditional form of legitimate domination. As Weber notes, 'personal charisma may be totally absent' when a leader assumes authority on a hereditary basis.[68] Weber was particularly concerned with hereditary charisma – which he also called 'familial charisma' or 'clan charisma' – in his studies of the religions of China and India.[69] Weber found that charisma attributed to kinship was especially strong in China with its 'great families', and in India, where 'charisma of the clans' contributed greatly to the establishment of the caste structure.[70]

In *Economy and Society*, Weber maintains the distinction between the original 'personal' charisma and those routinised forms that transfer authority into offices or traditions. Where a replacement charismatic leader is recruited by followers or administrative staff using tests of eligibility, their recruitment represents the discovery, rather than the manufacture, of charisma, which 'can only be "awakened" and "tested" in an individual; it cannot be "learned" or "taught"'[71] Weber thus emphasises the innate or personal charisma as the 'original basis' of charismatic authority, before the inevitable routinsation into traditional or rationalised forms.

Part Two of *Economy and Society* provides further detail, from a comparative world-history perspective, of the character and transformations of charisma. Weber discusses charisma at the beginning of the long Sociology of Religion section, in the context of terms used across cultures – *mana*, *orenda* and the Persian *maga* – to designate extraordinary powers. Weber offers 'charisma' to denote such powers, but adds that charisma may be either of two types. Where the term is 'fully merited', charisma is 'a gift that inheres in an object or person simply by view of natural endowment'.[72] The investment of charisma in objects, presumably referring to magical or sacred objects, is not developed by Weber: his sociological interest in *Economy and Society* is in charisma as possessed by individuals or as transferred into institutions. For Weber, innateness is a feature of 'primary charisma', which 'cannot be acquired by any means'. The secondary type of charisma 'may be produced artificially in an object or person through extraordinary means', although the germ of such powers needs to exist before they can be evoked or developed.[73]

In his sociology of religion, Weber makes a strong distinction between prophet and priest: the prophet is a 'purely individual bearer of charisma' who answers a personal call and exerts power 'simply by virtue of his personal gifts'.[74] The priest, by contrast, lays claim to authority 'by virtue of his service in a sacred tradition'; even if the priest possess personal charisma, legitimate authority is conferred by the 'hierarchical office'.[75] Prophets are also distinguished from religious teachers due to the emotional nature of their inspired preaching; Weber regards the prophets of ancient religions as precursors of demagogues and publicists, due to their emotional connection with a community.[76]

At the conclusion of the section on religion in *Economy and Society*, Weber applies his own theory of charisma to Jesus, whom he describes as the bearer of 'magical charisma' with a 'unique feeling of individuality'. For Weber, Jesus's extraordinary self-esteem derived from his knowledge that he 'possessed both the charisma requisite for the control of demons and a tremendous preaching ability, far surpassing that of any scholar or Pharisee'. Like all charismatic leaders, Jesus needed to have his extraordinary powers recognised by his followers: Weber notes Jesus's conviction that his power of exorcism 'was operative only among the people who believed in him'. Weber finds that Jesus's charismatic powers 'were the absolutely decisive components in Jesus' feelings concerning his messiahship'.[77] By focusing on Jesus as a classical example of the charismatic religious leader, Weber has thoroughly shifted the meaning of 'charisma' (as initially defined by Paul 20 years after Jesus's death) from divine grace available for the benefit of the community to innate power residing in extraordinary leaders.

The final section of *Economy and Society* in which charisma is elaborated concerns the transformations undergone by charisma throughout history; Weber provides many examples to illustrate this process, ranging from ancient religion to contemporary (1913) American politics. Weber specifies that charismatic figures appear as 'natural' leaders in 'moments of distress', manifesting to their communities 'specific gifts of body and mind ... considered "supernatural" (in the sense that not everybody could have access to them)'.[78] Weber expands the range of such charismatic figures to include doctors, prophets, judges, military leaders or the leaders of hunting expeditions: all exert an authority over their followers by proving their charisma through extraordinary feats. The charismatic leader responds to moments of crisis, 'especially political or economic situations';[79] that leader feels chosen by destiny or divinity and announces his calling to the community. Weber emphasises again the 'highly individual quality' of charisma and its inherence in the exceptional individual: 'the mission and the power of its bearer is delimited from within, not by an external order'. This means that charismatic domination is 'the opposite' of bureaucracy and 'methodical rational acquisition'.[80]

Weber associates charismatic domination with 'heroism', whether of 'an ascetic, military, judicial, magical' or other kind.[81] Charismatic rulership 'arises from collective excitement produced by extraordinary events and from surrender to heroism of any kind'.[82] In the initial stages of a charismatic domination, the sole administration consists of a 'charismatic aristocracy', such as disciples loyal to the leader. But the desire to convert the 'transitory gift of grace' into a 'permanent possession of everyday life' is perennial: every instance of charisma 'is on the road from a turbulently emotional life that knows no economic rationality to a slow death by suffocation under the weight of material interests'.[83]

The rest of Weber's analysis of charisma is devoted to the many forms of its routinisation. Much of this section adds further detail to the means, sketched in Part One, by which the revolutionary power of charisma is tamed as it becomes a part of everyday life. More accurately, Part One – written later – is a schematisation of the material presented in Part Two concerning the methods by which a ruling structure is built up around charisma. This process is the capture of a 'charismatic, and thus sacred, source of authority' for use as a legitimation of economic and social power. An administrative staff is founded (priests, knights, warrior councils); traditions are established, imbued – like charisma – with 'a religious aura'.[84] In this process, charisma and tradition – 'basically antagonistic' in their pure form – merge with one another. Although Weber states that such a fusion strips charisma of its revolutionary force, and is indeed 'alien to its essence', such a merger is nevertheless an 'ever recurring development'.[85] The twin consequences of this marriage are that traditions are endowed with a legitimacy, and that charisma may maintain a presence – however muted – in traditional or rationalised social formations.

In discussing the process of routinisation, Weber addresses the issue – which later troubled or at least puzzled some critics – concerning the historical sequence of the types of legitimate domination. Because, Weber contends, it is possible to identify instances of charisma even in contemporary political life, the three types of domination 'cannot be placed into a simple evolutionary line'; rather, they appear together, mixed in 'the most diverse combinations'. However, he then declares that it is the fate of charisma 'to recede with the development of permanent institutional structures'.[86] This universal 'fate' does suggest a temporal sequence in which an original charismatic authority necessarily becomes routinised into a traditional or legal structure. Weber points to 'the early stages of social life' in which magical forces were thought to inhere in 'things and men'; in such societies charismatic forces attended every extraordinary ability, act of magic or heroic quality. Routinisation occurred in such societies when the manipulation of deities by individual charismatics became a permanent cult: the charismatic prophet or magician then 'turns into a priest'. Similarly, when wars become especially difficult and require discipline (a form of rationalisation), the charismatic war hero 'becomes a king'.[87]

In this and the many other examples offered by Weber's comparative sociology, a 'simple evolutionary line' does seem to operate. The orientation is always from a 'pure' charismatic base towards the dilution of charisma as it is transferred into an institutionalised form. Weber details the 'depersonalisation' of charisma as it becomes attached to an office regardless of the occupant, or 'lineage charisma' – the belief in its 'transferability through blood ties'.[88] Charisma in such cases becomes 'impersonal': the monarchy or other office projects an extraordinary quality or aura, as charisma is transferred into an institution. This 'charisma of office' may even endure in a highly rationalised society in which that office itself has lost political power, as in the instance of the constitutional monarch, in whose name parliament functions.[89]

Weber's theoretical position concerning the historical sequence of the types of domination seems, then, contradictory, or at least unresolved. His charting of the process of routinisation repeatedly traces a line from primary charisma to the 'petrifaction' of tradition or rationalised order. Weber concludes the section on Charisma and Its Transformations with a final observation, drawn from the contemporary state of rationalisation, as manifest in the factory and the 'bureaucratic state machine': this 'universal phenomenon more and more restricts the importance of charisma and of individually differentiated conduct'.[90] Weber posits universal phenomena that invariably domesticate or vitiate the original charismatic impulse.

On the other hand, Weber also points to the persistence of charisma, in even the most secular and highly ordered societies. In such circumstances, charisma survives, in diverse and perhaps surprising combinations with traditional or rationalised forms. The massive bureaucratic apparatus of modern democracies may still accentuate the charismatic power of party leaders; this indicates a conflict between 'the charismatic hero principle and the mundane power of the party organization': Weber proposes Roosevelt's 1912 US presidential campaign as an example of this conflict.[91] Weber argues that all political parties have their origins in the charismatic following of 'legitimate or caesarist pretenders' or demagogues; if such followings develop into routinised and permanent organisations, they succumb to a bureaucratic apparatus that 'controls the party's course, including the vitally important nomination of candidates'.[92] Democratic elections are in reality a decision between candidates who have been 'screened' by party machines before being offered to voters. Enormous financial resources are required, particularly in the US, where quadrennial campaigns 'already amount to about as much as a colonial war'.

Yet despite the controlling power of bureaucratic party machines, charisma retains a role in the democratic political process: Weber nominates the 'charisma of rhetoric' evident in electioneering 'stump speeches'. The 'purely emotional' effect of charismatic rhetoric may occasionally build into a case of 'charismatic hero worship', where a political candidate or leader generates so much emotional appeal that even the party machine must fall into service of this charisma.[93] In rare cases such a 'hero' may attempt to break the 'technician's hold over the party' by imposing 'plebiscitary designation' and nomination within the party. However, Weber states, only 'extraordinary conditions can bring about the triumph of charisma over the organization'; the general rule is that the party organisation 'easily succeeds in this castration of charisma'.[94]

Finally, Weber's belief in the ongoing role of charisma in the contemporary Western world was made evident in his two 1918 speeches, 'Politics as a Vocation' and 'Science as a Vocation'. In the former speech, he offered a brief summation of his theory of charismatic domination as 'the absolutely personal devotion and personal confidence in revelation, heroism, or other qualities of individual leadership'. In the political sphere, such charismatic domination could be exercised by warlords, plebiscitary rulers, great demagogues or – within the rationalised democratic political system – 'the political party leader'.[95] In the latter speech, particularly in the famous passage quoted earlier in this chapter, Weber drew attention to the 'pulsating' force, corresponding to the ancient 'prophetic *pneuma*', apparent even in his contemporary rationalised milieu.[96] The tone of lament in this passage indicates the context for Weber's motivation in reinventing charisma as a form of authority. For Weber, the bureaucratic processes of industrial modernity brought with them a form of loss: they engendered a 'disenchanted' world. By positing charisma as a universal type of authority, Weber could expose contemporary Western societies to a critical perspective with at least two salient points. First, he could argue that Western modernity, for all its technological and economic progress, suffered from a diminution on the spiritual level by comparison with earlier, less sophisticated societies. One index of this loss was the taming or bureaucratisation of charisma, which, in its 'purest' form, represented a galvanising spiritual force. Second, Weber could maintain that despite all the rationalisation of contemporary social formations, something of the older, irrational forces survived: the 'iron cage' of modernity was not so repressive as to lock forces like charisma completely out of sight. Weber identified charismatic authority functioning even within the modern world of bureaucratic politics; for him, highly rationalised societies remained, despite all their efforts, fusions of the rational and the irrational or charismatic.

'Charisma' after Weber

Weber's treatment of charismatic leadership as a form of legitimate domination quickly gained purchase within sociology and political theory. Albert Salamon published an essay, 'Max Weber', in 1925, summarising Weber's historical world view as a struggle between rationalisation and charisma, in which the 'charismatic hero' fights 'unto death'.[97] One of Salamon's essays on Weber was translated into English in 1935, providing a definition of charisma faithful to Weber's conception:

> Charisma as a sociological category signifies not a value judgement but merely that quality of appearing as a leader because of extraordinary achievements, which must be legitimised by verification before his followers.[98]

Weber's theory of charismatic leadership was accurately summarised and applied to the rise of Hitler in Theodore Abel's *Why Hitler Came into Power*, published in 1938:

> The leader who is thus invested by all his followers with the attributes of a man of destiny may be designated a *charismatic* leader, following the terminology of Max Weber. Such a leader is one supposedly endowed with 'special grace' (Charisma), for the fulfilment of a given mission.[99]

The debates concerning Weber's political views, and the applicability of charisma to democratic and authoritarian political systems, will be considered later in the next section.

The Henderson and Parsons 1947 translation of *Wirtschaft und Gesellschaft*, and the essays and excerpts translated by Gerth and Mills in *From Max Weber* (1946), made Weber's elaboration of charisma available to English readers; by the 1960s Weber's definition of charisma as 'a certain quality of an individual by virtue of which he is considered extraordinary' had emerged from the sociological discourse into a much wider usage. This emergence entailed a slight shift in the word's meaning. In the late 1940s, charisma was understood, within the context of Weber's theory of domination, as a 'gift of leadership or power of authority'; by the 1960s, charisma connoted 'strong personal appeal or magnetism, especially in reference to political figures'.[100] The difference is only minor, a matter of emphasis. The focus has shifted a little from the innate gift or power of leadership enabling domination to the personal charm or appeal exhibited by special political figures.

The significant factor in this shift is the advent of John F. Kennedy to the American presidency, and the use of television in transmitting his personal appeal not only to American viewers but also to international audiences. Kennedy appeared youthful, vital and attractive on television, exuding a confidence and energy in his 1960 televised debate with Richard Nixon. The impact of this televised event heralded a new type of mass-mediated politician. Kennedy's appeal – conveyed through the

Figure 6.1 John F. Kennedy in the televised US presidential debate, 1960. Kennedy's appeal was described in media reports as 'the Kennedy charisma'.

medium of TV – was described as 'charismatic' by commentators in the press, and on the electronic media of radio and TV. After the assassination of President Kennedy, his brother Robert was also widely deemed to possess charisma, once again as mediated through television. In 1967, *The Spectator* reported: 'Like many of his generation, he succumbs to the Kennedy charisma'.[101] Even an encyclopedia of religion published in the mid-1980s acknowledged the secular form of charisma as 'a human quality ... as when one speaks of "the Kennedy charisma"'.[102]

With the political advantage of charismatic appeal firmly established by the Kennedy precedent, other politicians laid public claim in the 1960s to their personal stock of charisma. In 1966 the Greek politician Andreas Papandreou told the *New York Times*: 'After George Papandreou, I have the widest popular base in Greece ... I am the only other man in the party with such charisma'.[103] This declaration by a Greek politician to an American newspaper is revealing in several ways. Charisma is invoked not only as a desirable quality in a politician but as a form of legitimation: personal charisma is associated with wide popular appeal and a political power base. There is even a suggestion, in the reference to the charisma of Papandreou's father Georgios (Greek prime minister until 1965) that the innate gift of charisma resides in the Papandreou family as it did in the Kennedy family. Finally, the international range of charisma as a concept within political discourse is displayed in Papandreou's statement. By the mid-1960s, charisma is entrenched as a topic of political analysis in the media, on an international scale. The ancient Greek word, with a secular meaning derived from the writing of a German theorist, can be deployed in English by a modern Greek politician interviewed by an American newspaper. Charisma had become part of secular global culture.

Criticisms and modifications of Weberian charisma

The critical reception of Weber's theory of charisma has fluctuated wildly since the first publication of *Wirtschaft und Gesellschaft* in 1922. There have been several contributing factors in this process, including the political aftermath of the Nazi regime and the association of charisma with totalitarian demagogues, competing interests within political and social theory, differing interpretations of Weber's sociology within the Anglophone world, and the wide range of disciplines in which charisma has been accepted as a theoretical term.

Weber died in 1920, before the advent of Hitler to political power; nevertheless, the subsequent characterisation by political theorists of

Hitler as a charismatic leader had two consequences. The first of these was an intense scrutiny of Weber's concept of charismatic domination; the second was speculation regarding Weber's own political position. Italian Fascist intellectuals invoked Weber in the late 1920s to endow Mussolini with special charismatic powers.[104] In political theory, Theodore Abel made a persuasive case for Hitler as a charismatic leader in Weber's terms. Writing in 1938, Abel referred to Hitler as 'prophet' and 'hero' of the Nazi movement, commanding followers who held the belief that he possessed an 'out-of-the-ordinary, superhuman power', the basis 'of what Max Weber calls charismatic leadership'.[105] In Germany, the philosopher Karl Löwith, in 1939, offered a frank assessment of Weber's political influence: 'He prepared the way to an authoritarian and dictatorial leadership state positively by advocating, generally, irrational "charismatic" leadership and "rule of a leader with machine"'.[106]

After the war, a new generation of German academics and politicians undertook a reassessment of the recent past, including the political theory of Weber. Wolfgang Mommsen describes the intellectual climate of Germany in the 1950s: members of this generation, determined to make democracy work, and highly sensitive to the catastrophe of Nazism, challenged the prevailing view of Weber as one of the few ancestors of German democracy. Mommsen notes that Weber's notion of 'plebiscitary leadership democracy' and the benefits of charismatic leaders appeared 'dangerously close to the conception of Fascist leadership, which was still vivid in everybody's mind'.[107] Mommsen himself led the way with an appraisal of Weber in 1959, including the charge that with his theory of charismatic leadership, Weber 'helped, if only marginally, to make the German people inwardly willing to acclaim Adolf Hitler's leadership position'.[108] Mommsen argued that Weber's preference for a 'plebiscitary democracy', in which a charismatic politician could exert authority over the party and parliamentary bureaucracy, set a dangerous precedent. It was then 'quite possible' for Carl Schmitt to justify an authoritarian state in theoretical terms, and for the German state to yield to a 'pure plebiscitarianism'.[109]

This revisionist view of Weber met strong resistance in Germany and elsewhere. As Guenther Roth observes, the revisionism displayed a 'tendency to view Weber's sociological writings as indicative of his political views',[110] a tendency which Mommsen himself attempted to correct in the second edition of his book in 1974. By then, as Mommsen noted, democracy in West Germany was secure, and the problem of National Socialism less urgent.[111] The complexity of Weber's politics, and their historical context, could also be more calmly assessed. Mommsen pointed to aspects of Weber's political theory – such as his ethic of politicians' public responsibility – that positioned Weber as 'diametrically opposed' to Fascist rule.[112] He also remarked that Weber 'neglected the question of the limits and misuse of charisma' for the compelling reason that for Weber the enemy would always be bureaucratisation, leaving charisma as a purely positive force in Weber's political vision.[113] Mommsen concluded that the Nazi regime's 'charismatic-plebiscitary leadership' was a development completely different to that anticipated by Weber; had he lived to see it, Mommsen asserted, Weber 'would have fought National Socialism with all his might'.[114] Nevertheless Mommsen maintained his earlier conviction that a candid evaluation of the political ramifications of Weber's theory should be made. Achieving a compromise position, Mommsen modified his earlier 1959 assertion to the less provocative statement that Weber's theory of charisma 'helped, if only marginally, to make the German people receptive to support of a leader, and to that extent to Adolf Hitler'.[115]

Opposition to charisma as a concept in sociology and political theory continued in the 1960s. Arthur Schlesinger Jr, in a paper delivered in 1960, argued that 'Weber's typology neither derives from nor applies to a study of democratic society' and that the concept of charisma should therefore be discarded from political analysis.[116] In *The Politics of Hope* (1964), Schlesinger lamented the 'hypnotic effect' on subsequent analysis of Weber's theory of authority, particularly the 'mischievous' concept of charisma.[117] Schlesinger asserted the 'irrelevance' of charisma to the pragmatics of the contemporary democratic political order; for him charisma is 'mystical, unstable, irrational, and, by Weber's definition, incapable of dealing with the realities of modern industrial society'.[118] Another dismissal of the term – as an amorphous 'sponge' concept – was administered by the sociologist Peter Worsley in his 1968 book *The Trumpet Shall Sound*.[119] Weber also suffered at the hands of Marxist critics, whose critical assaults on Weber's 'bourgeois social science' included an attack by Herbert Marcuse at a conference in Heidelberg in 1964.[120] Other Marxists took aim at Weber's emphasis on the individual and his 'naïve and optimistic research liberalism', in the words of Wolfgang Lefèvre in 1973.[121] The decline of Marxism as an intellectual force in the West after the 1970s, however, left Weber's theory of legitimate domination largely undamaged; it has also been observed that Weber's analysis of rationalisation within modernity anticipated a strand of Marxist thought, as expressed in Marcuse's *One-Dimensional Man*.[122]

It could be argued that Weber has suffered more from his proponents than from his antagonists, particularly in the Anglophone world. Talcott Parsons provided a summary of Weber's 'systematic theory' in his *The Structure of Social Action* (1937), but Parsons's version of Weber has been severely criticised as a 'creative misinterpretation'.[123] Parsons invoked the sociology of Weber, and of Emile Durkheim, as the foundations for his own method of 'structural functionalism'; Parsons's 1947 translation of only the first – ahistorical – part of *Wirtschaft und Gesellschaft* furthered this cause. In *The Structure of Social Action*, Parsons attempts to yoke Weber and Durkheim together, despite acknowledging their differences and the complete lack in Weber of any reference to Durkheim.[124] In the context of religion, Parsons erroneously states that charisma is 'a term coined by Weber himself', and that because it represents an 'exceptional quality ... exemplified in such conceptions as mana', it is very close to Durkheim's theorisation of religion: the 'similarity of this concept to Durkheim's *sacré* is striking'.[125] This simplistic comparison denudes Weber's concept of charisma of much of its significance in his sociology of religion. In the sphere of social action, Parsons makes a similar theoretical connection: because charisma 'implies a specific attitude of respect ... like that owed to a recognised duty', such a function is 'clearly the ritual attitude of Durkheim: charismatic authority is a phase of moral authority'.[126]

Parsons's rendering of Weber and Durkheim in this manner created the impression that 'Weber was one of his intellectual forebears and a systems theorist manqué',[127] as Guenther Roth critically remarks. While a 'Weberian-Parsonian' approach enjoyed an ascendancy in American social theory in the 1950s, this construction of Weber was challenged in the 1960s and 1970s. Reinhard Bendix's 1960 book *Max Weber: An Intellectual Portrait* countered Parsons's systems approach with a demonstration of the 'historical substance of Weber's comparative sociology'.[128] Other theorists attempted to engage with Weber's 'political ideas in the perspective of our time', in the words of Karl Löwenstein in 1965. Löwenstein objected to Weber's identification of 'plebiscitarian' with 'cesarist' rule, but attempted to modify Weber's concept of charismatic leadership to render it more compatible with democratic government.[129] In the 1970s, the project of 'de-Parsonizing Weber'[130] in the Anglophone world continued. Anthony Giddens's 1971 study of Marx, Durkheim and Weber was part of a 'radical revision' of social theory, which also aimed to correct the 'failure in some secondary accounts to grasp the essential consistency in Weber's work'.[131]

By the 1970s, charisma as defined by Weber was accepted as a concept in numerous academic disciplines, most notably sociology, political science and psychology. In *Charisma: A Psychoanalytical Look at Mass Society* (1973) the Freudian psychoanalyst Irvine Schiffer proceeds from the premise that charisma, 'especially in the field of politics, is with us still'.[132] He rejects Schlesinger's contention that charisma is 'incapable of dealing with the realities of democratic culture'; for Schiffer, charisma 'lives on and continues to play, as it has in the past, that subtly seductive and at times infantilizing role in today's democratic processes'.[133] Schiffer, however, aims to modify Weber's concept of charisma. He notes that Weber's account of charismatic authority 'gives little attention to any specific dynamism operative in the group'; for Weber the followers of the charismatic leader are simply that: followers, 'totally captivated by the forceful magnetism of their leader'.[134] Schiffer contends that Weber has no recognition of a crucial factor in leadership, 'that all leaders, including the charismatic, are to a meaningful degree creations of the people'. Schiffer aims to correct the 'elitism' of Weber's account, which focuses on the leader at the expense of the people; his goal is 'to dramatize the significance of the masses in the choice of political leaders', including charismatic leaders.[135]

A similar movement to modify Weber's concept of charisma occurred in sociology. As Jack Sanders has observed, 'a number of sociologists have pointed out that a charismatic leader cannot be charismatic all on his own, that charisma depends as much on the situation and on the (willing) followers as it does on the leader himself'.[136] Robert Tucker wrote in 1968 on the interdependence of leader and followers: 'To speak of charismatic leaders ... is to speak of charismatic movements; the two phenomena are inseparable'.[137] Similarly, Bryan Wilson accentuated the 'charismatic demand' in his 1975 book *Noble Savages: The Primitive Origins of Charisma and Its Contemporary Survival*. Sanders remarks that this shift of emphasis from the leader to the role of the followers is a tilt towards Durkheim, who theorised that society will raise one individual above others if it finds in that person 'the principle aspirations that move it, as well as a means of satisfying them'. The 'charismatic demand' espoused by Wilson is a version of the view that charisma is a 'projection of a collectivity'; Charles Lindholm in his 1990 book *Charisma* shares this Durkheim-inspired corrective of Weber's theory of charisma.[138] The 'social construction of charisma', Roy Wallis wrote in 1982, reveals that charisma 'emerges out of a particular structure of social relationships'.[139]

In the post-Weber debate on charisma in sociology, psychology and religious studies, the relationship between leader and followers has received varying emphasis. Roy Wallis proposed that the notion of charisma 'has a greater role as an explanation of a *leader's* actions' than as an explanation of the followers' behaviour.[140] Writing in 2000, Sanders concludes that 'a leader's charisma can by no means be defined solely as something projected onto him by a collectivity'.[141] Although a leader needs followers, those followers do not choose their leader at random: the charismatic leader must repeatedly demonstrate extraordinary leadership qualities, a point emphasised by Weber. The role of social crisis in provoking charismatic leadership has been foregrounded in the discussion: for Wilson, the 'charismatic demand' is incited by a 'growth of anxieties and the disruption of normal life'. Tucker theorises that a 'state of acute distress' predisposes people to perceive an individual as their saviour from that distress. This situation provides the individual with a 'sense of mission', but as Tucker remarks, it is charismatic leaders' 'self-confident' assurance that they can deliver salvation that then generates the 'extreme devotion and loyalty' of their followers.[142]

A more critical sociology, however, rejects the idea of charisma as inherent in an individual. Pierre Bourdieu, writing in 1987, criticised Weber for succumbing 'to the naïve representation of charisma as a mysterious quality inherent in a person or as a gift of nature'.[143] Bourdieu attempts to demystify charisma by shifting the focus to the social formation; a charismatic leader merely embodies 'feelings and aspirations that existed before his arrival'. A time of social crisis throws up the possibility of a challenge to traditional value systems: Bourdieu quotes Marcel Mauss's remark that at such times individual leaders are the 'interpreters of such phenomena rather than their masters'.[144] Bourdieu's rigorously materialist analysis attempts to explain why 'a particular individual finds himself *socially* predisposed to live out and express' roles such as leadership.[145] By focussing not on the individual but on the social relationships impinging on that individual, Bourdieu disputes the notion of inner charismatic power as the driving force of leadership.

From the opposite perspective, several theorists have rejected the 'social construction of charisma' thesis. Prominent in this group is psychologist Len Oakes, who develops, in his 1997 book *Prophetic Charisma*, a psychological profile of charismatic religious leaders. Drawing on many years of study of charismatic leaders, Oakes declares that 'it simply beggars the imagination' to suggest that individuals such as L. Ron Hubbard, Bhagwan Shree Rajneesh and Sun Myong Moon are not, objectively, 'unusual people possessing exceptional abilities to inspire the kinds of mass followings they have achieved'.[146] Oakes defines a prophet as one who promotes a message of salvation opposed to conventional values, attracting followers who look to him or her for guidance; modern prophets apart from those mentioned above include Madame Blavatsky (Theosophical Society), Ann Lee (Shakers), Joseph Smith (Mormons) and the many less well-known founders of new religious movements, sects or communes. This conception of prophets commanding followers by virtue of their 'revolutionary personal visions' is very close to Weber's account of charismatic religious leaders; Oakes maintains that such charismatic leaders – one of whom he observed at close quarters for 16 years – possess distinctive personality constellations, 'radically different in essence' from their peers.[147]

Oakes developed methods of psychological testing to specify the 'distinctive personality constellation' of the modern charismatic prophet. Psychometric testing of 11 charismatic leaders revealed, surprisingly, no extreme or distinctive personality traits: these modern prophets were revealed as 'average' and 'ordinary' by standardised psychological tests. Oakes then pursued a more qualitative approach, based on observation and interviews with 20 charismatic leaders, as well as a survey of the literature on dozens of other modern prophets. From this information, Oakes constructed a list of their specific traits, as well as a developmental sequence of life stages undergone by the typical charismatic leader. Oakes concluded that prophets exhibit enormous energy and 'grandiose self-confidence', which can veer into delusion. They possess abilities for inspirational rhetoric, social insight and empathy, and supreme manipulative skills. They also tend to be self-contained, remaining aloof from others, including their followers.[148]

These characteristics lead Oakes to the conclusion that charismatic leaders are striking examples of the 'narcissistic personality'. Oakes draws on the studies in the 1970s by the psychoanalyst Heinz Kohut, which found strong similarities between charismatic personalities and patients with narcissistic disorders: both groups displayed 'grandiose self-confidence' and 'an extraordinary lack of self-doubt'.[149] For Oakes, Weber's 'mysterious' concept of charisma is illuminated by the studies of Kohut and other psychoanalytical theorists, disclosing a 'narcissistic explanation of charisma'.[150] From this foundation, Oakes builds his developmental 'natural history' of the charismatic prophet, whose first stage is a childhood narcissistic relationship, usually with a parent. As an adult, the prophet undergoes an 'awakening' and acceptance of mission, assuming a 'divine role' in order to receive love from others.

Charismatic leaders, according to Oakes's account, need the 'uncritical devotion' of followers, because this extreme form of love, echoing their childhood attachment, is the only form of love they can recognise.[151]

While Oakes's theory contains elements of generalisation and speculation, it is a considered attempt to add psychological insight to Weber's concept of charisma. Oakes is far more accepting of charisma as an innate quality in special individuals – 'the magnetic ability of some people to inspire and lead others'[152] – than are those psychologists and sociologists of the 'social construction of charisma' school. One other, idiosyncratic, contribution to the theorising of charisma has come from Philip Rieff, whose thesis may be gleaned from the title of his 2007 book: *Charisma: The Gift of Grace, and How It Has Been Taken Away from Us*. This work, originally written but abandoned in 1973, before its reassembly and posthumous publication by two of his former students in 2007, aims to rescue the original religious power of charisma from its modern debased secular version. Writing from an anti-psychiatry perspective, Rieff sets up a Weberesque dichotomy between the charismatic and the 'therapeutic' in a contemporary culture of 'spray-on charisma'. Within this scenario, Weber is indicted as the theorist who 'canned charisma for us'; by secularising the 'holy terror' of charisma, Weber created the means by which transgressive charisma is transformed into its anti-type, the normative therapeutic.[153]

Rieff's argument, however, is erratic and inconsistent. He traces charisma to the Hebrew prophets and then to the 'supreme effort' of the Pauline concept of charisma in the early Christian church – but he writes of the early Christians' 'high culture' based on their 'recognition of charismatic authority'.[154] Rieff avers that by 'lifting the concept of charisma out of the symbolic of Christianity, Weber unwittingly destroyed it'.[155] Yet despite his intention to 'resurrect theology from within modern sociology',[156] Rieff reproduces Weber's notion of charisma as a form of individualised authority, imposing it in an anachronistic manner on the Pauline charismatic community.

Critical assaults on Weberian charisma have been rare since the 1960s – and even Rieff appears to have absorbed Weber's refiguring of charisma while professing to oppose it. Much more typical is political scientist Ann Ruth Willner's 1984 book *The Spellbinders: Charismatic Political Leadership*, which dismisses critical attempts to reject or revise the Weberian concept as 'neither logically nor scientifically tenable'.[157] Wellner works with a concept of 'political charisma' adopted from Weber's 'classic classification of authority',[158] examining its operation in a number of democratic, socialist and authoritarian political systems.

Weberian charisma has been accepted into many disciplines and has been applied to myriad scenarios. In psychology, Doris McIlwain has studied the appeal of contemporary self-help gurus with reference to 'Weber's classic analyses of charismatic leadership'.[159] William Clark in *Academic Charisma* (2006) has chronicled the rise of the charismatic individual academic within the historical transformation towards the modern research university. Clark simply states that the 'notion of charisma comes from Weber'; he deploys Weberian vocabulary in summarising his theme, which 'casts light on bureaucratization and commodification – the twin engines of the rationalization and the disenchantment of the world'.[160] In a radically different field, the Australian museum collector Tom Griffiths uses the same vocabulary to articulate his dilemma on receiving Aboriginal sacred objects: 'Was I participating in the dispossession of a people and the disenchantment of the world?'[161] The cultural theorists Ken Gelder and Jane Jacobs situate this question concerning sacred objects within a discussion of 'repatriation and charisma' in a postcolonial context.[162] Within the disciplines of history and political theory, the continued viability of charisma as a theoretical term is demonstrated in the 2007 collection of essays *Charisma and Fascism in Interwar Europe*. As Roger Eatwell, one of the contributors, notes, charisma is employed throughout the book as a 'useful analytical concept', in the study of interwar Fascism, with modifications such as 'coterie charisma' and 'cultic charisma' proposed to meet the specific historical context.[163]

There are many other instances, in disparate disciplinary contexts, of the application of Weberian charisma. At the same time, the term has become a commonplace, since the 1960s, in media commentary and popular discourse. Critics such as Schlesinger may have rejected this 'mischievous' term as unsuited to modern political systems; Bourdieu may have demystified the concept and attempted to replace it with a rigorously materialist analysis. But these critical interventions have not deflected Weber's concept of charisma from its path to acceptance as a 'classic' term within modern social thought. Nor have they diminished the current everyday use of the word charisma, which retains much of its Weberian legacy.

7
Twentieth-Century Charismatics

The Charismatic Renewal movement commencing in the 1960s revived the Pauline belief that any individual Christian may be divinely empowered; the gifts of speaking in tongues, healing and prophecy – as well as other Pauline charismata – were thought to issue forth in moments of religious ecstasy. These twentieth-century charismatics – both Protestant and Catholic – returned to a literal interpretation of Paul's epistles concerning charisma as spiritual gift, as part of their project of reviving early Christian faith. But the charismatic renewal did not erupt in isolation. It emerged from within the Pentecostal movement of evangelical Christianity, which was established in the US in 1906. The Pentecostal faith in turn was the culmination of a number of evangelical movements that flourished in the nineteenth century.

The various movements and denominations feeding into Pentecostalism and charismatic practice had in common the belief in direct visitation of the Holy Spirit. They also shared a literal reading of Acts and the Pauline epistles concerning spiritual endowment: they believed in an apostolic Christianity – that is, one equivalent to the pneumatic faith delivered to the earliest apostles, including Paul.

The 'Corinthian Gifts'

One influential nineteenth-century figure was John Alexander Dowie, a Scottish-born minister of the Congregational denomination, who practised in Australia in the 1870s. Dowie took literally the passages in the gospels concerning the healing power of Jesus, and began to preach a healing evangelism, withdrawing from the Congregational church to form his own tabernacle. Dowie opposed the cessationist view of the mainstream Christian churches, which held that the spiritual gifts had been withdrawn from the church following the early apostolic period. For Dowie, healing through the laying on of hands by spiritually empowered ministers was still available: indeed this faculty had never been withdrawn.[1] Several other evangelical figures were practising the gift of healing in the 1880s in the US; Dowie joined the American divine-healing movement in 1888. By 1895 he had formed the Christian Catholic Church in Chicago with specific reference to the Pauline spiritual gifts (even if the words charisma or charismata were not used). 'We need the old time Christianity of the first century', Dowie proclaimed,[2] supporting his restorationist vision with the claim that all the gifts and offices detailed by Paul in 1 Corinthians would operate in his new church. 'We shall teach, preach and practice [*sic*] a Full Gospel', he announced, '[m]ay this Church be endowed with the nine gifts of the Holy Spirit'.[3] In 1900 Dowie expanded his vision of a new spiritual church into the reality of a Christian city called Zion, built on a large allotment of land near Chicago.

For the gifts to be properly distributed in the church community, however, the group needed an apostle with divine calling. Dowie declared that a modern-day apostle would be 'possessed of the Holy Ghost' and that this possession would be signalled by the demonstration of at least one of the 'Corinthian Gifts'. Dowie claimed in 1904 that he himself possessed four of the gifts. He publicly announced that he was an apostle ordained by God, and that through him apostolic office had been restored. His apostolic status ensured that devout members of his community could also be endowed with spiritual gifts, although they needed to display humility and hope that they may be granted one of those gifts.[4]

Dowie was in effect the leader of a theocratic community: Zion, which at its height had a population of 6000, was envisioned as a closed environment in which all activities were under church control. Dowie was uncompromising on matters such as health: he forbade citizens of Zion to consult doctors or use medicine. He asserted that because he had been imbued with the divine gift of healing, there was no need for secular medical science. His stance was extreme even compared to other exponents of divine healing, whom he denounced if they compromised on medicine or physicians. His proclamations assumed an apocalyptic tone: the restoration of the miraculous gifts and apostolic offices, he declared, heralded the imminent Second Coming.[5] His leadership became increasingly authoritarian, while the success of Zion encouraged grander ambitions: he planned many Zions around the world.

But by 1906 the original Zion City in Illinois was suffering financial difficulties. While Dowie was away attempting to found new Zion communities in Mexico and Jamaica, he was unseated from leadership of the church on the grounds of financial mismanagement and dubious morality (there were rumours that he advocated polygamy).[6] References to prophetic and apostolic functions were removed from Zion church offices. Dowie engaged Zion management in a legal battle, while the city was placed in receivership. The theocratic utopia of Zion had self-destructed. Dowie died in 1907; many of the citizens of Zion drifted off to other evangelical callings.

Dowie's Zion City is significant in a number of respects. At the beginning of the twentieth century, it played out a brief, densely packed narrative that would recur many times later in the century. The components of this narrative were to become hauntingly familiar: a self-contained utopian religious community on the fringes of the established church; a self-proclaimed leader, defected from the institutional church, now claiming direct divine authorisation; the community led to extreme views, rejecting mainstream secular values; the apocalyptic tenor of the leader's preaching; the destruction or self-destruction of the community, often with violent or tragic results. In the case of Zion City, disintegration of the community entailed little more than economic loss and hardship for its members. The followers of later self-decreed leaders would suffer far greater loss.

In the shorter term, Zion City served as inspiration, despite its failure, for other religious movements, including the Pentecostal Church. Dowie's literal interpretation of the New Testament, and his conviction that the pneumatic condition of the apostolic period could be restored, inspired many others to follow those principles. Dowie was adamant that cessationsim was a fallacy, and that the spiritual gifts endowed in the first century were just as available in the twentieth: in 1904, he wrote that 'the Gifts' would 'be made manifest increasingly in this Church'.[7] Dowie was quite literal in his references to the spiritual gifts: he listed the nine charismata detailed by Paul in 1 Corinthians.[8] This invoking of divine powers awakened, in those who heard it or heard of it, 'a desire for the supernatural and a longing for spiritual reality'.[9] The other pertinent – and perhaps ominous – aspect of Dowie's faith was that he was convinced not only of the currency of spiritual gifts but that he himself possessed several of them. This self-asserted faculty was the basis of his own authority. For Dowie, his possession of the 'Corinthian Gifts' was the bestowal of divine legitimation of his status as twentieth-century apostle and religious leader.

Pentecostalism

The Pentecostal movement came to prominence in 1906, when a gathering in Los Angeles known as the Azusa Street Revival organised itself into the Apostolic Faith Mission. Yet there were many instances of Pentecostal activity in the US prior to this event. The theologian William Arthur, in his book *The Tongue of Fire*, published in 1856, called on the Spirit to 'renew the Pentecost in this our age'.[10] The Holiness Movement in the 1860s used the term 'Pentecostal', referring to the spiritual outpouring on the day of Pentecost described in Acts, and practised spiritual baptism. The leading figure in the early twentieth century was Charles Fox Parham, who led prayer meetings in Topeka, Kansas. Parham visited Zion City in 1900 and took inspiration from its restorationist mode and emphasis on the Spirit; however, he found Dowie lacking in the fullness of Holy Spirit.[11]

The distinctive features of Parham's revivalist preaching were an emphasis on spirit baptism, and the belief that successful baptism in the Holy Spirit was signalled by speaking in tongues. He defined 'tongues' as recognisable languages otherwise unknown to the speaker. Parham thereby elevated one of the Pauline charismata – the one ranked lowest by Paul – to a lofty spiritual function. Glossolalia in Parham's Pentecostalism was the manifestation guaranteeing authentic visitation by the Spirit.

Speaking in tongues occurred in Parham's Topeka prayer meetings from 1901; he left the Methodist denomination to practise a revival ministry. In 1905 he returned to Zion City, where he took 25 into spirit baptism – with the spirit-evidence of a range of languages from Norwegian to Chinese.[12] Parham's student, an African American named William J. Seymour, led the Azusa Street revival that firmly established the Pentecostal movement; Parham himself, dogged by allegations of sexual misconduct, became alienated from the growing Pentecostal movement. A feature of the early years of Pentecostal worship was the interracial composition of the community, although a racial divide later emerged in the 1920s, evident in white-only Pentecostal churches.

As an evangelical movement, Pentecostalism imputed final authority to the Bible. It found validation for its variant of Christian faith in Acts' account of spiritual manifestations and in Paul's elaboration of the spiritual gifts infusing the community. The early proponents also inferred an eschatological imperative from these sources: the current-day signs and wonders, including tongues, were thought to herald a 'latter-day rain of the Holy Spirit', restoring fractured Christianity and preparing for the Second Coming.[13]

Pentecostal fervour was greeted with resistance or scepticism by the Protestant denominations in which it first appeared: undeterred, the Pentecostals formed their own churches and denominations, such as the Assemblies of God. The liturgy performed in these churches devalued creed and emphasised spirit-filled communal worship. As they grew in size, the Pentecostal churches attempted to avoid a corresponding decline in spiritual awareness: church offices were meant to be accountable to the group. Members of the community were regarded as peers of the ministry; in the Pentecostal model, every member was considered a minister of the church. Because they had been baptised in the Spirit, they were considered capable of manifesting any of the spiritual gifts.

Throughout the first half of the twentieth century, the mainstream churches maintained their negative judgement of the Pentecostal movement as a 'false cult'.[14] Pentecostals were variously considered 'emotionally disturbed, mentally limited, inherently sociologically deprived', while the pneumatic displays celebrated by the Pentecostals were judged inauthentic.[15] The major twentieth-century theologians Dibelius, Barth and Bultmann evinced a disdain towards mysticism that could trace a pedigree back through nineteenth-century theology and indeed further back to Luther and Calvin.[16] Bultmann's rationalist theology left no place for the supernatural in the mid-twentieth century: 'It is impossible', he wrote in 1953, 'to use electric light and the wireless and to avail ourselves of modern medical and surgical discoveries, and at the same time to believe in the New Testament world of daemons and spirits'.[17]

Despite this disregard and mainstream opposition, the growth and diversification of the Pentecostal movement in the twentieth century was astounding. By the middle of the century, many different forms of Pentecostal evangelism had emerged, including the 'Latter Day Rain' movement, as well as distinctive styles developed by individual preachers. Notable among those individuals were William Branham, who claimed the power of diagnosing illness through interpretation of auras, and Oral Roberts, who pioneered the 'slaying in the Spirit' method in his tent meetings, whereby those worshippers possessed by the Spirit fell to the ground.[18] Roberts and other mid-century evangelists spoke of their calling in terms reminiscent of the ancient prophets and early Christian apostles. In books such as *The Call* and other publications, Roberts described the direct divine command given to him: 'From this hour your ministry of healing will begin. You will have my power to pray for the sick and to cast out devils'.[19] Possession by the Holy Spirit, Roberts believed, granted him 'a new world-wide emphasis on healing and supernatural deliverance'.[20]

By the end of the century, there were an estimated 11,000 Pentecostal church groupings, while there were claims that Pentecostals, charismatics and other revivalists comprised up to one-fifth of organised global Christianity.[21] Growth was most rapid among the poor and in the developing world, in South America, Africa and parts of Asia, notably South Korea, whose Yoido Full Gospel Church is Pentecostal and considered the world's largest Christian church.

Charismatic Renewal

The charismatic movement, which emerged in the 1960s, was inspired by Pentecostalism, but differed from it in one important respect. While Pentecostals left their initial Protestant denominations and formed their own churches, charismatic worshippers tended to remain within their denominations, whether Protestant or Catholic. Charismatic Christians also tended to place less emphasis than did the Pentecostals on glossolalia as the initial evidence of baptism in the Spirit.

Precursors of the charismatic movement emerged in the 1950s in the US and Britain, in the form of groups such as the London Healing Mission and the Nights of Prayer for Worldwide Revival. Several individual preachers placed a special emphasis on Acts, such as the American Methodist minister Tommy Tyson.[22] Charismatic worship first came to public attention within Protestantism, when Dennis Bennett, a rector of the American Episcopalian Church in California, declared to his congregation in 1960 that he had received outpourings of the Holy Spirit, including the gift of tongues.[23] Facing opposition from within his church, Bennett resigned, took up a position as vicar of the small St Luke's church in Seattle, and openly preached on the visitations of Spirit resulting in the manifestation of spiritual gifts. His outspoken stance within the Protestant church was deemed newsworthy in the early 1960s: his ministry and the conflict it generated within the church were covered in the American media, including *Time* and *Newsweek*. Bennett's new congregation grew rapidly, while the national media attention spread awareness of ecstatic worship occurring within an established Protestant denomination. This form of worship quickly spread to other denominations, including Methodist, Presbyterian, Baptist and Lutheran.[24] In Britain, the Anglican minister Michael Harper made similar public claims of spirit-filled worship from 1963; by 1965 the charismatic movement had spread to Germany, Kenya, South Africa, New Zealand and Australia.[25]

Bennett himself is unclear regarding how and when the term 'charismatic' was applied to this type of Christian worship:

> As the good news began to spread, the word 'charismatic' came to be used to refer to folks from old-line denominations who were receiving the freedom of the Holy Spirit while continuing in their respective traditions.[26]

The term had been used as early as 1936 as a description of Pentecostal worship. E. Underhill, in his book *Worship*, defended 'charismatic worship' of the Pentecostal type against the claim that it represented nothing more than 'the passing effect of unbalanced enthusiasm'.[27] The plural noun 'charismatics' had been used even earlier, in reference to the early church, in *Harnack's Constitution and Law of the Church* (1910), in which apostles, prophets and teachers were described as 'charismatics', while a 1947 *Encyclopedia Britannica* reference to the high authority of the 'charismatics' in the early church reveals that the term was active in the Christian context in the middle of the twentieth century.[28]

Noting the various forms of confusion surrounding the term in the early 1960s, Bennett provided his own definition:

> A Charismatic parish is one in which the individual members are baptized in the Holy Spirit and are daily praying in the Spirit (in the language or 'tongue' provided by the Holy Spirit) in their private prayers.[29]

This definition is extremely close to Pentecostal worship: indeed early charismatic Christianity was also known as neo-Pentecostal. The substantial difference in the early years of the 1960s was that such worship, following baptism in the Spirit, was conducted within the traditional – or 'old-line' – church denominations.

The first recorded use of the term 'charismatic' to describe this form of Christian worship is from 1963, in a letter to the religious magazine *Eternity* written by Harald Bredersen and Jean Stone Willans.[30] Bredersen was an American Lutheran pastor who received the Pentecostal Spirit Baptism in the 1940s, but unlike other Pentecostals, stayed within his mainstream denomination. In the 1963 letter, Bredersen and Willans coined the term 'Charismatic Renewal' to designate Pentecostal-style worship within the traditional Protestant denominations: this became the general connotation of the 'charismatic' renewal or movement by the mid-1960s.[31] Although he did not attract the wider public attention of Bennett or the individual 'star' preachers who soon became associated with the charismatic renewal, Bredersen was often called the 'father' of the charismatic movement, and later hosted a television programme *Charisma* on the Christian Broadcasting Network.

By 1966, 'charismatic renewal' and 'charismatic movement' had become accepted terminology within Christian discourse. W. A. Criswell, in his book *The Holy Spirit in Today's World* (1966) referred to the 'charismatic movement' while admitting that it 'bewildered' him. In 1967 the Presbyterian General Assembly in New Zealand heard of the 'charismatic renewal', with the observation that whereas this form of worship had long been regarded as the sole prerogative of 'Pentecostal sects', it now affected 'some of our own church people'.[32] Young Catholic university students in Pittsburgh came into contact with Protestant charismatics in 1966 and received the Pentecostal baptism. One hundred Catholic Pentecostals gathered in 1967; by 1972, their number had increased to 11,500, and their movement was known as Catholic Charismatic Renewal.[33] In 1973, 30,000 Catholic charismatics gathered at Notre Dame, Indiana, for a national conference, while in 1975, 10,000 charismatics gathered at St Peter's in Rome with the endorsement of Pope Paul VI.[34]

The Roman Catholic Church accepted the charismatic movement as a form of renewal: Pope John Paul II extended a papal blessing and encouragement in the 1980s. Inroads into the Eastern Orthodox Church were less extensive, despite the precedent of charismatic monks such as Symeon the New Theologian. Individual church leaders adopted a charismatic position, but resistance was strong from within the Orthodox faith. In general, the charismatic movement received least resistance from the Roman Catholic Church, but encountered opposition within some Protestant denominations such as the Presbyterians and Lutherans.[35] By the late 1960s, independent charismatic groups and ministries arose, often identifying themselves as 'non-denominational'. As this independent sector grew in the 1970s, the charismatic movement assumed a broader base, encompassing followers in the Catholic and Protestant churches, as well as these independent groups.

The flourishing of charismatic practice within Protestant and Catholic churches – in contrast to the earlier Pentecostals, who had no choice but to practise their faith outside the mainstream – was the result of a number of factors. One was the 'crisis of identity' experienced by the institutionalised churches in the 1960s, particularly the Catholic

Church, which suffered a significant exodus of priests in that decade.[36] The joyful celebration of Spirit embraced in charismatic gatherings was regarded by some Christians as a healthy antidote to the 'sin-centred piety' found in much Catholic and evangelical theology.[37] The 'singing in the Spirit' – a collective and spontaneous singing in tongues – that became a feature of charismatic worship, was regarded as evidence of a direct emotional engagement with the Spirit. Such spontaneous religious experience had cast off the 'second-hand' dependence on prayer books and other forms of received liturgy.[38] The emphasis on direct and immediate experience of the divine had more in common with eastern Christianity than with the guilt-centred doctrine of Catholicism and Protestantism; the charismatic renewal appeared to infuse a new spiritual energy into a jaded Western Christianity.

Another contributing factor was the turbulent cultural environment of the 1960s. The appeal of charismatic worship to the youth of Western societies corresponded to the rise of youth culture and the radical countercultural movement of the late 1960s. American Christianity adapted quickly to this cultural condition. In 1966 a new Bible translation was published as *Good News for Modern Man*, successfully marketed as 'a Bible for the young and disaffected': five million copies were sold. This success encouraged other versions such as the *Living Bible*, and *The Way*, which featured psychedelic lettering, shaggy-haired youth and a Jesus described as 'the greatest spiritual Activist who ever lived'.[39] In their pursuit of accessibility, these translations were less literal, included more paraphrase and used far simpler vocabulary than previous Bible translations. Rock musicals *Jesus Christ Superstar* and *Godspell* depicted Jesus as a long-haired rebel, an icon for the counterculture. The anti-hierarchical and spontaneous nature of charismatic worship resonated within the non-conformist character of late-1960s youth culture.

The charismatic movement in the 1970s appealed largely to middle-class Protestants and Catholics, occasioning some misgivings from Pentecostalism, which had always been associated with the poor and socially marginalised. Harvey Cox, in his sympathetic account of Pentecostalism, has recounted his distaste for the charismatics of the early 1970s, whose services he found 'tepid and derivative' of Pentecostal practices. For him, and for many within the Pentecostal movement, charismatic Christianity was a 'milder and more domesticated version', contained within the traditional churches, of Pentecostal worship.[40]

Owing to all these factors, the charismatic movement grew quickly on an international scale, from various bases. James Dunn has noted that in the 1970s, the renewal shifted from its early 'neo-Pentecostal' phase to an emphasis on keynote words 'charisma' and 'community'. By the early 1980s, the energy associated with the charismatics was recognised as a source of renewal for the traditional church: in 1981 the World Council of Churches published a report entitled *The Church Is Charismatic: The World Council and the Charismatic Renewal*.[41] In South Africa, David du Plessis, initially a Pentecostal, promoted the charismatic cause. Charismatic worship became popular with Filipino Catholic communities in the US, before spreading to the Philippines, where the gift of faith healing was prominent.

In the 1990s a further renewal in the US announced itself as 'the third wave of the Holy Spirit', following the earlier Pentecostal and charismatic waves. Also known as 'power evangelism', this third wave maintained belief in the availability of the charismata, but de-emphasised the miraculous and spectacular gifts such as healing and glossolalia, affirming the importance of the non-miraculous gifts of ministry and service to the church.[42] By the end of the twentieth century, there were an estimated 3000 charismatic denominations,[43] while the boundary between Pentecostal and charismatic was often blurred: some Pentecostal churches adopted elements of charismatic worship.

Charismatic faith within these denominations and churches was commonly experienced as a communal act, with a strong lay character and emphasis on an 'every-member' form of ministry.[44] However, a different version of charismatic Christianity – as practised by star preachers and televangelists – attracted greater public attention and controversy. Neo-Pentecostal evangelists such as Oral Roberts took advantage of radio and television as those broadcast media – and their mass audiences – became available. Televangelism emerged in the 1960s in the US, attracting a brand of evangelist – often fronting newly formed churches removed from the Protestant mainstream – whose televised preaching emphasised the flamboyant and spectacular. Many of these preachers professed possession of charismatic abilities, including the gifts of healing, prophecy and the ability to perform miracles. Roberts announced in the 1980s that God had granted him the power of raising the dead,[45] while others claimed to be able to heal the sick and dying through the medium of television. The televangelist Dr Gene Scott, for example, claimed to have cured his own cancer by doing communion every day; he provided guidance, through his TV programme, for his followers to achieve the same feat. Communion in a meditative state supervised by Scott was meant to connect deeply to Spirit and its healing power. The scandals and controversies surrounding several of the most flamboyant – and wealthy – televangelists in the late twentieth century was lamented by the practitioners of communal charismatic worship: the high-profile ministries of several televangelists were at least partly responsible, it was thought, 'for the tawdry reputation of charismatic religion'.[46]

The charismata in Charismatic Renewal

The charismatic movement has not, in general, followed a programmatic order of the Pauline charismata; rather, it is thought that individuals and gatherings experience various spiritual gifts as the Spirit may deign at any particular time and place. Charismatic worship has tended to emphasise the ecstatic nature of Spirit possession. 'Ecstasy' here is understood in both its senses: the technical 'standing outside oneself' denoted by the original Greek word, which was used to describe the abandon and delirium exhibited by those in states of religious frenzy; and the more general sense of great joy or rapture. Experience of charismatic worship has been described as 'the feelings of joy and ecstasy expressed by means of glossolalia, joyful music, raising of hands, dance, and, in extreme cases, spirit possession to the point of losing consciousness'.[47] The pursuit of spontaneity has also generated innovations such as 'singing in the Spirit', a form of communal glossolalia described above. The charisma of miraculous healing is considered one of those gifts available either to a community of charismatic worshippers or to an individual blessed with the 'ministry of healing'.

Testimonies by individual practitioners – some of them well versed in mainstream theology and secular thought – provide some insight into the charismatic experience. Tom Smail, a Presbyterian minister intellectually formed by the anti-mystical theology of Karl Barth, recounts that his charismatic renewal in 1965 was signalled by his glossolalia, followed by 'other gifts', specifically prophecy and 'a little healing'. By prophecy he appears to mean predictions concerning particular people and events. Smail is rationalist enough to acknowledge that in some instances the prophecies were proven incorrect, and that some attempts at healing produced 'no observable response'. But success on other occasions has persuaded him that he experienced 'genuine manifestations of the Spirit'.[48] Likewise, Nigel Wright, a Baptist minister with theological training, experienced a charismatic renewal in 1982 which he has recounted: many members of the congregation 'were trembling and shaking, speaking in tongues, calling on the Lord, prophesying', while some 'were flapping up and down like fish upon the floor'.[49]

Charismatic Renewal, experienced as a fervent spiritual empowerment, has been celebrated by its proponents as a necessary corrective to the overly intellectual and emotionally arid state of the institution-alised church.[50] This emphasis on emotion at the expense of intellec-tual rigour has, unsurprisingly, fostered an imprecision concerning the biblical charismata. Although the charismatic movement takes its name from the Greek word used by Paul to describe spiritual gifts, twentieth-century charismatics have interpreted Paul very loosely. Prophecy as elaborated by Paul as one of the charismata did not mean the prediction of future events: it simply referred to utterance directly inspired by God. Modern-day charismatics professing the ability to predict future events are not, therefore, operating in the spirit of the original charismata. Similarly, other phenomena in charismatic worship identified as 'words of knowledge' cannot confidently be equated with the utterance of knowledge described by Paul as one of the charismata.[51]

The one Pauline charisma in shortest supply in the charismatic renewal is the gift of discernment of spirits. The ability to 'distinguish between spirits', which Paul included in the nine charismata outlined to the Corinthians, was important in that context due to the Corinthians' eagerness for 'manifestations of the Spirit' (1 Cor 14: 12). Their previ-ous revelling in ecstatic states had included exhortations condemned by Paul as distinctly un-Christian: 'no one speaking by the Spirit of God ever says "Jesus be cursed"', he cautioned members of the Corinthian congregation (1 Cor 12: 3). Distinguishing between spirits was accord-ingly a valuable charisma in that it could separate manifestations of the Holy Spirit from other forms of spirit possession or intoxication. The neglect of such discernment within the twentieth-century charismatic movement has been noted even by those who have practised char-ismatic worship.[52] The sheer enthusiasm of charismatic worshippers has re-created the eagerness for manifestations of Spirit about which Paul counselled the Corinthians. Tom Smail has criticised the 'over-credulous' zeal of many contemporary charismatics in their uncritical acceptance of alleged miracles and spirit-possession. In such instances, there is no discernment between what may be accepted as a divine gift and imagined phenomena or products of human invention.[53] Andrew Walker has made a similar assertion concerning the overeager belief in healings and other miracles in charismatic renewal circles: he has called for 'what we might call "quality control" of alleged charismata'.[54]

The other deviation from Paul apparent in the charismatic renewal concerns the function and status of glossolalia. Charismatics share with Pentecostals the celebration of glossolalia as a sign of Spirit visitation, and have made 'tongues' a central part of charismatic worship. Even those theologians maintaining a sceptical perspective on aspects of charismatic renewal have celebrated the liberating – and intoxicating – sensation accompanied by the initial experience of speaking in tongues. Andrew Walker has described his experience of 'merrily pealing away with a fresh triple of the tongues', and the aftermath of 'feeling drunk' with Spirit,[55] while Tom Smail has acknowledged, based on his own experience, the 'releasing and renewing' spiritual charge of speaking in tongues.[56]

Glossolalia is revered in the charismatic movement as a manifestation of the Spirit, and as a form of joyous bonding in communal worship. Yet there is no corresponding emphasis on interpretation of the tongues, which often are celebrated in their unintelligible state. 'We don't understand the verbiage, but we know we're in communication', one charismatic church minister has enthused.[57] This practice is strictly counter to Paul's instruction in 1 Corinthians, where he declared that speaking in tongues without interpretation is useless to the community and serves only the self-esteem of the speaker. Such a person, he asserted, speaks 'into the air' and provides no 'edification' for the church (1 Cor 14: 10). For Paul, intelligibility was paramount for the upbuilding of the church; untranslated glossolalia offered no community benefit and for that reason was ranked lowest of the nine charismata in 1 Corinthians. The twentieth-century charismatics, for all their literalness of interpretation of Paul, appear largely to have ignored his admonition in this regard.

Christian critics of the Pentecostal and charismatic emphasis on glossolalia have placed the practice under further scrutiny. If the tongues are not recognisable languages able to be translated, they represent nothing more than 'gibberish',[58] while speaking in tongues may be nothing more than learned behaviour within an emotionally excited group.[59] Other explanations for the tongues phenomenon have included 'motor automatism', 'ecstasy', 'hypnosis', 'psychic catharsis', 'collective psyche' and 'memory excitation'.[60] These psychologically based analyses of the phenomenon have been deployed by sceptics within the Christian church to defuse the enthusiasm associated with glossolalia. Ultimately, however, Christian sceptics point to the disruptive nature of the practice within many church congregations – a point first made by Paul in Corinth.

How many charismata and how do you know which ones you have?

There are so many variants of charismatic faith and so many individual preachers claiming charismatic empowerment, that interpretation of the charismata varies wildly. This confusion pertains even to the number of charismata thought to be available to contemporary Christians. Some Pentecostal and charismatic exponents have adhered strictly to the nine 'Corinthian gifts' elaborated by Paul at 1 Corinthians 12. James Dunn has argued that this unnecessarily narrows the range of charismata by treating the 1 Corinthians 12 list as definitive rather than representative;[61] this view seems sound given Paul's provision of a different list of charismata to the Romans in Romans 12. Following this principle, other commentators have combined the charismata listed by Paul in 1 Corinthians and Romans with the church offices and roles he mentions at 1 Cor 12: 27–30 and Ephesians 4: 11, resulting in an expanded list of gifts that could number – depending on the means of calculation – 21, 23, 24, 25 or 27. This extremely loose interpretation of Paul, which erases the distinction between charisma and office, has had the effect of increasing the obfuscation regarding the charismata. Furthering this confusion, some preachers have added to the biblical list of spiritual gifts, some commentators have combed the New Testament for other phenomena that can be added to the ranks of charismata, while others have maintained that the number of charismata cannot be determined because new gifts could arise to fit particular circumstances.

One attempted means of simplifying this complexity is the 'spiritual gifts test', which has been developed as a 'discovery instrument' by several charismatic and evangelical organisations. The most well known was originally devised in 1976 by Richard Houts from the North American Baptist Theological Seminary. Later modified by Peter Wagner of the Charles E. Fuller Institute of Evangelism and Church Growth, the test is entitled the Wagner-Modified Houts Questionnaire, available for download on the World Wide Web.[62] The questionnaire is a form of psychometric testing, offering 125 statements to which the participant responds with the choice of MUCH, SOME, LITTLE OR NOT AT ALL. The answers are assigned a numerical value and tabulated with reference to a list of 25 spiritual gifts. This list is an expanded compendium of spiritual gifts compiled by combining the Pauline charismata at 1 Corinthians and Romans with the church offices such as pastor, evangelist and missionary mentioned in the New Testament. The Wagner-Houts list of gifts also contains 'voluntary poverty' and 'intercession', discussed by Paul (1 Cor 13: 3 and Colossians 1: 9–12) but not otherwise acknowledged as spiritual gifts, and exorcism, described in the New Testament but not by Paul.

The test comprises five statements relating to each of the 15 designated spiritual gifts, resulting in the total of 125 statements. The gifts of 'service', 'giving' and 'hospitality' are represented by modest statements such as 'I enjoy being called upon to do special jobs around the church' and 'I find I manage money well in order to give liberally to the Lord's work' and 'My home is always open to people passing through who need a place to stay'. The more spectacular or supernatural gifts are denoted by 'In the name of the Lord, I have been used in curing diseases instantaneously' (healing) and 'I cast out demons in Jesus' name' (exorcism). Tongues and interpretation of tongues are also accorded five statements each, as are the gifts of miracles and discerning of spirits.

The participant is invited to compile a list of the three highest-scored gifts, termed 'dominant', and three 'subordinate' gifts of the three next-highest scores. With the 'gift cluster' thus determined, the participant is asked to consider which ministry roles are most appropriate. As further assistance, the Fuller Institute offers Spiritual Gifts 'Mobilization Workbooks', 'Implementation Videos', study manuals and other spiritual gifts tests: the Wesley Spiritual Gifts Questionnaire, which tests for 24 gifts, and the Networking Assessment Booklet, designed by Bruce L. Bugbee, testing for 23 spiritual gifts.

These tests, designed and promoted by Christian churches and institutions, have reduced the idea of charismata to the level of the instant do-it-yourself questionnaires found in great abundance elsewhere on the web and in popular magazines. The normal topics of such tests are 'How Passionate Are You?' or how honest, ambitious, sexy or trustworthy. The simplistic and quick-fire nature of the 'spiritual gifts' test is far removed from Paul, who gave the first – sober and cautious – expression to the charismata, and from the later church fathers who spent many years deliberating on their status and function. At least the Wagner-Modified Houts Questionnaire states the proviso that the scores constitute only a 'tentative evaluation of where your gifts may lie'; confirmation of the gifts needs to be pursued with 'your pastor and elders in the Lord'. In addition, the test is reflective to some degree of Paul's emphases in its accentuation of the gifts' role in the church's growth, and in its allocation of equal importance to tongues and the interpretation of tongues. However, the shaky foundations on which the test is founded – including the unquestioned constitution of the list of 25 gifts – are likely to produce a superficial theological understanding of the charismata. The emphasis is on the 'thrilling experience' of discovering one's gifts, as the test announces, rather than on any reflection on the purpose, hazards or nature of the spiritual gifts themselves.

Criticisms of the Charismatic Renewal

The most visible exponents of charismatic Christianity – televangelist preachers claiming supernatural gifts – have also been the most heavily deprecated. Critics within the traditional churches – as well as secular critics and media commentators – have attacked many of the televangelists for their pecuniary focus, and for their unregulated promotion of a personality cult, exploitation of poor and ill-educated viewers and hypocritical morality. The spectacular falls from grace in the late twentieth century of Jimmy Swaggart, Jim Bakker and other televangelists attracted keen media attention, which highlighted the personal wealth accumulated by such preachers through the lucrative business of televangelism. Criticism from within the mainstream churches has emphasised the theological flaws of these self-appointed ministries, which, it has been claimed, stray so far from orthodox Christian dogma that they deserve the charge of heresy.[63]

It is not difficult to notate the televangelists' many deviations even from the principles of the early church, whose apostolic faith – articulated primarily by Paul – they claim to revive. The central flaw is the absolute authority claimed by many evangelists as modern-day prophets: like Dowie at the beginning of the twentieth century, many televangelists have asserted their own religious authority based on their claims to direct divine inspiration. The failure of such charismatic church leaders to submit their prophetic words to testing within the Christian community is a violation of Paul's instructions in 1 Corinthians, where he states that the words of prophets must be 'weighed' by others in the community (1 Cor 14: 29). Paul himself tested his own preaching with church leaders to ensure he was not 'running or had run in vain' (Gal 2: 1–2).[64] This example of humility and self-assessment has not in general been followed by the televangelists. Their claims of receiving direct and private revelations from God have instead engendered, in many cases, an unchecked hubris.[65] In addition, there is of course no precedent in Paul or the gospels for great personal wealth to be earned in the name of prophecy or preaching; indeed, the opposite idea is prominent in Jesus's sermons.

The ministry of healing and other miracles conducted by some preachers has also concerned critics within the traditional church. Many charismatic preachers and televangelists rose to prominence through their claims to heal the sick in their congregations, yet none of these assertions has ever been verified by objective scrutiny.[66] Other claims to have worked miracles have been proven fraudulent, while publicly announced prophecies (predictions) have failed.[67]

Various explanations have been proposed for the belief that modern-day miraculous healings take place during evangelical services and prayer meetings, most centring on the intensity of emotional experience of participants. The group dynamics of a congregation willing to believe in miracles, brought to a pitch of excitement by an impassioned speaker, may create an atmosphere of heightened suggestion. Music, dancing, projected visuals and lighting have the effect of intensifying audience excitement and expectation in some of the large-scale events.[68] Many supposed healings may be the result of hysteria; or the alleged ailment may have been psychosomatic in the first place, allowing an immediate response triggered by suggestion.[69] Certainly many individual worshippers claim to have been healed of ailments and diseases, and some documentation of such cases has occurred;[70] yet substantial research verifying the healings – and their permanence – has not eventuated. The many fantastic claims made by televangelists, ranging from minor healings to the raising of the dead, have been condemned as 'preposterous' within the church, and have attracted widespread ridicule outside it.[71]

None of this criticism, however, has deterred the leading televangelists and their followers. The most successful 'healing evangelists' such as Benny Hinn travel the world with their crusades, supported by television and web outlets, all the time accumulating large donations to their churches. Hinn leads his 'miracle crusades', complete with 250-voice choir, with the promise of miraculous healings to be imparted to members of his audience. Critical analysis of a Hinn crusade event for 8000 in Australia in 2008 was made by Uniting Church minister and academic David Millikan, published in an Australian newspaper. Millikan summarises Hinn's anti-cessationist argument, delivered as part of his 'healing time' sermon: Jesus healed people in the gospels; Jesus is the same today as yesterday; so he is healing today. 'I don't care what your pastor says', Hinn proclaimed. 'I don't care what your doctor says ... Jesus is here tonight and is waiting to heal you'.[72] Hinn's brand of evangelism, like that of many other practitioners before him, claims self-justification – or 'anointing' – through the display of the charismatic gift of healing.

Millikan recounts the procedure by which Hinn's assistants selected members of the audience for healing: any person exhibiting serious disability or infirmity was ignored: Hinn's operatives 'were not interested in the profoundly ill'.[73] Preliminary prayer sessions were held by the assistants with those professing lesser ailments: if these audience members displayed signs that could be construed as recovery, they were led to the stage where, under a dazzling light, they were slain in the spirit by Hinn, with the assistance of his minders, who pulled each audience member back and to the floor. Despite the lack of any empirical evidence for healings or long-term recovery, the Hinn organisation continuously reports the success of its healing mission. The official Hinn website claimed that 'powerful miracles' were achieved at events on the Australian tour.[74] Millikan reserves his most stringent criticism for Hinn's pursuit of wealth: 20 minutes of Hinn's oratory were devoted to the 'cajoling' of large sums from the audience; Hinn's three shows in Brisbane were reported to have raised about $AUS800,000. Apart from the funds invested back into his ministry, Hinn's 'parsonage' reportedly cost $US3.5 million, incorporating seven bedrooms and garage space for ten cars. The self-proclaimed charismatic healer has 'recast Jesus in his own image',[75] turning humility into luxury.

Away from the singular realm of televangelists and star preachers, the more humble and communal practice of charismatic worship has also received trenchant criticism from within the church. A stern Greek Orthodox dismissal of charismatic Christianity was issued by John Zizioulas in 1990:

> Only in our day do we have a superabundance of 'charismatics' who are active and carry on their spiritual work simply by right of their priesthood or their 'gifts', without it being clear that everything in the Church is done in the name of the bishop.[76]

From this Orthodox position, the church community is 'episcopocentric', centred on the bishop in the manner first enunciated by bishops Clement and Ignatius in the early second century. Charismatic worship, if not approved by the bishop, is therefore unauthorised and lamentable.[77]

There has been criticism of charismatic practice even from those within the charismatic faith. Tom Smail has observed that the initial strength of charismatic worship – the reaction against the sin and guilt emphasised in the traditional church – became a weakness. Because charismatic worship maintained no regular place for repentance, it created an impression of superficiality and 'unreality'.[78] Smail adds that the charismatics' rejection of all liturgical constraints, again initially celebrated as a liberating factor, has often resulted in self-indulgence, or in the adoption of liturgical formulas, so that spontaneity has diminished over time.[79]

One of the most sustained attacks on the charismatic movement has been launched by the pastor and broadcaster John MacArthur, who bemoans the 'chaos and doctrinal confusion' unleashed within

Christianity by the twentieth-century charismatics.[80] For MacArthur, the extremism and confusion resulting from the charismatic renewal stem from the 'errors' inherent in its doctrine, which he summarises:

> [T]he idea that God is still revealing truth beyond Scripture; the teaching that Spirit baptism is subsequent to and separate from salvation, thus creating two classes of believers; and the mysticism that is innate in charismatic teaching, which encourages people to denigrate reason, elevate feeling, and open their minds and spirits to powers they cannot understand.[81]

The charges of mysticism and of the divisive creation of 'two classes of believers' recall the accusations of heresy brought against Montanism by the church in the second century. Indeed, MacArthur notes with displeasure that the charismatic movement could be designated 'neo-Montanism', and that at least one charismatic writer has claimed Montanism as part of the charismatic tradition.[82] MacArthur articulates the cessationist view: the canon closed with the completion of the New Testament; divine revelation ceased with that closure, as did the performance of miracles, including healing.[83] Any claim to the contrary is 'fantastic', fraudulent or deluded, resulting from a desperate emotional need for the 'new and esoteric' in religious experience.[84]

MacArthur draws on other critics of the charismatic movement, one of whom has disparaged it as 'the zenith of mysticism'.[85] This charge of mysticism from within mainstream Christian theology echoes the long history of denunciations, beginning in the second century, of Gnosticism and many other variants of faith deemed heretical. Yet the terms of the charge – that charismatics pursue an anti-intellectual, non-dogmatic faith, overemphasising personal experience and direct divine revelation – are also the factors which have made the charismatic renewal, like countless revivals before it, intensely popular for a minority of Christians. The craving for Spirit possession, received as 'sensational experience',[86] animated Pentecostals in the early twentieth century, energised charismatics in the later part of that century, and continues to inspire the many hybrid forms of such worship in the twenty-first century.

Charismatics and charisma

The term 'charismatic' was applied from the early 1960s to the type of worship, conducted within the mainstream churches, that would once have been labelled 'Pentecostal'. The book published in 1972 by

Walter Hollenweger – *The Pentecostals: The Charismatic Movement in the Churches* – reflects this usage. However, there appears to be little or no connection between charismatic worship and the Weberian sense of charisma, which also had attained wide currency in Western culture by the 1960s.

Christian theologians and historians of religion writing in the late twentieth century preserved the distinction between charismatic Christianity and the secular notion of charisma. Paul Hiebert, in an article on the charismatic movement published in 1985, wrote that founders of new movements within Christianity 'are often charismatic leaders (in the Weberian sense)', noting that Weber 'produced a classical study on types of leadership'.[87] Andrew Walker, in 1995, discussed the phenomenon of miraculous healing within charismatic Christian congregations, observing the effect on large groups of 'charismatic personalities (using "charismatic" in the popular, secular sense)'.[88] In these instances, the Weberian notion of charismatic leader is kept strictly separate from the charismatic worship of the late twentieth century. *Charisma* magazine, an interdenominational Christian publication commencing in 1975, took its name from the Christian derivation of 'spirit-gift', not from the Weberian definition of the word.

The emphasis on community within the 1970s charismatics, noted by James Dunn, certainly drew on the first-century Pauline conception of the charismata, and ran counter to the individualistic notion of charisma – as form of leadership – proposed by Weber. 'Charismatic' as the descriptive term for ecstatic Christian worshipers in the 1960s appears to have been taken directly from the Greek word for spiritual gift, without recourse to Weber or his theory. The primary motivation behind the introduction of this term to Christian discourse was the need to distinguish this increasingly popular form of worship from the Pentecostalism from which it was derived. 'Neo-Pentecostal' could scarcely serve as a descriptor for a type of worship that had been tolerated within Protestant churches; nor, a little later, could the Pope be expected to accord his blessing to a practice known as 'neo-Pentecostal'. Charismatic worship may well have been accepted within the traditional churches because it represented – as Harvey Cox asserts – a milder, domesticated version of Pentecostalism; the term 'charismatic' served to distinguish it from its forbear, and to align its particular form of revivalism with an impeccable Pauline antecedent.

However, it is remarkable that the two usages of 'charisma' – Christian and secular – should both occupy high public profiles from roughly the same period: the 1960s. The emergence of charismatic Christianity in the 1960s paralleled the emergence of youth culture, including the phenomenon of rock stars commanding delirious audiences. At the same time, major political figures – such as John F. Kennedy – were described as 'charismatic' by media commentators.

These cultural developments shared at least two common features. The first was the role of the mass media. Kennedy appeared a glamorous, 'charismatic' politician largely due to his photogenic presence, widely distributed through television coverage as well as magazines and newspapers. Evangelical Christian preachers, some professing charismatic powers, adapted to the medium of television in the 1960s, reaching huge audiences as 'televangelists'. Billy Graham toured the world in the 1950s and 1960s, holding revival meetings in large auditoriums, extending the reach of his mission through media outlets. Even the minor controversy within a small American church in 1960 – Dennis Bennett's Episcopalian church – received national media coverage, generating interest far beyond the local milieu.

The second pertinent feature was the search for intense emotional experience. From the 1960s, mass audiences in large auditoriums or stadiums acted as if possessed – shouting, screaming, swooning, fainting – whether the subject of their devotion was an evangelist or a rock star. Charismatic Christianity valued experience over structured religious rite; charismatic worshippers sought a heightened spiritual state, culminating in a transforming, emotional, moment. Many other young people sought such extremes of emotional or spiritual experience in the 1960s and 1970s, whether achieved through the stimulus of music, drugs or religion.

The secular and the religious crossed over at many points: 'soul' music was a secularisation of the gospel music of southern Baptist churches; non-Western, non-traditional religious forms were eagerly adopted by experimental Western youth. The extreme emotional condition pursued by the curious or the unconventional was condemned as irrational by traditionalists, both Christian and secular. The power of 'charisma' – an irrational force in Weber's sociology – was celebrated by its supporters in both Christian and secular contexts. Evangelical preachers such as Oral Roberts, Billy Graham and Pat Robertson were considered charismatic in both its senses: magnetic and commanding of an audience (Weberian) and spiritually empowered (Pauline). Although the two meanings were kept apart within Christian discourse, they began to blur together in wider usage. Primarily this was due to the high levels of exposure gained by the televangelists and other revival-style preachers capable of attracting and maintaining a large audience.

Charisma in Weber's sense is an individual attribute, displayed by a leader able to galvanise a crowd of followers: increasingly, evangelical preachers were seen performing in this way. They were 'charismatic' as they entranced huge stadium audiences; their individual charisma was thought to transmit itself to even larger unseen audiences through the medium of television. Some of the charismatic Christian leaders created family dynasties (Billy Graham, for example, nominated his son Franklin as successor at Billy Graham Ministries), in a manner reminiscent of the Kennedy 'family line' of charisma. In this manner, the individual star preachers achieved greater prominence as bearers of (Weberian) charisma than did the communal charismatic worshippers, revelling in their revivalist Pauline charismata.

8
The Age of Media: Charisma and Celebrity

The words 'fame' and 'celebrity' derive from the Latin *fama* and *celebritas*. For the Romans, *fama* meant news, public opinion, a person's reputation, or the glory and renown of a figure known to the public. *Celebritas* meant the state of being busy or crowded, as in a crowded festive day; its meaning was extended to the reputation or renown of a person celebrated by the public.[1] Fame for the Romans was a public virtue, the celebration of great achievements – such as military victories – wrought by individuals who embodied the glories of the Roman state. The contrast between this conception of fame and twenty-first-century celebrity – in which, it is widely known, an individual may be 'famous for being famous', with no great or even notable achievements – is stark.

Yet the two cultures, two millennia apart, have some common features: the central role of media technology in promulgating fame; and the self-conscious willingness of the individual to seek public acclaim, to project an image of the self into the public order. Julius Caesar and Augustus had books, portraits and even coinage to promote their greatness; the contemporary celebrity has a publicity machine functioning through mass media broadcasting and the Internet. All of them have moulded a public persona – with an eye to the greatness of the past or to posterity or simply to their enduring popularity – that bears a complex relationship to their private selves.

There is a singularity to modern celebrity, however, that relates directly to the apparatus in which it operates: consumer capitalism and a media technology adept at the reproduction and transmission of images, sounds and text. The twentieth-century celebrity was a commodity, a construct produced in factories of light and sound to be sold to the public at enormous profit, an image endlessly repeated, reproduced and promoted. This interpretation of modern celebrity as a commercial machine is not simply a conceit of critical theory, an academic overstatement. American popular culture was already reflecting back on itself by the early 1960s. Andy Warhol's screen prints from that period – some of the most well-known Western art works of the second half of the twentieth century – reproduced images of Marilyn, Elvis, Elizabeth Taylor and other celebrities in the same manner as were reproduced Campbell's soup cans and Coke bottles. Warhol exposed the mechanics of celebrity as serial repetition. The celebrity was revealed as a fabricated object with the qualities of a commodity: alluring, exciting, manufactured, mass-produced, advertised, consumed. The modern star was made to shine but it was primarily made to sell.

Writing in 2002, the journalist Andrew Anthony equated contemporary celebrity with the shaping force of consumerism and mass media: 'You could make the crude equation that fame + the consumer society = celebrity'. Anthony pointed to the crucial role of the media edifices built by Hollywood: 'The history of 20th century fame is the history of Hollywood. And the history of Hollywood ... is all about the triumph of celebrity'.[2] Hollywood has generated stars of unprecedented glamour and appeal. The word 'charisma' was not part of the general vocabulary as Hollywood's star system took hold in the 1920s and 1930s; it would not enjoy prevalence until the 1960s. But the Hollywood stars were rapturously praised for their magnetic charm; stars attracted devoted followings in the manner of charismatic leaders. Looking back from 2001, the film historian Samantha Barbas wrote of the Hollywood stars of the 1920s: 'Wealthy and charismatic, successful and adored, they became the nation's most prominent spokespeople for modernity'.[3] The challenge for a history of charisma, then, is to determine the relationship between charisma and celebrity: in the parade of twentieth-century stars, does charisma reduce to a mere synonym for celebrity?

From Alexander to Barnum: A brief history of fame

In ancient civilisations, fame resided at the top of the social hierarchy: pharaohs, kings and queens, great military leaders. The fame attached to monarchies and dynasties corresponds to the Weberian concepts of charisma of office and familial charisma, discussed in Chapter 6. Glory resulting from military deeds could be used as a means of attaining political power and fame, as achieved by Julius Caesar; otherwise, great military feats could be immortalised in epic poems, legends or written histories. In his book *The Frenzy of Renown*, Leo Braudy traces a history of fame that finds the desire for recognition a 'culturally adaptive trait',[4] taking different forms throughout ancient and modern civilisations. For Braudy, the history of fame begins not with the grand god-kings of Egypt or the great dynasties of Persia or China, but with the act of 'self-naming' by Alexander the Great.[5]

Braudy's history of fame in Western culture (which can only be summarised here) begins with Alexander because his fame was based not on his inherited place in society, but on his own achievements, the publicising of which was 'stage-managed' to a remarkable degree. Alexander's military adventures self-consciously echoed those of the Homeric heroes; he made himself 'Great' not only through his conquests and the cities named after himself, but through management of the media of his time – in this case the writers and artists who travelled with him. Alexander was depicted in paintings and sculptures, while his feats were narrated by his own historian-publicist Callisthenes. For Braudy, Alexander exhibited an 'urge to be unique' that extended beyond military glory into 'cultural and imaginative domination'. Callisthenes functioned as a form of 'press agent', promoting Alexander's achievements to the Greek city-states in Homeric terms, representing Alexander as the legitimate heir of Greek culture.[6]

Alexander's career then survived as a guide for later Roman leaders. The intensely public culture of Rome upheld fame as 'action in public for the good or ostensible good of the state'.[7] Braudy argues that fame assumed another dimension for the Romans, whose religion lacked a developed concept of the afterlife: fame for public action was 'the only way to live beyond death'.[8] Pompey wore Alexander's cloak and emblem, modelling his aspiration on Alexander the Great, while Julius Caesar took Alexander's 'self-naming' to the next level, writing his own war memoirs. Cicero, 'intemperately fond of his own glory' in the words of Plutarch, sought fame for himself, but also helped define fame as a Roman 'national program', inseparable from political virtue.[9] For Cicero, fame was an 'exalted reputation', an honour and glory that carried an almost physical presence: Pompey, he wrote, conquered by reputation as much as by prowess.[10] The shift from Republic to Empire entailed enhanced means of propagating the Emperor's fame: Augustus made extensive political use of coinage, which bore not only his image but also 'catchwords' of his regime, such as *Libertas augusti*.[11]

The Christian era introduced a radical counter to the Roman notion of public fame. In his *Confessions*, Augustine rejected his earlier aspiration to 'ignominious glory' through public displays of eloquence, devoting himself instead to an inward spiritual relationship with God.[12] Renown in Christian culture was bestowed on saints of exceptional spiritual purity, often in ascetic mode. Athanasius's fourth-century biography of St Antony extolled his spiritual discipline in the desert, redolent of an inner purity. But if Christianity in its first few centuries turned away from the display of hollow public glory, public grandeur grew as the church expanded its power and privilege. Bishops, popes and patriarchs evinced ceremonial pomp as well as spiritual rectitude. The conflict between inner truth and public display continued within European culture throughout the medieval period and into the Renaissance.

Braudy notes the ambivalent attitude to fame in the works of Dante and Chaucer. In the *Inferno*, Dante has the power to determine the reputations of the dead, while also bestowing fame on himself as poetic creator; yet the *Divine Comedy* as a whole also represents a spiritual aspiration to 'inner virtue'. Braudy contends that Dante resolves the contradiction between, on the one hand, the Roman urge to public fame and, on the other, the Christian rejection of such fame's emptiness, by defining an 'exemplary true fame' inspired by God. This virtuous fame has a spiritual character beyond 'mere public show'.[13] Chaucer's poem *The House of Fame* stands, according to Braudy, 'at a crux in the warring traditions of Roman and Christian fame'.[14] Chaucer displays both fascination with fame and repulsion from it: in the poem he sees Fame herself, dispensing favours arbitrarily, but when asked if he has come for fame, Chaucer replies that he has not. Distrusting the urge to worldly acclaim, Chaucer declares that he seeks instead love's tidings, and is led out of the House of Fame.

The Renaissance rediscovery of posterity is exemplified in the writing of Petrarch, whose *The Fates of Illustrious Men* was intended both to reveal the lessons offered by the past and to disclose the power of fame: posterity, he wrote, could transform even the deformed into 'handsome, illustrious, and revered' men.[15] Renaissance portraiture promoted, in Braudy's phrase, 'the dissemination of the unique' through paintings of esteemed individuals, while a reading public began to grow in the wake of the printing press.[16] The gradual growth of readerships, audiences and markets for artistic works, corresponding to a decline in the importance of royal and aristocratic patronage, was highly significant in the history of fame. By the seventeenth century, John Milton could describe fame as 'the spur' prompting his 'laborious days' of writing; Braudy observes that while Milton still accorded true glory to God, this could be reflected by 'enhanced fame on earth'.[17] In the eighteenth century, the book became a 'new place of fame': in Alexander Pope's *The Temple of Fame*, Pope emphasised books that promoted their authors, affording a moral fame deemed acceptable by Pope.[18]

The meaning of 'celebrity' as a condition of being widely extolled or celebrated was available in the eighteenth century: Samuel Johnson could write of his own 'celebrity' in 1751.[19] The notion that one could create one's own name, without the advantage of inherited class privilege, was especially favoured in the United States, where Benjamin Franklin fashioned his own public profile partly by means of his *Autobiography*. Jean-Jacques Rousseau struck a 'wholly modern note' in the history of fame, Braudy remarks, because of his determination to be recognised for what he 'really' was. Rousseau's *Confessions*, an account of his developing feelings and beliefs, promoted a 'natural fame', based on inner qualities and without the props of social privilege.[20] Yet Rousseau found his own celebrity oppressive: he wished to avoid the fate of Voltaire, who, he wrote, was 'weighed down by fame and prosperity'.[21] David Hume wrote in defence of Rousseau, whose contradictory persona as the reclusive social philosopher, Hume admitted, was 'extraordinary'. It was not true, Hume asserted, that Rousseau practised 'an art to gain celebrity'; Rousseau in reality possessed a 'love of solitude'.[22] Braudy suggests that this paradoxical condition of Rousseau, which perplexed his contemporaries, was an early instance of the modern 'shy star',[23] the celebrity who publicises his or her uniqueness, yet shrinks from the public gaze.

Rousseau's commitment to writing as self-expression fed the Romantic movement, which also developed the cult of genius: fame now belonged to the unique, the inspired, whether artists or great military leaders such as Napoleon. The fascination with Lord Byron in the early nineteenth century signalled, for Braudy, the effective end of aristocracy as the purveyor of fame: Byron was an aristocrat who wanted to be famous for his works and his deeds.[24] By the mid-nineteenth century, Braudy notes, the 'marketplace of fame' had become so crowded that both Thomas Carlyle and Ralph Waldo Emerson devised typologies of greatness.[25] Carlyle's *On Heroes and Hero-Worship* (1840) distinguished various hero types, listing Prophet, Poet, Priest, King (including Napoleon) and Man of Letters (including Johnson and Rousseau). Emerson's *Representative Men* (1850) differed slightly with its categories of Mystic, Philosopher, Skeptic, Man of the World (Napoleon) and Writer (Goethe). Carlyle's belief in the crucial importance of the Great Man also included the observation that such a figure can plot his own demise through a self-conscious focus on fame. For Carlyle, this process of 'Lionism' turned a hero into a mere celebrity.[26]

In the second half of the nineteenth century a distinction between celebrity and fame could be observed, in which celebrity was ranked lower than fame. Matthew Arnold wrote in 1863: 'They [Spinoza's successors] had celebrity, Spinoza has fame.' The meaning of 'celebrity' as a celebrated person had also emerged by the mid-nineteenth century, at first in inverted commas – 'Did you see any of those "celebrities", as you call them?', Dinah Mulock wrote in 1849 – and then without: Emerson wrote of 'the celebrities of wealth and fashion' in 1856.[27] The 'engines of fame' gathering momentum in the late nineteenth century included the use of photography in newspapers and magazines; publicity; and specialist publications such as *Who's Who*, founded in the United States in 1898.[28] In the prehistory of twentieth-century celebrity, the last significant nineteenth-century figure was P. T. Barnum, the impresario whose travelling circuses showcased an array of natural and spectacular talent. Barnum's methods prefigured those of the twentieth-century Hollywood studios in many ways: the importance of promotion, no matter how outlandish; the cultivation of show-business excitement; the involvement of the audience; and the staging of entertainment as a 'democratic theater', in Braudy's phrase, holding out the promise of the 'democratization of fame'.[29]

'Star' was used in the language of the theatre in the nineteenth century to describe an exceptionally brilliant performer. It was noted in the Scottish press in 1827 that 'stars' was a term found in 'theatrical language';[30] the press frequently made use of the term in referring to the most famous theatrical performers of the day. Although cinema was first publicly exhibited in 1895, the term 'star' could not be applied to a film actor before 1910, because the performers in films remained uncredited and anonymous until that date, despite audience requests to the studios to identify their actors. One incident in 1910 is often cited as the beginning of Hollywood film celebrity: studio head Carl Laemmle revealed to the press the name of his new leading actress, Florence Lawrence. This first publicising of a film actor's identity was also one of the first publicity stunts orchestrated by a film company: Laemmle planted a false press report that Lawrence had died, only to refute the claim – in the press – shortly afterwards. As a result of this media chicanery, the silence surrounding film actors was broken and, in the words of Samantha Barbas, 'the movie star system was born'.[31] In the blunter terminology of the philosopher and sociologist Edgar Morin, the star system was 'grafted to the production system after 15 years of anonymous evolution'.[32]

An important technical development was the technique of the close-up, used regularly by D. W. Griffith in his films by 1910, allowing viewers an intimacy with the screen actor not possible in the theatre.

The term 'star' was soon applied to film actors: 'movie star' appeared in the press in 1913, and the motion-picture industry in America was already celebrating its 'greatest film stars in the world' in 1914.[33] Actors quickly shifted in the public consciousness from being anonymous members of stock film companies to glamorous performers. The film star differed from the earlier 'picture personality' because the actor's private life became part of the discourse around the film actor; from 1914, articles in film magazines such as *Photoplay* focused on actors – a 'New Type of Hero' – rather than on their roles.[34] After 1910 other film-making nations, notably Italy, Russia and Denmark, produced their own film stars.[35] The tight control of the representation of actors' public and private lives – the shaping of their public image – did not emerge, however, until the rise of the Hollywood studio system in the 1920s.

The star factory

In his history of world cinema, David Robinson notes that by the early 1920s, the most popular film actors in Hollywood had assumed enormous significance, both artistically and economically. The biggest stars of the silent-film period – Mary Pickford, Douglas Fairbanks and Charlie Chaplin – were, Robinson records, 'the most famous and the highest salaried people in the world'. The stars' function in the economic system of Hollywood, particularly its distribution mode, was paramount: 'it was their faces and their fame which assured the market for American films from Siberia to Africa, from London to Tokyo'.[36] Morin posits the star system as 'a specific institution of capitalism on a major scale', contrasting the Western film system with that of the Soviets, who attempted to eliminate the star from their cinema (at least before the advent of Stalinist hero-worship).[37] Carl Laemmle was explicit concerning the importance of stars to the economic viability of Hollywood: 'The production of the stars is a prime necessity in the film industry'.[38]

The Studio System of Hollywood, which dominated American cinema from the 1920s until the early 1950s, has been characterised as an 'assembly-line of greatness', a 'star machine' and a 'rational paradise' for the manufacture of entertainment, glamour and celebrity.[39] This system, driver of the 'Golden Age' of Hollywood, has frequently been construed as a form of factory: a dream factory, a star factory, the Hollywood machine. The film star – the actor deemed to occupy the top echelon of film celebrity – was a product of this system, a property of the film studio; Joshua Gamson remarks that film performers by the 1920s 'were essentially studio owned-and-operated commodities'.[40]

The factory metaphor is an appropriate choice to designate the range of manufacture conducted by the major studios: films, promotional campaigns, publicity, celebrities. However, 'factory' is a less accurate descriptor of these studios than the admittedly more cumbersome 'vertically integrated production and distribution monopoly'. The studios' domination of the American film industry was enabled by vertical monopolies through which the studios owned their own distribution wings and cinema chains. Studios controlled the creative process through contractual hold over creative practitioners: writers, directors, actors, cinematographers, producers, composers, editors, set designers, make-up artists and other technicians. In the highly rationalised studio system, every effort was made to eliminate the unpredictable elements of the artistic process.[41]

This integrated system became fully entrenched in the few years following the advent of sound cinema in 1927, coinciding with the early Depression, which caused further rationalisation within the industry.[42] By 1930, almost all film production in the US was by eight studios, including the five majors – M-G-M, Paramount, Warners, Fox and RKO. Efficient production systems and tight scheduling generated around 40 films per year at M-G-M, Paramount and Warners (contracted actors were expected to complete three or four films per year). Films released by each of the majors could be identified by their particular style, genre, and their stable of stars. M-G-M boasted 'more stars than there are in heaven', including Garbo, Jean Harlow and Clark Gable, and favoured extravagant, opulent films; Paramount's stars included Cary Grant and Claudette Colbert, and the comic performers Mae West, W. C. Fields and the Marx Brothers, hence their speciality of sophisticated comedy; Warner Brothers' main stars – Bette Davis, James Cagney and Humphrey Bogart – were used in darker, grittier dramas; Fox actors John Wayne and Spencer Tracey were featured in various genres, especially the Western.

The extraordinary capacity of a major studio extended to its role in creating, sustaining and regulating celebrity. As Ellis Cashmore has remarked in his book *Celebrity/Culture*, actors were the 'primary materials' of the studio's economic system, whose machinery functioned to convert certain actors into stars.[43] These primary resources came equipped with their own raw materials: aspiring actors needed to be physically attractive and photogenic. Talent scouts sought them out around the country; hopefuls arrived in Hollywood hoping for stardom. Aspirants were photographed and screen-tested; if promise was detected, they would be taken in by the studio and physically modified if necessary (facial alteration such as teeth or nose straightening was common). Acting and diction lessons were provided, as well as instruction in social manners. For Morin, this process, particularly in the case of female aspirants, could be bluntly encapsulated: the 'manufacture of stars essentially consists of inflating the original pin-up with personality'.[44] The studio allocated the actor minor roles, which became larger if audiences responded favourably. Barbas notes that M-G-M in particular was known for its ability to transform 'nondescript actors' into 'brilliant, captivating celebrities'.[45] If the actor attained prominence, his or her public appearances would then be controlled by the studio's publicity department.

This aspect of the studio's power has the most direct bearing on the shaping of celebrity. In the wake of scandals surrounding actors in the early 1920s – most notably Fatty Arbuckle in 1921 – the studios resolved to maintain a tight control over information released to the public. Actors' private lives were removed from public scrutiny; public appearances were stage-managed by the studio publicity departments. Potentially damaging incidents in an actor's private life were concealed by any means – including bribery – by industrious publicity teams. The effect of this effort by the studios was to produce a positive, benign public image of the Hollywood celebrity. Film critic David Denby has remarked that the Hollywood stars were essentially public figures; and their public displays and pronouncements were designed to portray them as 'helpful, kind, grateful for their enormous luck'.[46] There was nothing shocking or even tawdry revealed of the celebrities' private lives; any glimpse into their home life was regulated to show a wholesome, admirable aspect to their personalities. Barbas states that in many cases, studio publicity departments penned 'semifictional' biographies of new stars, whose allegedly authentic private lives were 'largely fabricated'.[47] Morin describes this function as the 'systematic organization of the private-public life of the stars' so that even stars' ostensibly private romantic rendezvous were orchestrated, 'illuminated by moonlight and flashbulbs'.[48]

As part of this process, the media outlets were largely complicit with the studio publicity departments in promoting a sanitised, constructed version of film actors' private lives. Most journalists and magazine writers were happy to accept the releases issued by the studio publicity departments, or conspired with them to generate 'anemic stories' of the stars.[49] The enormous quantity of cinema gossip columns and magazines constituted, in Morin's words, 'the nutritive plankton of the star system'.[50] From the 1920s, film actors' public profiles were enhanced by their frequent use in advertising, so that film celebrities became entrenched in American consumer culture.[51]

Of these Hollywood celebrities, the most glamorous and dazzling were the stars. The devotion of fans to their favourite stars – spectacularly evident in the riot surrounding the funeral of Rudolf Valentino in 1926 – provoked critical responses from the traditional social elites. Barbas records the rueful observation following this event in the *New York Times*, that films had 'created a new mental attitude in vast multitudes of people'. A favoured film actor was, the *Times* observed, 'a household name in millions of homes where a mere writer of books could never hope to enter'.[52] Barbas concludes that by the late 1920s, movies 'seemed to impress the people more deeply than literature or religion', and that the stars commanded greater respect and attention than political leaders.[53] The intensity of devotion remained strong in the 1950s, as revealed in the analysis in 1957 by Edgar Morin. One of the first scholars to make a serious study of fandom, Morin scrutinised film fans' letters to magazines, studios and fan clubs to explore the 'cult' of stardom from the perspective of the devotee. Morin interpreted the fans' devotion to their favourite stars as a kind of love, a 'matter of adoration', that at times assumes a religious dimension: 'the star is like a patron saint to whom the faithful dedicate themselves'.[54] For these devoted followers, the star 'hovers at the level of the divinised hero', straddling 'sacred and profane, divine and real'; the stars are 'anthropomorphic gods' in the eyes of their fans.[55]

If this 'divinised' aura surrounding the stars was a feature of film stardom, its construction by the studios was given historical perspective, as well as critical analysis, by the German critic Walter Benjamin in 1936, in his famous essay 'The Work of Art in the Age of Mechanical Reproduction'. Benjamin celebrated the general capacity of mechanical reproduction (primarily photography, printing and film) to emancipate the work of art 'from its parasitical dependence on ritual':[56] the production of many copies, he proposed, would diminish the reverence associated with the original artwork. Benjamin's assertion was: 'that which withers in the age of mechanical reproduction is the aura of the work of art'.[57] When the masses could handle or own copies of celebrated works, the near-religious 'aura' which had previously imbued these works with authority and value would evaporate. Yet Benjamin also observed a counter-impulse within the sphere of mechanical reproduction. The film industry, he noted, responded to the 'shriveling of the aura' with the 'cult of the movie star'. This fabricated cult comprised the 'artificial build-up of the "personality" outside the studio', made possible by 'the money of the film industry'. For Benjamin, the movie star was not a manifestation of 'the unique aura of the person'; it was rather a form of commercial manufacture: the '"spell of the personality", the phony spell of a commodity'.[58]

Benjamin's insights anticipate the Warhol screenprints of Marilyn and Elvis suggesting the manufactured aura of celebrities, as does the observation of Morin in 1957 that the star has 'all the virtues of a standard product adapted to the world market, like chewing gum'. For Morin, 'star-merchandise', unlike other forms of commodity, 'neither wears out nor diminishes upon consumption'. Rather, the 'multiplication of a star's images, far from impairing, augments her worth and makes her more desirable'.[59] The fabricated aura enveloping film stars, capable of inspiring near-religious devotion in their admirers, was nevertheless the result of a commercial imperative employing technological means: Morin concludes that stars were 'endowed with magic or mystical value ... [and] sold at prices far in excess of their production costs'.[60]

The inner gift of the stars

If the stars projected an aura, casting a spell over their adoring fans, was this aura the equivalent of charisma? Was the irrational, near-religious devotion of fans to their favourite stars the equivalent of followers' devotion to a charismatic leader? While the word 'charisma' was not available to describe the height of film stardom from the 1920s to 1950s, the discourses around film stars – press reports, magazine coverage, publicity, critical writing – provide an indication, using different vocabulary, of the qualities attributed to the stars.

'Personality' was the term used in the discourse surrounding early Hollywood to describe qualities later associated with charisma. Samantha Barbas comments that 'personality' denoted 'a particular set of characteristics: charm, attractiveness, magnetism'.[61] As early as 1910, at the very beginning of the star system, film actor Mabel Trunnelle was praised in the trade journal *Moving Picture World* because from her first picture, 'her personality stood out prominently'.[62] 'Magnetism' was a term also applied to exceptional film actors from the 1910s and 1920s: an M-G-M executive described to a movie magazine the impression made by ingénue Lucille LeSueur (later renamed Joan Crawford): 'I knew that she had that rare thing – personality. She is beautiful, but more essential than beauty is that quality known as screen magnetism'.[63] Barbas records that fans adopted this vocabulary – personality, magnetism, charm – while praising film stars in their fan club journals or in letters to magazines and studios. A fan in 1927 wrote of Mary Pickford that she was blessed with 'magnetic personality – that so called indescribable something – which colors and vitalizes everything she does'.[64] The 'indescribable something' was also known as 'It', loosely defined in 1926 as 'one of the rarest gifts in the world', to be found only in special stars such as Gloria Swanson. 'It' also took on sexual connotations in the jazz age, personified in 1927 in the 'It-girl', Clara Bow; the indefinable 'It' was tagged a 'jazz name for personality', or, more directly, 'sex magnetism'.[65]

The publicity surrounding the major film stars also perpetuated the idea of natural talent or giftedness. Joshua Gamson, considering Hollywood film stars in the context of Braudy's history of fame, argues that the commercial discourse around stars (film magazines, publicity, press coverage) fostered a 'fame meritocracy'. A film star arose, according to this discourse, not through public virtue and action, but due to his or her 'authentic, gifted self'. Luck may be involved in the rise of a star, as in the 'lucky break', but what ultimately counted were the inner qualities of the individual, who needed to have 'what it takes'. Talent was important but not sufficient to ensure the rise to stardom. *Photoplay* magazine advised in 1919 that the stars who survived 'had that rare gift designated as screen charm or personality, combined with adaptability and inherent talent'.[66] The precise quality possessed by these rare individuals remained mysterious: it was described as 'ineffable' in a magazine article of 1940.[67] The stars' success, according to this discourse, was 'based on an indefinable internal quality of the self'.[68] If the word 'charisma' had been available in the 1930s and 1940s, it would certainly have been invoked to articulate this special ingredient, this inborn quality, possessed by these stars.

Edgar Morin, writing in 1957 on the international cult of the film star, pinpoints the mystery built into the very premise of the star. For Morin, the discourse around the star, and the possibility of becoming a star, emphasises the utter unlikelihood – indeed the impossibility – of an ordinary person making it to the pinnacle. And yet this same discourse reminds aspirants of those rare 'Cinderella' success stories. The handbooks with 'promising titles' such as *Tu seras star* insist that there is no 'recipe' for stardom; what matters is the gift, 'the gift of oneself as much as that miraculous and transcendent gift, the gift of grace'.[69] Morin's reference to the 'gift of grace' suggests the original religious meaning of 'charisma'; indeed, the idea of divine gift as explanation for the stars' 'miraculous' careers can be traced in the discourse surrounding stardom. Film mogul Samuel Goldwyn stated the idea boldly when he declared: 'God makes the stars. It's up to the producers to find them'.[70]

By the 1970s, the term 'charisma' – in Weber's sense of a special quality of individuals thought to be extraordinary or gifted with 'exceptional powers' – was in wide usage, and applied to film stars. The film critic Molly Haskell, writing in 1974, argued that certain female stars had transcended their demeaning roles 'through sheer will and talent and charisma'.[71] Richard Dyer, in his book *Stars* (1979), addresses the issue of the applicability of charisma, as defined by Weber, to film stars. Rather than identifying stars' special quality as charisma, however, Dyer situates 'star charisma' in the specific social framework that has generated the need to revere film stars, a framework that has generated the stars themselves. Dyer's perspective is that of the 'social construction of charisma', as developed in sociology and other disciplines in the 1960s and 1970s. According to this account, the image of Marilyn Monroe embodied 'the very tensions that ran through the ideological life of fifties America', so that her 'charisma' was in effect the 'apparent condensation' of conflicting currents of sexuality and innocence.[72] Much more common than this ideological reading of charisma, however, has been the simple description of stars as charismatic. Writing in 2007, film critic David Denby described the stars of the Hollywood studio system era as 'charismatic, indelibly idiosyncratic people, who transcend celebrity and mean something emotionally powerful to the audience'.[73] The stars appeared, in the words of Ellis Cashmore (2006), as 'ordinary people who were gifted with a little something extra: charisma, magic, *je ne sais quoi* – an indefinable quality that made them stars'.[74]

The meaning attributed to 'star' in the film industry and its related discourses – publicity, fan magazines, critical writing – has been inconsistent since 'film star' and 'movie star' were introduced soon after 1910. At times it has been used broadly to denote any famous film actor; at times the industry's box-office-related definition of a star as a 'reliable big earner'[75] has been primary. But the most commonly accepted meaning of 'star' has been the elite film actor, the most famous of the famous, the most celebrated among celebrities. The 'true star', it has been suggested, 'gracefully' combines huge box office draw with high celebrity; a *Time* article in 2008, following this definition, proposed that only one such star remained.[76] The elite figures – Garbo, Gable, and others in the history of cinema, including Joan Crawford, Gary Cooper, Rita Hayworth – have been considered to stand apart from their peers in the milieu of famous film actors. They are the few rare performers 'who transcend celebrity', possessing some special quality that has elevated them above all others.

In contemporary terminology, that quality is charisma, as deployed by Denby to denote the egregious nature of these exceptional stars.

In previous decades, this quality has been termed 'personality' or the 'It' factor. The language used to designate this quality, from as early as the 1910s, has emphasised two characteristics: rarity and innateness. It is not, then, possessed by all film stars, but only by a very small minority. It is 'that rare thing', the 'indefinable something' known as 'personality', 'magnetism' or 'screen charm'; it is a 'rare gift', an 'internal quality of the self'. By these discursive means, a distinction has been made between the general cast of stars and a special elite possessing a peerless gift. In the highly artificial industry of Hollywood, a place was reserved for exceptional individuals who had that 'rare thing' transcending fabrication; that quality would later be called charisma.

The advent of celebrity

The Hollywood studio system began to break down in the late 1940s. In 1948 the Supreme Court broke up the production-distribution-exhibition monopoly enjoyed by the Big Five studios. Some actors had already begun forming alternative management structures: in 1947 Burt Lancaster, for instance, formed a partnership with the agent Harold Hecht and producer James Hill. In 1950 the actor James Stewart set an example by successfully negotiating the terms of his contract for the film *Winchester 73*. The grip of the studios weakened in the 1950s, as actors, represented by powerful agents, demanded more financial control (including percentage points of film profits) and exercised greater freedom of choice in their screen roles. Increasingly, film actors became 'proprietors of their own image';[77] but their freedom from the hold of the studios also meant that they were no longer protected by those studios' publicity departments.

Exposure of the stars' private lives, once rigorously patrolled by the studios as part of their actors' public image, became increasingly difficult to manage. Photographers hired by the press and magazines, armed with telephoto lenses, began feeding the celebrity gossip industry with previously unattainable images of stars' private lives (the plot of the 1954 Alfred Hitchcock film *Rear Window* tuns on the properties of the telephoto lens owned by a press photographer played by James Stewart). Intrusive press photographers were given the name 'paparazzi', after an annoying celebrity-chasing photographer in Federico Fellini's 1960 film *La Dolce Vita*. Television, which in the 1950s and 1960s replaced cinema as the dominant leisure activity, offered a new site for generating and consuming celebrity, generally of a smaller and less glamorous variety than the stars of Hollywood's golden era. The publicity apparatus attending all celebrities – great and small – escalated in the years following World War II.

While the word 'celebrity' meaning a celebrated person had been available as early as the mid-nineteenth century, it was not in common use during the first half of the twentieth. In his book *Common Fame* (1985), Richard Schickel remarks that in the 1940s the word 'celebrity' was almost never used in the press, radio, magazines or everyday conversation: instead, one heard or read about 'successful' or 'famous' individuals.[78] By the early 1950s, the machinery of fame in American consumer culture – publicity and television – had begun to develop a culture of celebrity. This new aspect of public life was satirised in the 1954 George Cukor film *It Should Happen to You!*, in which a 'nobody', played by Judy Holliday, plasters her name – Gladys Glover – on billboards across Manhattan. As a result of this simple act of self-promotion, she literally makes a name for herself: she is soon swamped by fans seeking her autograph. Famous merely for having a well-known name, she is signed by a television producer, becoming better known through undignified – but popular – TV appearances.

It Should Happen to You! is partly a Hollywood critique of the new TV-driven celebrity culture: in the film Jack Lemmon plays a conscientious documentary film-maker, under whose influence Gladys eventually rejects her new social status as inauthentic. Yet despite the film's vested

Figure 8.1   It Should Happen to You! Dir. George Cukor. In this 1954 film satirising the emerging celebrity culture, a 'nobody' becomes a celebrity by making a name for herself – literally.

interest in deriding the influence of television, its satire exposes the cultural effects of the expanding publicity machine and the voracious appetite of TV. In this emergent celebrity culture, one does not need great achievements to be socially eminent; one does not even need talent or good looks, as possessed by the Hollywood film stars. One merely needs to be before the public, to 'have a name'. *It Should Happen to You!* also discloses that the vocabulary of celebrity, and the distinction between stars and celebrities, had become entrenched by the early 1950s. In the film, a team of advertising men, working on methods to exploit the new 'ordinary' celebrity figure, come up with this campaign: 'Stars use it, celebrities too, but more important, it's the favourite of average American girls such as Miss Gladys Glover'.[79] Modern fame, according to the perspective satirised here, has reduced to a hierarchy of the star; the celebrity; and the ordinary person, who may yet be transformed into a celebrity.

In 1959 the *Celebrity Register* was published in America, comprising over 2200 biographies. The editors of this volume proclaimed its superiority to previous publications such as *Who's Who* due to the new simplified empirical approach taken in assessing individuals' status. While it is impossible to truly determine a person's social standing, the editors claimed, 'you *can* judge a man as a celebrity – all you have to do is weigh his press clippings'.[80] This culture of celebrity, which valued public figures simply on the basis of the volume of their publicity, received a scathing critique in Daniel Boorstin's book *The Image*, published in 1962. For Boorstin, the celebrity is a 'human pseudo-event', a product of mass media and publicity departments. Boorstin made the observation – later repeated and rephrased many times by others – that the celebrity 'is a person who is known for his well-knownness'.[81] Expanding on this theme, Boorstin asserted that 'anyone can become a celebrity, if only he can get into the news and stay there'. As 'mere figments of the media', celebrities' 'chief claim to fame is their fame itself. They are notorious for their notoriety'.[82]

Boorstin traces the history of celebrity-construction to around 1900, when the Western world 'discovered the processes by which fame is manufactured'.[83] Citing studies of popular American magazines, he notes a transition in the first three decades of the twentieth century: between 1901 and 1914, roughly three-quarters of biographical articles concerned politicians, business and professional figures. After 1922, more than half such articles featured entertainment figures; by the early 1960s, nearly all biographical magazine articles were drawn from 'light entertainment, sports, and the night club circuit'.[84] Boorstin contrasts the eminence of these figures with the fame based on great or heroic achievements of earlier ages. Whereas heroes were 'self-made', modern celebrities are 'mass-produced', 'fabricated on purpose to satisfy our exaggerated expectations of human greatness'.[85] Celebrity for Boorstin is a form of artificial fame generated in the media through 'simple familiarity, induced and re-enforced by public means'. A celebrity is merely a 'big name', as the *Celebrity Register* attests: celebrities are 'the "names" who, once made by news, now make news by themselves'.[86]

Boorstin makes the further observation that the modern celebrity, having been made by publicity, can also be destroyed by publicity in the form of adverse gossip propagated through media outlets. In the age of TV and radio, the rise and fall of a celebrity can be so swift that it leaves little trace and negligible emotional impact: celebrities are made more quickly than ever before, and 'they die more quickly than ever before'.[87] On the other hand, some efforts to debunk a celebrity can have the adverse effect of enhancing popular appeal, on the grounds that 'as much publicity yardage can be created one way as another'.[88] Boorstin makes the final assertion that unlike heroes, who represented an ideal or could be admired for great achievements, the modern celebrity is 'usually nothing greater than a more-publicised version of us'.[89]

This tendency of the celebrity culture to favour common or ordinary individuals with passing, minor incarnations of fame – noted by Boorstin in 1962 – has only intensified in the decades since the publication of *The Image*. In the book's twenty-fifth-anniversary edition, Boorstin observed that new communication technologies – such as VHS and Cable TV – had 'multiplied and vivified pseudo-events', while their 'unimaginable successors' would no doubt further accelerate this process.[90] Those successors – primarily the Internet and the reality TV genre – have spread 'artificial fame' much wider, and much more thinly, than Boorstin had witnessed in 1962 or 1987.

Braudy concluded his history of fame, published in 1986, with the rueful observation that in contemporary culture 'the concept of fame has been grotesquely distended'.[91] This distending reached new proportions in the late 1990s with the worldwide popularity of the reality TV genre, featuring reality programmes such as *Big Brother* and *Idol*. These and other reality shows proved hugely popular with young audiences, from which were drawn the programmes' eager participants. The thousands of young adults auditioning to appear on these programmes hope first to be chosen by the show's producers, and then to perform to the satisfaction of their peers, who, as viewers, determine the participants' fate. The eventual winners of such programmes enjoy a minor celebrity for a time, especially if they are able to exploit their status in other media appearances. Even non-winners may experience at least negligible celebrity, for as long as they remain on the show, or for as long as they are recognised once they have left it. The urge to renown has become the urge to be on television; it is as if the mere presence on TV coats the participant with a temporary aura, the sheen of minor celebrity.

This new form of television has generated a new form of celebrity. Ellis Cashmore characterises this novelty in the terms of the old Hollywood star system: 'it was as if extras had been upgraded to headline players: people that would previously have gone unnoticed were promoted to a status comparable to movie stars and rock singers'.[92] The democratisation of fame, which Braudy posited as the last phase in the history of renown, reaches its conclusion on the Internet, where individuals publicise themselves via webcams and blogs. In addition, specific websites are dedicated to the democratisation of fame: in 2005 the UK talent management firm Wannabe Famous declared on its website that 'absolutely everybody has the chance to become a star!'. The website proclaimed that as a result of reality TV, 'the barriers have come crashing down', so that an aspirant's talent, combined with the firm's 'expertise and advice', creates a new formula for stardom: 'Whether you have lots or little talent ... Wannabe Famous Ltd will supply you with the chance to realise your dreams and ambitions'.[93]

Sites such as this take seriously Warhol's prediction that everyone will be world famous for 15 minutes; the promise made in the early twenty-first century seems to imply fame for everyone who wants it, and for longer than that quarter-hour time frame. The iWannaBeFamous website declares its mission: 'we feature one ordinary person at a time'; aspirants are invited to take 'the challenge of having fame'. One candidate in 2008 states her ambition: 'I don't want to be the average girl, I want to stand out. Have people know my name. Have fans that will support me. I want to be known'. This drive to be known, satirised in 1954 by George Cukor – the nobody creating a name through the medium of billboards – has a more potent medium in the Internet. This website assures contributors that their very presence in the form of postings has inaugurated their path to celebrity: *x is Famous!* is the reassuring heading above every declaration of intent by a contributor.[94]

If almost everyone has at least the opportunity to achieve some degree of fame, the corollary of this development is the devaluing of actual celebrities. In contrast to the Golden Hollywood era, when stars' detachment from their public engendered a kind of awe in their fans, contemporary celebrities are treated as much closer to the average. David Denby notes the 'abusively familiar tone – chummy, coarse, knowing' in which the media reports gossip and scandals concerning celebrities. A regular feature in *Us Weekly* magazine, he remarks, is called 'Stars – They're Just Like US!', and there is an inexhaustible supply of paparazzi photographs to prove this assertion.[95] Celebrities' private lives, including their most mundane activities, are continually featured in such magazines and websites; the professional paparazzi are now complemented by amateur photographers able to post their digital photographs of celebrity activities to the Web. As a result of this development, Denby concludes that the 'the magical aura around movie actors has vanished'.[96] There remain some movie stars in the old sense, Denby states, but 'there are fewer stars than in the past, and they have come down in the world'.[97] This observation is often expressed – as a lament – in newspapers and magazines: a 2007 article in a weekend newspaper supplement averred that 'today's celebs aren't a patch on the thoroughbreds from the old star system'.[98]

The lowering of celebrities to the level of ordinary citizens may take the form of a probing beneath the artifice of celebrity manufacture. An article in *New Weekly* magazine, 2007, begins by itemising the means by which 'Hollywood stars' artificially preserve their youth, before noting that 'there are still a few celebs who … are comfortable enough with themselves to look as old as they really are – crow's feet, saggy bits, wrinkles and all'.[99] This article is typical of the celebrity weekly magazine's propensity to expose the fallibilities of celebrities, revealing their ordinariness beneath the surface glamour. 'Stars' Secrets Exposed!' is the refrain found in magazines and TV shows of this type, accompanied by images of overweight, underweight, intoxicated, embarrassed or plain mediocre celebrities. At times this coverage veers into a sadistic voyeurism; at other times the admiration for celebrities is rejoined, as they are shown in a more flattering – glamorous – light. The sheer volume of celebrity coverage – both complimentary and exposing – testifies to the condition of modern celebrity as articulated by Denby: 'every part of a star's existence, including the surgical scars and the cellulite deposits, belongs to the media – and to the public'.[100]

The scholarship on celebrity since the 1990s has shifted emphasis from the manufacture of celebrity – as critiqued by Boorstin in 1962 – to a focus on the role of audiences in the process of constructing celebrity. Audience involvement assumes a number of expressions: the direct contribution to celebrity as voters in reality TV shows; the positive or negative response, given greater prominence via the Internet, to putative celebrity figures; and the ways in which fans relate information on celebrities' lives – including gossip and scandal – to their own emotional lives.[101] Celebrities are construed, in such theoretical writing, as the 'projection of a collectivity', in Durkheim's terms – or, in contemporary terminology, as constructions or productions of an actively engaged audience. The audience thus 'negotiates' celebrity, making use of celebrity narratives and gossip for their own purposes. Much of this theoretical writing, however, following a 'demotic turn' in media studies, lacks critical judgement concerning the cultural significance of celebrities, or even a discernment between different forms or levels of celebrity.[102]

Other forms of commentary, particularly in journalism, are more critical of modern celebrity. Journalist Bernard Zuel has remarked that the dream of everyone attaining some degree of fame is not only a 'big lie' but may be psychologically harmful to those given such extravagant hope.[103] Even contemporary celebrities have been publicly critical of the modern version of fame: 'I think celebrity is a vulgar thing', the actor Rachel Weisz has stated. 'It is so easy to be famous. Turn up in a certain frock, present a show, take your top off.'[104] The one issue not in dispute, however, is the sheer ubiquity of contemporary celebrity, and the foregrounded – or 'distended' – role it has come to occupy in Western culture.

Celebrity, but not charisma

If modern celebrity is dispersed so widely, credited to more entertainers and public figures than ever before, has there also been a corresponding increase in the number of public figures deemed charismatic? Has charisma been liberally spread across the populace to match the dispersal of fame?

On this matter, media commentators are adamant: there is a clear distinction between celebrity – which is constructed within the apparatus of mass media – and charisma, which does not depend on such an apparatus.[105] In a 1999 weekend newspaper supplement article on charisma, 'The It Factor', it is claimed that 'As any showbusiness insider will testify, celebrity and charisma do not necessarily go together'.[106] The authors of this article quote Australian celebrity agent Harry M. Miller: 'you can sometimes meet big rock stars or movie stars … you see them without all their trappings [and] they have absolutely no charisma'.[107] Many reviews of performances by pop stars, sportspeople, even politicians, remark on these individuals' lack of charisma, often in derisory terms, thus drawing a sharp contrast between charisma and celebrity. A review of a pop concert finds that the popular singer 'has all the charisma and stage presence of a sandwich shop attendant'.[108] A newspaper article reports a golf tour official's remarks concerning a successful, but decidedly uncharismatic, golfer: when the official overheard journalists' complaints that the golfer lacked charisma, she replied, 'We can't make her something she's not'.[109] Another newspaper article on charisma in politics dismisses a high-profile Australian politician as 'Celebrity mistaken for charisma'.[110]

The success of reality TV has made the process of celebrity construction increasingly transparent, as pop stars and other celebrities are 'manufactured' on prime-time television. This has engendered a degree of cynicism in critics and media analysts concerning those celebrities who are 'famous for being famous' while exhibiting no appreciable talent, and exuding zero charisma. Journalist Andrew Anthony quotes the novelist Martin Amis: 'You can become famous without having any talent (by abasing yourself on some TV nerdothon)'.[111] Journalists frequently comment on the distinction between the fleeting celebrity status of reality TV personalities and other, more enduring, forms of celebrity. For example, journalist Laura Demasi, recording that a woman's magazine devoted four pages to the wedding of a former *Big Brother* contestant, remarks that the magazine 'seems to have mistaken' this person 'for someone with the same celebrity status as Princess Diana', before caustically concluding that 'no one actually cares about the former reality TV star. Not even just a tiny bit'.[112] It may be argued that such sardonic criticism is merely the condescending reportage of popular culture within a quality newspaper. However, the distinction between the recent, obviously manufactured celebrities, and those of more lasting – and significant – fame, is also held by fans.

In 2007 a book of celebrity photographs taken by a long-term fan was published. Richard Simpkin compiled his photographs of celebrities taken over a 20-year period into the book *Richard & Famous*; in promoting this publication, he made critical observations on the contemporary 'cult of celebrity'. 'It's out of control', he claimed. 'Now you have people like Paris Hilton, who is famous for being Paris Hilton'. Simpkin, who photographed actors, musicians, politicians, sports performers and even religious figures simply as a fan, was critical of contemporary manifestations of celebrity: 'I call today's celebrities disposable celebrities. They're the plastic celebrities that will dissolve in the future'. He discriminated between these figures and the stars of an earlier generation: 'that's why the legends like Gregory Peck or Audrey Hepburn are so important. They'll never be forgotten'. Simpkin also preserved a distinction between mere celebrity and charisma. Despite attaining proximity to hundreds of celebrities over two decades, he was sparing in his designation of these figures as charismatic. In an interview publicising his book, he used the word only once, in describing his encounter with rock star Michael Hutchence: 'I spent five or 10 minutes talking to him. He was the most charismatic person I'd ever met'.[113]

The distinction between the media-constructed reality TV celebrity and the charismatic performer is especially pronounced in the field of pop music. The international success of the *Idol* reality TV concept has generated numerous *Idol* winners (or near-winners) who have subsequently enjoyed commercial success as pop performers. However, an 'anti-Idol snobbery' has been evident in the pop music industry, which withholds respect for winners of a 'TV talent quest' deemed to lack credibility.[114] A review of the Australian record industry awards (ARIA) night in 2007, by a newspaper TV reviewer identifying herself as an *Australian Idol* fan, is telling in this regard. For reviewer Ruth Ritchie, the juxtaposition of an *Idol* episode with the broadcast of the ARIAs awards night produced a vivid contrast. The 'artificiality of the process' behind the 'sensible, average, manufactured *Australian Idol* product' became 'blindingly clear' after only a few moments of the first song performed at the ARIAs. The performer was the 'impossibly charismatic, unfeasibly talented' Daniel Johns of the rock group Silverchair. Ritchie declares that such a talent 'can't be formed or farmed on a talent show', and that any musical utterance by Johns would be 'more musical than anybody who has ever graced an *Idol* stage'. Observing that even a talented *Idol* performer had 'felt a fraud at the ARIAs', Ritchie concludes with a question that appears to set limits to the quality – and authenticity – of successful *Idol* contestants: 'can we really ever worship any Idol we are stupid enough to create and vote for ourselves?'[115]

In coverage of popular culture in the media, the descriptor 'charismatic' is applied only to those rare individuals who seem to transcend normal celebrity. Charisma is considered a special quality innate in exceptional individuals, as posited by Weber. Such figures are thought to emanate charisma in person, without the need of media technology to fabricate a celebrity aura. This rare, authentic quality – a special presence – is stipulated as the factor separating 'true celebrity' from the manufactured kind. Journalist Richard Jinman describes a press conference appearance by Michael Hutchence in these terms, the rock star's arrival 'triggering the slight shift in air pressure that accompanies true celebrity'. In the specific context of rock music, this charisma is deemed to 'exude rock's key ingredients: sex and danger'.[116] A similar presence and effect on others has been noticed, with different characteristics, in politicians. A former staffer says of former Australian politician Jeff Kennett: 'the mood of a whole room of people would change when Kennett walked in'.[117]

Charisma is understood as an unmediated presence. In 'The It Factor' article, Liz Porter and Sue Williams contend that charisma is a 'genuine' factor that was evident before the advent of mass media: 'Lord Byron ... managed to be famous for his charisma without the help of the modern media. As did Ned Kelly'. In the modern world, charisma exists independent of media artifice: the authors report a former football coach's opinion on the presence of charisma in non-celebrities: the 'genuine quality [of charisma] can be spotted in sportspeople who have never graced a magazine cover'.[118] This 'genuine quality' is indeed most powerfully experienced in a live environment, without the filter of mediation. One former footballer turned TV celebrity is described as possessing such charisma that a room full of 'supposedly blasé TV industry types' is inspired to 'swivel its collective head and gawp' when he enters the room. According to Porter and Williams, such native charisma may be 'aerated' by media exposure, allowing the charismatic presence to be projected to a much larger audience. But the genuine attribute announces itself without the props of media: the same individual is described, as a young footballer, as someone exuding presence: 'His whole bearing was fantastic. He was the sort of person people looked at'.[119] The designation of rare talented performers as possessing innate gifts is made not just by media commentators. Producers, talent agents and other professionals regularly judge performers in this light. For example, television producer Laura Waters has said of actor/writer Chris Lilley: 'he's gifted. I feel like he was born with – and given – these amazing gifts ... It's not manufactured, that's just who he is'.[120]

Celebrity, then, is understood as a form of invention, while charisma is not. An individual, it is generally assumed, can be made into a celebrity, with the aid of cameras, lighting, publicity machines and marketing. But charisma cannot be manufactured. It is a 'genuine quality' that existed well before the advent of mass media and public relations, and endures as an innate gift. In the assessments made of the legions of contemporary celebrities, charisma is deployed as an index of authenticity. There may be tens of thousands of celebrities, but only a tiny minority are considered 'true' celebrities, bearers of charisma. Very few Hollywood stars were deemed to possess the 'rare gift'; in the age of ready-made media celebrities, that quality has become even rarer.

9
Charisma Past, Present and Future

In recent years, an article in the *China Daily* mentioned charisma as part of leadership skills; a Japanese film was titled *Charisma*; a Bollywood actress was named Karisma Kapoor.[1] The international spread of the word charisma has proceeded largely by phonetic transliteration (the Japanese equates to 'karisuma' with meaning close to the Western sense of charisma) or direct use of the Western word (as in Mandarin). Polish has imported the word as 'charyzma' or 'charyzmat', the latter connoting the religious domain, as in charisma of prophets. Ukrainian, using the Cyrillic alphabet, pronounces the word as *kharyzma*. Other languages have similarly added 'charisma' to their vocabulary, adapting the word to fit their orthographies. The appropriation of the word into many languages suggests that no exact equivalent already existed in those languages; to express the thing called charisma, it was necessary to use 'charisma', in transliterated form.[2] Yet even as the word has gained international currency, the meaning and proper use of 'charisma' in Western culture have remained ill-defined.

From a survey of current media usage of the term, I attempt in this chapter some small speculation regarding the future of this enduring word and its associated meanings. Also surveyed are the dissections of charisma undertaken in disciplines such as leadership theory and psychology, while the role of charisma as a term in contemporary politics is examined. The first task, however, is to ascertain the current general flavour of charisma.

The 'It' factor

What exactly is the contemporary meaning of charisma? A simplified definition reduces charisma to 'compelling charm',[3] also expressed as 'personal magnetism' or drawing power. Weber's definition – 'a certain quality of an individual personality by virtue of which he is considered extraordinary' – remains the base on which the current popular understanding of charisma is built. 'Charisma' has certainly been modified and extended from Weber's specific conceptualisation of charismatic leadership as a form of legitimate domination: charisma is now just as likely to be attributed to a pop star as to a religious or political leader. Yet the contemporary meaning of charisma in general usage derives from Weber's sociology, not from Paul's religious discourse. Charisma is considered not as a spiritual gift dispersed throughout the community, but as an exceptional quality possessed by certain remarkable individuals. There is more, however, to charisma – as used within a wide range of contemporary discourses – than can be rendered in a reductive definition such as 'compelling charm'.

Writing in 1990, the anthropologist Charles Lindholm observed that '"charisma" is now a part of the vocabulary of the general public, and obviously fills a felt need to conceptualize and categorize ... cultic commitment and extraordinary crowd phenomena'. Lindholm also noted that the meaning of charisma had been extended to cover

> the admiration offered to glamorous movie stars, exciting sports heroes, and Kennedyesque politicians – adulation which goes far beyond mere admiration of someone with special expertise.[4]

For Lindholm, placing the 'discourse about charisma' into a theoretical framework is difficult because the term is applied to a diversity of individuals in divergent contexts. Leaders of religious cults are frequently described as charismatic figures (Lindholm analyses Jim Jones and Charles Manson as charismatic cult leaders), but the meaning of charisma has been expanded to include celebrities, sports performers and any figure thought to manifest a special 'extraordinary' quality.

An appreciation of the contemporary usage of charisma may be gleaned from an analysis of the word's appearance in recent media reportage.[5] Charisma is regularly attributed to certain politicians, actors, musicians and others by journalists, critics, commentators and members of the public. The attempt to determine the current meaning – or range of meanings – of charisma is greatly assisted by media discourse, which is fond of asking – and answering – questions of this type.

An Australian Sunday newspaper supplement of 1999 devoted its front cover to the theme of charisma. Underneath photographs of 12 individuals deemed charismatic – and beneath the word 'charisma' – were

Figure 9.1 Sun-Herald, SundayLife! Front page, 7 November 1999. This weekend newspaper supplement nominated a mix of charismatic individuals: politicians, actors, television personalities, a religious leader, a boxer, and a writer.

three questions: 'What is it? Who's got it? And why?'. The supplement provided pictorial assistance in answering the second of these questions: its 12 chosen ones included politicians – British Prime Minister Tony Blair, former Australian Prime Ministers Bob Hawke and Paul Keating and politician Cheryl Kernot; a religious leader – the Dalai Lama; actors Audrey Hepburn and Cate Blanchett; boxer Muhammad Ali; writer and academic Germaine Greer; and two current television personalities. This combination of individuals considered charismatic – male and female, politicians, religious leaders, actors, sportspeople and media celebrities – is supplemented within the article by additional photographs of individuals, including Nelson Mandela, Mahatma Gandhi, Bill Clinton, Imran Khan, Humphrey Bogart, Judy Davis and historical figures Ned Kelly and Lord Byron.[6]

The authors of this cover article on charisma, Liz Porter and Sue Williams, claim that determining 'who's got it?' presents no difficulties: 'It's easy to tell who has it and who never will'. Answering the question 'What is it?', however, is a different proposition: 'it's very hard to define charisma, the quality possessed by those who inspire us'.[7] Porter and Williams make several attempts at a definition, including a one-line tag on the contents page: 'The "it" factor: why some people will always stand out from the crowd'. Yet the 'it factor' is such a vague summation that the authors seek more precise characterisation of charisma from a number of specialists: celebrity agents, public relations practitioners, journalists and opinion pollsters. Charisma is 'physical presence combined with an ability to persuade – and great charm', according to one public relations consultant. Charisma 'is to do with a vitality', in the opinion of a celebrity agent; it derives from an 'energy', observes a political staffer. It is a 'personal magnetism and capacity to sway a mass audience', Porter and Williams suggest. It is a 'gift' for 'imparting a sense of inclusive intimacy', a gift that endears the individual to others, even if they may find aspects of that individual 'infuriating'. This gift for 'inclusive intimacy', remarks a political staffer, is 'always talked about with Bill Clinton'.[8]

This feature article is consistent with other media reports in its determination that charisma is easy to identify but very difficult to define. Another newspaper article in 2002, concerning charisma in politics, refers to 'that elusive something called "charisma"'.[9] In that same article charisma is termed 'drawing power', and a 'certain magnetism'. Another media report on individuals considered charismatic portrays charisma as that ability to walk into a room and 'command attention without even trying'.[10] The power of charisma in one instance – referring to a film director – is deemed 'frightening' and 'all-devouring'.[11]

The range of characteristics attributed to charisma – from charm to frightening intensity – in part proceeds from the diversity of individuals to which the term is ascribed. On one day in 2007, different newspapers analysed 'one-man charismatic dictatorships' as in Tito's Yugoslavia, and the 'once-in-a-lifetime … incredible charisma' of a golfer.[12] A letter to a newspaper warns of the 'power of charismatic leaders such as Osama bin Laden' over 'gullible and ignorant members of society'; in the same year, readers of the same newspaper are told of a visit by 'one of the world's most charismatic dancers'.[13] In one issue of the *London Review of Books* may be found discussion of the 'whole new level of charm and charisma' imputed to Stalin in a recent biography, and description of a speaker at a Slow Food meeting as 'charismatic' in delivering a 'fiery speech'.[14] A newspaper report describes a Chechen 'terrorist leader with charm and charisma' in terms suggestive of Weber's account of the charismatic leader's relationship with his followers: 'they fear and respect him in equal measure and are prepared ... to sacrifice their lives for him'.[15] Yet that same quality of charisma is also liberally applied in the media to dancers, pop stars, actors and golfers.

Charisma itself remains largely mysterious for most media commentators. Although several of the interviewees in the 'It Factor' article associate charisma with strong physical presence or attractiveness, others insist that neither of those attributes is essential to charisma. The Burmese political leader Aung San is described in a magazine article as 'not a physically imposing presence', yet he 'had a strange magnetism, the charisma of a man who cannot be deflected from his purpose'.[16] A newspaper columnist 'mulling over the phenomenon of charisma' in 2007 states that it cannot be equated with 'just beauty and glamour', supporting this claim with the declaration that of the two charismatic men she has met, one – Tony Blair – was 'certainly no beauty', while the other – Bob Dylan – was at the time 'a fairly wizened little prune'.[17] The columnist, Maggie Alderson, reports that both men emanated a powerful presence, Blair via 'extraordinarily intense' pale-blue eyes, Dylan by creating the impression that 'for the whole time ... he was looking at you – and only you'.

In this column, Alderson deploys charisma as an index of authenticity in assessing famous individuals; her use of charisma is consonant with the practice analysed in the previous chapter, whereby charisma is distinguished sharply from celebrity. She contends that 'in 25 years as a journalist I've met a lot of wildly famous people, but I've only ever come across three truly charismatic ones'. The third individual in her triumvirate of charisma is Princess Diana, of whose physical presence Alderson reports: 'she really had a glow about her' and 'she somehow seemed to occupy more space than an average human'. On a second, later, physical proximity to Diana, Alderson draws a distinction between her charisma and the artifice of the celebrity industry: 'I thought a layer of lacquered Hollywood-style gloss had grown over the more pure, naked charisma I had seen before'. Yet that 'naked charisma' had not been effaced by cosmetic application: 'she still had a glow that went far beyond what even Clarins Beauty Flash Balm can achieve'.

Figure 9.2 Princess Diana, described as the bearer of 'pure, naked charisma'.

Drawing on her memory of her encounters with these three 'truly charismatic' individuals, Alderson attempts to pinpoint the nature of charisma. The title and subtitle of her column offer the phrases 'a kind of magic' and 'rare and breathtaking aura'; the columnist is unable to articulate the subject with any greater clarity. Noting that no other meeting with famous individuals generated the 'frisson' she experienced in the proximity of Dylan, Blair and Diana, she declares: 'I still don't understand what creates the effect'. She counters the possibility that her perception of these three individuals was purely subjective by quoting the *Sunday Times* reporter Christina Lamb's impression of Diana: 'She had something I'd only ever seen before from Nelson Mandela, a kind of aura that made people want to be with her'. Inferring from this and other accounts of rare charismatic individuals such as Bill Clinton that 'it's definitely not just me', she concludes that charisma must constitute an intrinsic quality: 'If not fame, beauty, power, wealth and glory then what? It must be innate. I find that quite thrilling'.[18]

Alderson, like other media commentators, concludes that there is something unfathomable about charisma; the authors of 'The It Factor', in a similar manner, found charisma 'very hard to define'. 'True, naked charisma' for Alderson is such a rare entity that it must be an innate quality in certain very special individuals; for other observers, charisma is a 'gift' granted to exceptional individuals. The contrast between this rare quality and the demonstrably fabricated fame of celebrities reinforces the conviction that one is born with charisma: it cannot be manufactured. Weber's definition of the charismatic leader as an individual considered to be 'endowed with supernatural, superhuman, or at least specifically exceptional powers or qualities' remains germane, even in an age when charisma is regularly ascribed to entertainers. From the recent media usage of charisma surveyed in this and the previous chapter, the following definition may be inferred: charisma is broadly understood as a special innate quality that sets certain individuals apart and draws others to them.

There is very little deviation in the media from this accepted meaning, even in the coverage and analysis of contemporary politics (detailed later in this chapter). If the signification of 'charisma' contains a degree of ambiguity, that lack of semantic precision constitutes part of its meaning. While 'it's easy to tell who has it' (and while newspaper and magazine articles delight in nominating those who have it), charisma is yet 'very hard to define'. There is, then, a consensus view that charisma exists, and that it describes the special aspects of certain individuals – yet it retains an ineffable, or at least vaguely defined, character.

The charismatic sandwich

The term 'charisma' has attained such prevalence in Western culture that the enigmatic quality associated with the word may contribute to a blurring of its meaning. The future of 'charisma' and its associated meanings may be determined by the increasing range of applications to which the word is put. Weber applied the term strictly to leaders; its contemporary meaning has broadened due to its range of applications. In the near future, 'charisma' may suffer from its profligate usage in a media environment increasingly powered by public relations, marketing, self-help books and websites, all featuring hyperbolic statements. The term has become increasingly elastic since attaining wide popular usage in the 1960s; further indiscriminate usages may stretch that elasticity until the concept loses recognisable shape.

As early as 1960, Arthur Schlesinger, critical of Weber's concept of charisma, could complain of the slippery semantics of the word, used in a 'metaphorical' manner as 'a chic synonym for "heroic" or for "demagogic" or even just for "popular"'.[19] In the early twenty-first century, charisma is applied to such a range of individuals – and objects – that further slippage of meaning has occurred through use, or overuse, of the word. The sense of charisma as an innate quality may dissipate if the word is used frequently in self-help books and classes as an attribute to be acquired. For example, a 2007 book issues advice to fathers of adolescent girls:

> Be a charismatic adult for them. Be a source of strength to make those little girls, as they grow up, feel safe, valued and listened to. There is a very strong correlation in research between having a charismatic adult with those characteristics and resilience long term.[20]

This advice urges fathers to be 'a charismatic adult' for their daughters. Charismatic attributes are, according to this expert, something to be obtained by any father; they are not the mysterious qualities held by only certain special individuals. The characteristics of charisma in this context are strength, the offering of security and encouragement, compassion, sensitivity. These qualities may also be described as those of traditional parenting, or even good parenting; they have not generally been associated with charisma. The adjective 'charismatic' here appears to function as a synonym for 'inspiring' or 'compelling'. While the charismatic individual, in the Weberian sense, has been aligned with the ability to inspire and compel, 'charismatic' is drained of much of its distinctive meaning when it is applied to fathers of teenage girls. This article's other marked departure from received ideas concerning charisma is the assumption that charisma may be acquired after due diligent effort. Whereas charisma has been widely understood as a rare, innate quality that cannot be manufactured, here it is advocated as a skill that a father would be wise to obtain (by reading the book).

Charisma has also been attributed to inanimate objects, in such a manner that the word is denuded of much of its meaning. A city (Berlin) has been praised for its charisma by an architecture critic, who comments on 'the real street life ... the zany shops and bizarre cabarets that give Berlin its charisma'.[21] A lake (Lake Como) has been celebrated as 'sheer charisma'.[22] A play (Pinter's *The Homecoming*) has been described as possessing charisma by a theatre critic: 'I was drawn to the charisma of the work'.[23] Even an organ of the body (the heart) has been lauded for its charisma. A review of the book *A History of the Heart* finds that it concerns 'far more than the changing representation of this most charismatic organ'.[24] Attributing charisma to a city, a lake, a play or a body part makes little sense when charisma is understood as the special quality of an exceptional individual. It makes even less sense when applied to a sandwich. In the food pages of a weekend newspaper supplement in 2007, the subject is the iceberg lettuce. The subtitle of this column encourages readers to 'Revisit a retro classic with dressings that add charisma to its crunch'.[25]

The subeditor of this supplement has bestowed charisma onto a lettuce. More accurately, the salad dressings are deemed to endow the iceberg lettuce with charisma, thereby enhancing the lettuce's native property, crunchiness. When this dressed lettuce is shredded in a sandwich, the dressing adds the vital ingredient: the result is a charismatic sandwich. Such a sandwich is lovingly portrayed in a close-up photograph, in which the essential ingredient – the charismatic lettuce dressing – is prominent. It is unlikely that this salad dressing is charismatic in the Pauline sense of possessing spiritual gifts such as prophecy or speaking in tongues, nor does it display exceptional powers of leadership as stipulated in the Weberian definition. It is indeed difficult to imagine how a salad dressing or a sandwich can possess charisma. The sandwich is not in any way 'gifted', or blessed with intrinsic qualities. 'Charisma' in this subtitle is presumably intended as a synonym for 'zest' or 'tang', or possibly 'character'. Perhaps the alliteration of 'charisma' and 'crunch' is a feature of this subeditor's art. Whatever were the reasons behind charisma being ascribed to a salad dressing and included in a sandwich, 'charisma' here is employed in very strange territory.

Usages such as these threaten to drain meaning from the term, reducing 'charismatic' to a synonym for other words such as 'outstanding', 'impressive', 'punchy', 'exceptional'. If the general use of charisma were to become as indiscriminate as in the examples collected here, the career of this term would enter a new, nondescript, phase. Overuse of the word in journalism, marketing and advertising would produce a similar effect. One pop music critic in 2008 noted the 'diminished' status of the word charisma, presumably due to its overuse. This critic resorted instead to a lengthier description of a performer, describing her 'strength of character, depth, charm and sensuality' rather than use the 'diminished' term charisma.[26]

Misuse and overuse threaten to dilute the singular character of 'charisma'. If that were to occur, 'charismatic' would come to mean little more than 'special'. But for such a semantic change to eventuate, Western culture would need to relinquish the particular cultural role it has reserved for charisma. It would no longer require a word to signify individual aura, magic, magnetism, even 'the It factor', of certain rare individuals. This future may possibly eventuate, in which case 'charisma' will cease to connote these qualities, and will instead quietly take its place as a synonym for 'extraordinariness', or even fade from use altogether. Judging from the evidence of contemporary media usage, however, the cultural function performed by charisma is significant, and is unlikely to decline into disuse. It is needed, in contemporary culture, to perform a number of functions: to distinguish the artificial from the authentic in the realm of fame; to explain why only very few individuals generate a frisson for those who come in contact with them; to denote the magnetic appeal exerted by certain special individuals.

Teach-yourself charisma

Since the late 1990s, motivational books teaching techniques for success in business have expounded on charisma. Some titles (and their explanatory subtitles) include *The* New *Secrets of Charisma: How to Discover and Unleash Your Hidden Powers* (1999), *Charisma: Seven Keys to Developing the Magnetism That Leads to Success* (2000), *The Charisma Effect* (2002) and *Executive Charisma: Six Steps to Mastering the Art of Leadership* (2005). Projects such as these break with the sense of charisma as innate: they promise to impart charisma to readers of the books. Because they often retain the idea of charisma as an extraordinary quality setting great business leaders apart, these books at times generate contradictory messages concerning charisma. Yet as specimens of the self-help genre, they need to persuade their readers that charisma can be taught, or at least cultivated.

Doe Lang's *The* New *Secrets of Charisma* conveys the conviction that charisma is both innate and present to some degree in everyone, and therefore able to be 'unleashed'. '*Intrinsic* charisma is a birthright', she avers. 'Some of it is inborn, some must be developed, and some must be rediscovered'.[27] *The* New *Secrets of Charisma* presents itself as the means of developing this inner power. In her Introduction, Lang provides a brief historical perspective on the growth of popular usage of charisma as a term from the 1960s to 1999. Most people, she claims, remember 'the word *charisma* in connection with the Kennedys' – but Lang argues that the term had made little penetration in the 1960s. Only with the communications explosion of the 1990s, she insists, did the word enjoy prevalence: in the decade to

1999, 'use of the word *charisma* has increased over 100 percent in the United States alone', according to a search of 70,000 publications. Lang concludes that due to its inclusion in leadership studies courses as well as its general currency, 'charisma has become a respectable part of the landscape'.[28]

Lang also draws on her experience teaching courses on public speaking: 2000 respondents to the question 'What is charisma?' produced a stream of synonyms and associations, including 'allure, appeal, attraction, charm, dynamism, presence, magnetism, personality, confidence', and the descriptions 'larger than life, original, instantly familiar yet mysterious'.[29] This articulation of popular opinion on the meaning of charisma – consistent with the descriptions in recent media coverage – is the starting point for Doe's own segmentation of charisma into 'thirteen kinds', which are mostly the areas of achievement of famous charismatic individuals – 'sports charisma', 'money or business charisma' – with the exception of 'intrinsic charisma'. This innate quality does not depend on celebrity or achievement, as it is a 'basic energy force of nature' that each person can 'tap into' with the correct guidance.[30] The rest of this book contains instructions and exercises – 'charisma-cises' – for the 'care and maintenance of your charisma'. Doe cannot allow charisma to be so 'mysterious' that it cannot be cultivated; the instructions in her book pertain generally to confidence and esteem building, delivered with a New Age tinge.

Executive Charisma, by D. A. Benton, demonstrates – according to its back cover – 'that charismatic executives are not just born, they are made'. Benton defines Executive Charisma as *'the ability to gain effective responses from others by using aware actions and considerate civility in order to get useful things done'*. Admitting that this definition is 'a bit nebulous', the author assures her readers that 'Executive Charisma is a tangible thing. You know "it" when you see it. You remember times when you have had this intangible thing yourself'.[31] The confusion arising from these sentences – is Executive Charisma tangible or intangible? – is not alleviated by continued reference to the ineffable 'it' possessed by leaders: 'The leaders people choose to follow have "it."' The implication seems to be that these are born leaders, blessed with the 'it' of charisma – but such an assumption cannot be upheld by this book, whose purpose is to teach the skills of Executive Charisma. Hence readers are assured that '[w]ith Executive Charisma, you raise your stock in yourself. You're inspiring'. An element of self-contradiction resurfaces, however, with the assertion that 'You can't fake Executive Charisma'. Readers are encouraged to believe both that they can learn the techniques to make them charismatic in business and that their charisma is authentic and cannot be faked. Benton's resolution of this contradiction is to claim that 'ideally', Executive Charisma is 'an extension of your true personality', so that her book will help the reader 'embellish what you have'.[32]

The strategies proffered by Benton to this end include 'The Sacred Six Steps to Executive Charisma';[33] along the way, this book offers specific advice on Clothes and Executive Charisma – 'select a dominant colour' – and how to perform handshakes, smiles, humour, public speaking and listening. As the parade of self-help instruction proceeds, charisma – whether innate or to be acquired – recedes as a presence, obscured beneath a standard catalogue of leadership tips.

Tony Alessandra's *Charisma: Seven Keys to Developing the Magnetism That Leads to Success* makes a similar promise to its readers. The 'praise' from reviews reprinted on the first page includes: 'You don't have to be born with charisma. You can learn how to get it'.[34] The back cover urges potential readers to believe that '[w]hether you're a CEO or a clerk … charisma is something that can be learned, and learned fast'. Alessandra's approach to charisma, however, is more reflective than Benton's. He quotes Charles Lindholm's argument that while charisma is thought of as intrinsic to the individual, it is revealed only in the relationship between leader and followers.[35] Alessandra condenses – into one paragraph – the history of charisma from the early Greeks to Weber, and provides some perspective with the observation that both Roosevelt and Hitler were considered charismatic, as were the Reverends Billy Graham and Jim Jones.[36] Alessandra posits that charisma is 'easy to spot but hard to describe', before offering his own definition: *'the ability to influence others positively by connecting with them physically, emotionally and intellectually'.*[37]

This ability, he states, is possessed by the most effective managers, but it is 'not an effortless gift from the gods, not necessarily something they were born with'. Rather, charisma should be understood as 'a constellation of social skills' that produces a personal magnetism. The reader is assured that those skills 'are within you, too, just waiting to be developed'; the purpose of the book is to draw out that 'latent charisma' from within every reader.[38] The method is to maximise the seven elements of charisma;[39] by breaking charisma down into these components or 'keys', Alessandra proposes to demystify charisma, while at the same time allowing readers to 'harness its power'. This book attempts to counter the common assumption that charisma is 'elusive, something difficult to study or learn'; yet at the same time it retains

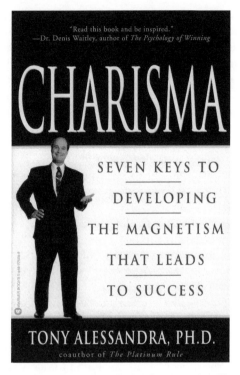

Figure 9.3   Charisma: Seven Keys to Developing the Magnetism That Leads to Success
by Tony Alessandra, one of several self-help books promising to impart the
secrets of charisma to their readers.

the belief in the intrinsic nature of charisma. Remarking on the 'special
sparkle' and 'magic' surrounding charismatic individuals, Alessandra
assures the reader that *'You* do *have these innate abilities'*, waiting to be
developed. If the reader follows the book's instructions on developing
that inner potential, he or she will 'become a catalyst, not just one of
the cattle'.[40]

One final example of this teach-yourself-charisma publishing sub-
genre, Desmond Guilfoyle's *The Charisma Effect*, follows the common
assertions that charisma 'is not a genetically inherited or God-given
trait'[41] and that it is a quality innate – to varying degrees – in everyone.
His means of determining the reader's '"It" quotient' is to administer
a 15-question test to ascertain the 'charisma building blocks' resident
in the reader. Guilfoyle's other strategy is to argue that 'charismatic communication and persuasion are ultimately determined by

the perceptions of audiences'; therefore, one's charisma may be enhanced by managing the impression made on others.[42] Starting from that premise, the book delivers advice on 'renovating your public personality', 'triggering the "yes" response' and other edicts of self-improvement.

These books have installed charisma as the star ingredient in their particular variant of the self-help genre. 'Charisma' could easily be replaced by 'confidence' or even 'how to influence people' in books such as these; indeed, the interchangeable nature of the key ingredient means that charisma is often forgotten in the later stages of these books. The authors tussle with a self-contradictory position, in that they accept the popular understanding of charisma as a mysterious, unfathomable quality, yet they claim the ability to impart – or at least develop – this quality through easily followed techniques. The cumulative effect of this type of publication may be to stretch the perceived meaning of charisma, demystifying the term by superimposing the belief that charisma is an attribute to be acquired by measured means. It is more likely, however, that these books will represent one episode in the history of self-help pop psychology, to be replaced by a new wave of books trumpeting the next super-ingredient in the formula to create a better you.

Apart from motivational books such as these, lessons on charisma may be obtained from 'communications gurus' who offer their services to business leaders and politicians suffering from a perceived lack of it. The American 'communications strategist' Richard Greene – designated a 'master of charisma' by *The Times* – was brought to the House of Lords in 1999 to 'inject some charisma' into the peers' speeches, to make them a 'little more Clintonesque'. Like the authors mentioned above, Greene has his own categorisation of charisma, breaking it down into four types of communication that can all be improved with motivational guidance. For Greene, 'words, tone of voice and body language are the "golden secrets of charisma"' which can, to some degree, be taught or imparted.[43] His claim that aptitude in these skills equates to charisma runs counter to the perception shared by other media commentators that charisma cannot be taught or invented. His method, in common with that of the self-help authors, is to improve individuals' communication skills, thereby boosting their ability to influence people. Charisma in this instance is the name given to the sum of those skills, which can be 'pepped up', by communications gurus, in those unfortunate public figures in need of help.

Charisma in lab conditions: Leadership theory and psychology

A much more scholarly analysis of charisma's role in business management has taken place, since the 1990s, in academic research. The
components of this interdisciplinary field include management theory,
business studies, organisational behaviour, applied psychology and
social psychology. In their survey of the literature in 1998, Conger and
Kanungo trace an escalation of scholarly interest in charisma in the
1990s that echoes the growth in the charisma self-help genre sketched
above by Doe Lang. Conger and Kanungo remark that their 1988 book
Charismatic Leadership stood virtually alone in the area of leadership
studies; in the ensuing decade interest boomed as reflected in the 'several
dozen' empirical studies of charismatic leadership in organisations.[44]
This 'flowering of research' was in part stimulated by the 'relative uniformity' of findings in these empirical studies, which found that leaders
perceived to be charismatic received higher performance ratings than
other managers, were regarded as more effective leaders, and generated
highly motivated followers. In brief, the empirical research indicated
that charismatic business leaders (or at least those perceived to be charismatic) generated 'charismatic effects' in organisations.[45]

Research in this field, and in the related discipline of psychology,
subjects charisma – as defined largely in Weberian terms – to empirical
testing in a manner never envisaged by Weber himself. Following
various forms of methodology, researchers in leadership theory, organisational behaviour and psychology have proposed testable hypotheses
on charisma; they have 'operationalised' these theoretical models and
tested them in experiments, sometimes in laboratory conditions. The
goal, as expressed by Conger and Kanungo, is to replace the 'naïve
theory of what constitutes charismatic leadership' that 'most of us carry
in our heads' with 'a more precise and scientific understanding of the
phenomenon'.[46] Research on charisma has been undertaken within a
broader theoretical framework established in leadership theory, which
has incorporated, since the 1980s, conceptual models including a distinction between management and leadership; a distinction between
'transformational' and 'transactional' leadership; and debates on
institutional context and the relation between leader and followers.[47]
Conger and Kanungo outline the four dominant theoretical models
as the transformational leadership theory, the charismatic leadership
theory, the visionary leadership theory and the attributional model.[48]
The latter, developed by Conger and Kanungo, posits that 'charisma

must be viewed as an attribution made by followers' and that 'it can and should be subjected to the same empirical and behavioural analysis' as other inferred dimensions of leadership behaviour.[49]

Conger and Kanungo operationalise their model through six empirical studies which inform their 'charismatic leadership measure'.[50] Their method, which includes detailed questionnaires of subordinates concerning their managers, is insulated with statistical techniques guarding against 'errors and disturbances',[51] yielding finely calibrated empirical data. The results are used not only to support the validity of 'the Conger–Kanungo scale for measuring charisma' but also to correlate this statistical method with Weber's conceptualisation of the charismatic leader. The authors claim that a 'five-factor formulation' of their model provides evidence for two key aspects of charismatic leadership as theorised by Weber: the followers' perception of 'the exceptional nature of the leader' and the charismatic leader's sensitivity to the needs of the followers.[52] This empirical approach, which rationalises charisma by breaking it into component parts and testing perceptions of management behaviour, endorses Weber's concept of charisma. The authors sound a warning note, however, concerning the function of charisma in business organisations: while charismatic leaders may be beneficial for business in many cases, some charismatic individuals may prove to be self-serving, even delusional, thus turning charismatic qualities into business liabilities.[53]

Bernard Bass employs a similar method in his *Transformational Leadership* (1998), with the difference that he incorporates charisma as only one component of transformational leadership. Bass deploys a Multifactor Leadership Questionnaire to measure factors associated with charismatic leadership.[54] He considers that such methods have improved on Weber's conceptualisation of charisma by adding empirical information: Weber's criteria for charisma were, Bass notes, 'relaxed'. Once they have been 'operationalized, measured, and included as one of the four dimensions of transformational leadership', these criteria become useful in the analysis of the behaviours exhibited by leaders perceived as charismatic.[55] Bass adds the further qualification that charismatic leadership in industry and the military needs to be 'socialised' rather than 'personalised'. The latter form of charismatic leader exhibits personalised dominance, aggression, narcissism and impetuosity – and is therefore not to be encouraged within organisations. 'Socialised' charismatic leadership, by contrast, 'serves collective interests, and develops and empowers others' while using 'legitimate established channels of authority'.[56] Although he does not acknowledge it, Bass is advocating 'routinised' charisma – in Weber's terminology – as a component of a productive transformational leadership.

Other research projects conducted within the discipline of leadership theory have claimed to vindicate charisma as an element of leadership – although different approaches have yielded differing conclusions. In 'A Laboratory Study of Charismatic Leadership' (1989), Howell and Frost argue that 'charisma can be empirically isolated, identified, and distinguished from other leadership styles'. Their empirical study leads them to the conclusion that charisma cannot be reduced to 'the sum of a number of leadership elements already well known': charisma, they claim, is 'a qualitatively different phenomenon'.[57] Howell and Frost make the further assertion that 'charismatic leadership can be studied under controlled laboratory conditions', and that therefore 'charisma is not as elusive as some scholars have thought it to be'.[58] Their experiment involved actors performing in three leadership styles – charismatic, considerate and structuring – setting a two-hour task for university students.[59] Analysis of the task data revealed that individuals working under a charismatic leader had the highest task performance, including the number of courses of action suggested.[60] One feature of this experiment, however, was that actors were taught to perform in a charismatic manner, prompting Howell and Frost to conclude that 'individuals can be trained to exhibit charismatic behaviour'.[61] The results of this experiment, then, do not support the notion of charisma as an intrinsic quality; rather, they endorse the proposition of Conger and Kanungo that charisma is relational – that is, attributed by followers to a leader.

One final study of note was conducted by Roberts and Bradley, published as 'Limits of Charisma' (1988). This project used the case study method to test the function of institutional context in charismatic leadership. Roberts and Bradley preface their study with a categorisation of charisma into three different levels, based on common usage. The first is charisma as social category, articulated in the belief that particular individuals possess 'inexplicable powers of persuasion' that are 'in some special way magical or mystical in nature'. The person thought to possess these powers is 'set apart from everyone else'. The second is charisma as social relationship, reflecting the 'powerful, all-encompassing' connection between charismatic leader and followers. The third is charisma as a distinctive form of social organisation, referring to the 'explosive levels of collective energy' in a revolutionary charismatic structure.[62]

Roberts and Bradley find all three levels active in their case study, which concerns a female school district superintendent in the United States.

In her superintendent role, this individual is considered by teachers and parents to be a 'visionary' with extraordinary talents, earning her a 'cult-like' following in the district.[63] Her widely perceived charismatic leadership energises the local community into a productive charismatic organisation, which allows creative measures to be made in response to a difficult budgetary situation. As a result of her outstanding success, the superintendent is promoted by the governor to the position of commissioner of education. However, in this new role, the individual's charisma is not evident at any of the three levels.

Roberts and Bradley explore the possible reasons for this failure of charisma to transfer from one position to another. All are related to the organisational framework of the second, much larger office. As superintendent, the leader was able to respond to a funding crisis by galvanising local support; as commissioner, she faced no crisis calling for restructure but rather an agenda calling for stability. As superintendent she could make bold decisions; as commissioner, she answered to the governor and exercised limited authority. In addition, the office of commissioner needed to balance conflicting stakeholder demands, which militated against a productive energy of 'communion'. The commissioner spent much time and resources 'learning the ropes', 'putting out fires' and dealing with bureaucratic procedure, so that her personal touch was limited. Her public speaking, now on a much larger scale and with media coverage, lacked spark and vitality. The commissioner's office, far from an inspired charismatic community, experienced reports of low morale and resignations.[64]

Roberts and Bradley conclude from this case study that charisma is 'an emergent process' requiring a complex set of interactions.[65] The organisational context is revealed as a major contributing factor to charismatic leadership. Although the authors make only limited reference to Weber, their case study illustrates two key elements of his conceptualisation of charismatic authority: the initial triggering effect of social crisis, to which the leader responds; and the inevitable diminution of charisma within bureaucratic apparatus. Roberts and Bradley draw additional conclusions that counter the findings of other leadership researchers. Because the superintendent's charisma could not be re-created in a different context, the authors postulate 'severe limits to efforts aimed at the deliberate creation of charisma'. They argue that charisma 'cannot be manufactured by a leader or an organization', contrary to the claims of Bass and other leadership theorists (as well as the many charisma self-help authors and motivational gurus). They also maintain, against Howell and Frost, that charisma cannot be 'simulated or fabricated in a laboratory'.[66] Ultimately, Roberts and Bradley accept the irrational character and function of charisma as defined by Weber: it is, they argue, 'beyond the reach of purposeful, "rational" action'; it is 'charged with explosive, unpredictable potential'.[67] Indeed, such is its unpredictability and its destructive potential (in the instances of charismatic cult leaders such as Jim Jones) that the authors urge caution: 'Do we really want to deliberately risk unleashing its darker side?'[68]

One dissenting view in the academic scholarship concerning charisma is that of John Kotter. In his essay 'What Leaders Really Do', originally published in 1990, Kotter has no interest in the irrational or unpredictable nature of charisma as theorised by Roberts and Bradley. In his theoretical model of leadership, Kotter dispenses with charisma altogether:

> Leadership isn't mystical and mysterious. It has nothing to do with having 'charisma' or other exotic personality traits. It is not the province of a chosen few.[69]

Kotter instead outlines a distinction between leadership and management that can be simply and rationally defined: leadership involves setting direction, aligning people, motivating people and leading change.[70] Kotter's pragmatic approach – reflected in the 'what leaders really do' expression and in his use of successful leadership case studies as examples – leaves no place for anything intrinsic or mysterious by the name of charisma.

Other recent researchers in psychology do not so much dismiss the 'mystery' of charisma as attempt to illuminate it. Psychologists, including Ronald Riggio and Frank Bernieri, are closer in this regard to the approach of Len Oakes (discussed in Chapter 6) than to the curt rejection of charisma found in Kotter. Bernieri's research has linked charisma to the 'synchrony' or rapport between speaker and audience, often triggered subconsciously by physical gestures. The charismatic speaker, according to this approach, is finely attuned to the audience, able 'to play the crowd like improvisational jazz'. For Bernieri, the charismatic individual is skilled in the necessary gestures, but he also 'has the innate ability to play any given audience'.[71] For this reason, Bernieri considers that 'charisma itself can't be taught'; charismatic individuals are natural 'attractors' with the ability to make others synchronise to them. Bernier suggests, however, that charisma can be 'approximated' through techniques of communication, so that even those without the 'attractor' ability may develop similar skills as 'second nature'.[72]

Riggio makes a similar conclusion that 'charismatic people are essentially brilliant communicators' who combine expressivity with high levels of empathy. Finding – like many of the other researchers and commentators surveyed in this chapter – that students and audiences could always nominate charismatic individuals (most often John F. Kennedy and Martin Luther King Jr) yet always struggled to define charisma, Riggio devised his own measurement technique. His Social Skills Inventory questionnaire yielded six descriptors linked to charismatic individuals: emotionally expressive, enthusiastic, eloquent, visionary, self-confident, responsive to others. Despite breaking charisma down to these constituent elements, Riggio preserves something of the enigma associated with charisma: 'It's not clear that having all these skills makes you charismatic'.[73]

Charisma in contemporary politics

While specialists in leadership theory, organisational behaviour, psychology and other disciplines have debated many aspects of charisma – how best to dissect it or analyse it, whether it is a viable concept, whether it even exists – the discourse on contemporary politics is a much less contested domain. Media coverage of politics, both domestic and international, regularly makes reference to charisma. Although journalists and other political commentators sometimes mention the 'elusive' or ill-defined character of charisma, it is rarely questioned as a factor relevant to the contemporary political milieu.

It is not just journalists who apply the concept to political developments: academics, consultants, independent political analysts, politicians and members of the public all cite charisma as a significant political element. Analysts may attribute a political party's success to its charismatic leader; or the lack of charisma in a party's leadership ranks may be deemed the cause of the party's poor electoral fortune. Political parties conduct their own opinion polls and focus groups on matters concerning their leaders, including appeal to voters. At times newspapers hire opinion pollsters to conduct focus groups on similar issues, publishing the results. One Australian media report in 2007, for example, was based on such a focus group, in which a participant stated of the politician in question: 'He's not projecting charisma and an image of a leader'.[74] At times there is general reflection in the media on the state of the political culture, and whether charisma is able to survive within the modern machinery of politics. At other times – when a leading politician is widely deemed charismatic – the 'X-factor' of politics is brought to the foreground of media commentary.

Kennedyesque

The touchstone for political charisma remains John F. Kennedy. Any contemporary politician considered charismatic will at one stage be compared to Kennedy, or will have the adjective 'Kennedyesque' applied. Kennedy's charisma was noted by many observers, including political journalists working at the time of his presidency. The journalist Helen Thomas, for example, described Kennedy as 'inspiring and magnetic', someone who 'radiated that onward-and-upward good feeling'.[75]

An appreciation of Kennedy's impact– both emotional and political – in the early 1960s may be gained from the comments of the American artist Robert Rauschenberg, an admirer of the President. Rauschenberg stated that 'Kennedy and his presidency had merged to become fact.

Figure 9.4 Robert Rauschenberg, *Retroactive 1*, 1964. In this silkscreen work, Rauschenberg evoked the special, 'larger-than-life' quality of President Kennedy, even endowing him with a God-like status.

He re-established what a President is supposed to be – somebody special, not somebody you're comfortable with'.[76] Kennedy's heroic persona was represented by Rauschenberg in a series of silkscreen paintings in 1964. The curator and critic Roni Feinstein observes that the image of a pointing Kennedy calls to mind the President's televised press conferences, in which Kennedy's personal appeal and eloquence were demonstrated; the juxtaposition of this shot with other imagery enhances the 'larger-than-life' aspect of the President.[77] In *Retroactive 1*, for example, Kennedy appears to assume a God-like stature, his finger pointing authoritatively towards smaller human figures in a manner reminiscent, as Robert Hughes has remarked, of God expelling Adam and Eve.[78]

Because 'Kennedyesque' refers in part to Robert Kennedy as well as to his more famous brother, the word implies a degree of familial charisma. As discussed in Chapter 6, from as early as the mid-1960s, other politicians – notably Andreas Papandreou – proclaimed that the vital quality of charisma ran within their politically engaged families. Other political dynasties which have claimed – or have had claimed for them – familial charisma include the Bhutto family in Pakistan. After Benazir Bhutto was assassinated in 2007, it was remarked that she had possessed 'the famous Bhutto charisma' that had been evident in her father.[79] The assertion that charisma may 'run in the family' is an instance of the transfer of charisma thoroughly delineated by Weber; it may also be regarded, more cynically, as a political strategy designed to boost family members' political fortunes.

However, it should also be remembered that charisma needs to be perceived and affirmed by observers, particularly political followers and media analysts; a politician cannot become charismatic simply by making the claim. Certainly, journalists are quick to identify the lack of the quality in politicians with familial links to the charismatic. When Fidel Castro stood down from the presidency of Cuba in 2008, journalists noted the charisma void of his successor, brother Raul. Indeed, it was questioned whether Raul, 'lacking his brother's charisma', could sustain the Cuban communist system.[80] While Fidel Castro's 'vast charisma' was credited as a powerful political force that 'enabled' him to 'hold on to power for nearly half a century', his brother's lack of the same quality was considered, at least in the American media, a significant factor in Cuba's future.[81]

In Western politics, the politician most frequently deemed to possess the Kennedyesque quality of charisma has been Bill Clinton, whose leadership appeal has been analysed in a book entitled *The Clinton Charisma*.[82] So common was the attribution of charisma to Clinton

Figure 9.5   Benazir Bhutto, bearer of a familial charisma reported as 'the famous Bhutto charisma'.

Figure 9.6   Fidel Castro, widely credited as a charismatic leader. His brother and successor Raul, however, is thought to lack the quality of charisma.

Figure 9.7 Bill Clinton, whose commonly attributed charisma during his presidency inspired the epithet 'Clintonesque'.

during his presidency that he inspired the epithet 'Clintonesque'. In his post-President years, Clinton was even consulted as an expert on the charisma levels of contemporary politicians. In 2007, the *Guardian* sought Clinton's views on the charisma of British Prime Minister Gordon Brown, as compared to that of his predecessor Tony Blair. Asked if he thought Brown less charismatic than Blair, Clinton replied that 'there are different ways to be charismatic'. Clinton suggested that Brown's qualities of intellectual brilliance and authenticity each 'carries its own charisma'.[83] In the post-Kennedy world, Clinton became an iconic figure and reference point of political charisma. Even when he was not directly consulted, charisma was invoked in his name: the communications expert and 'master of charisma' – mentioned earlier in this chapter – was brought to London to render peers 'more Clintonesque'.

The decline of charismatic politicians

Despite the eminence of figures such as Bill Clinton, media analysis often comments on the dwindling of charismatic leadership in Western democracies. Several reasons have been advanced to explain this decline. One is the perceived rareness of the quality: a truly charismatic, successful politician is considered a 'once-in-a-generation' proposition, as embodied in the former Presidents Kennedy and Clinton. Another factor is the erratic nature of charisma, a perceived instability rooted in the association of charismatic appeal with dictators, demagogues and cult leaders. The political biographer David Barnet has stated that charisma is 'one of the most dangerous concepts in a democracy that you can find'. For Barnet, 'the most charismatic personality in history was undoubtedly Adolf Hitler'.[84] The historian Paul Ginsborg made a related observation concerning the dangers for democracy in the early twenty-first century stemming from 'media-based populism', evident in the 'more or less charismatic figures' of Menem in Argentina, Berlusconi in Italy and Shinawatra in Thailand.[85]

If the charisma projected by populist politicians such as Berlusconi is considered – by Ginsborg and other analysts – a danger to democratic values and institutions, a more common assertion, at least in the Anglophone democracies, pertains to the increasingly bureaucratic nature of contemporary government. Politics in the affluent and stable Western democracies, it has been argued, is largely 'technocratic' rather than ideological;[86] this prevailing condition is likely to reduce the incidence of charisma within the leadership of major parties. Even a review in 2007 of a biography of Julius Caesar could contrast Caesar's grandeur with the modern-day 'charismatically challenged leaders on the political stage'.[87]

The Australian political commentator Paul Lyneham has suggested that 'most people now think running a nation is like a large exercise in being a certified practising accountant'. Lyneham poses the rhetorical question: 'And have you ever met an accountant with charisma?'[88] Coincidentally, another newspaper article dealing with the 'charisma game' made the observation that John Howard, Prime Minister of Australia from 1996 to 2007, has 'all the charisma of a tax accountant'.[89] Howard's charisma vacuum was widely noted as a contrast to his predecessor Paul Keating, who declared that 'politics is about leading people'.[90] Keating was generally considered a charismatic leader, visionary but also divisive. In that context, Howard's charisma void could even be hailed as a political strength by another analyst, who found that the 'key to Howard's appeal lies in his very lack of charisma'. The 'appearance of ordinariness' was this politician's 'greatest political asset', creating a reassuring sense that 'we recognise our own frailties' in the leader.[91] A similar observation of American politics was made concerning the popularity, early in his presidency, of George W. Bush, who was the candidate, according to one opinion poll, 'people would most like at their barbeque'.[92] These triumphs of the ordinary 'folksy' politicians in modern democracies echo Weber's gloomy prediction concerning the fate of charismatic leadership in an age of rationalisation.

One other contributing factor to the decline of the charismatic politician concerns the paradoxical impact of television. On the one hand, John F. Kennedy became known as the charismatic President largely because of his mastery of television, which had only recently become an important mediator of politics. The first televised presidential debates were those in 1960 between Kennedy and Nixon: many of those who heard them on radio thought Nixon the winner; the majority of TV viewers, struck by the telegenic and youthful Kennedy, regarded him as the victor.[93] Kennedy's charm and galvanising appeal were broadly disseminated on an international scale through the medium of television. Yet the general effect of television's mediation of politics since the 1960s has encouraged not Kennedyesque politicians but rather their opposite. Media theorist Joshua Meywrowitz has characterised the impact of television coverage as 'lowering the political hero to our level'.[94]

Meywrowitz argues that the medium's emphasis on close-ups, its intrusion into public figures' private lives, its seizure of any 'contaminating acts' (slips, errors or unfortunate gestures) has destroyed the possibility of a great leader. A politician must make as few mistakes as possible in front of the camera, and must appeal to as many voters as possible. The focus of TV (and of the web) is not on grand public presence but on the previously hidden, private aspects of behaviour. The best a political party can hope for is to install a leader who is likeable, or at least not offensive to the majority of voters (TV viewers). This imperative has fostered the ascendancy of cautious, personable politicians whose public image is geared to the level of ordinary people. The charismatic politician, who may display visionary, flamboyant, unpredictable or divisive behaviour, does not fit this prescription.

Barack Obama's charisma of rhetoric

While Weber predicted that charisma would recede in the face of bureaucratic political party machines, he also held that an element of charisma could survive in such an inhospitable environment. The US presidential campaign of 2007–8 attracted great media attention, much of it focused on the theme of political charisma. An analysis of the Democratic nomination campaign and the subsequent presidential contest provides the opportunity to determine how much of Weber's analysis of the American political system – which he made in 1913 – remains valid in the early twenty-first century.

Weber's claim in 1913 that the US presidential quadrennial campaigns 'already amount to about as much as a colonial war' was made before the age of mass media, and before television advertising in particular. An estimated $US720 million was spent on the 2004 presidential campaign, a figure well exceeded by the 2008 campaign. Even the party nomination campaign for 2008 required a minimum $US100 million 'entry fee', according to the Federal Election Commission. Those candidates whose campaign for party nomination extended into many months needed to raise funds well in excess of $US100 million: it was reported that Democratic Party candidate Barack Obama raised $US32 million in the month of January 2008 alone. Other candidates have supported their nomination campaign with their personal wealth: one Republican candidate withdrew from the 2008 nomination campaign after spending an estimated $US35 million of his own funds.[95] Much of this fund-raising is spent on advertising on television and other media. A presidential campaign in the early twenty-first century, therefore, requires expenditure equivalent to the cost of a postcolonial war; Weber's comment on the restricting force of this cost on the range of party candidates remains pertinent. The enormous cost also heightens the need for efficient party machinery to administer such campaigns: apart from the necessary organisational and fund-raising skills, public relations and media management are crucial components of a contemporary political campaign. Another reason for the tight control exerted by party machines over candidates is the ever-present danger of mistakes or contaminating events being captured and transmitted by the media.

Weber asserted that despite this regulating power of bureaucratic party machines, charisma may retain a role in the democratic political process. He contended that the 'charisma of rhetoric' evident in electioneering would continue to exert a significant influence. His prediction that the 'purely emotional' effect of charismatic rhetoric may occasionally forge an instance of 'charismatic hero worship' was supported in 2007–8 by the example of Barack Obama's successful campaigns to gain the Democratic Party nomination and the presidency. Weber claimed that the charisma of rhetoric was manifest in 'stump speeches'; in the age of mass media, the emotional force of galvanising speeches is also transmitted via television, radio and Internet.

In 2007, Obama was the only candidate from either party deemed charismatic by journalists. He was described as 'by far the most exciting candidate', 'a charismatic speaker' and a politician promising 'a new style of politics'.[96] His charisma was linked to an authenticity considered rare in contemporary politicians, revealing that 'not all politicians are manufactured'.[97] His campaign message that 'change is possible' was delivered in passionate stump speeches around the country, where he 'work[ed] his audience into a kind of religious frenzy'.[98] Media coverage emphasised the contrast between Obama and his Democratic Party opponent, Hillary Clinton. A *Washington Post* article previewing this contest quoted a Democratic strategist who spoke of the opposition between Obama's 'magic' and Clinton's 'muscle'. This strategist expressed the dichotomy in almost Weberian terms: 'This is going to be a titanic fight between energy and charisma on the one hand and money and organization on the other'.[99]

Obama was portrayed in media coverage as a charismatic politician operating outside the entrenched party machinery, while Clinton was depicted as a conventional politician dependent on traditional methods and support. One report in *Time* declared that she 'seemed to be shedding her private dismay that she could never be a charismatic politician like Obama or Kennedy, or her husband', adopting instead a pragmatic, if compassionate, persona.[100] The Clinton campaign accentuated her experience and organisational abilities, in contrast to Obama's untested visionary appeal. Her stolid political image came to function as a form of counter-charisma, earning Clinton media support when aspects of Obama's inspirational campaign were subject to journalists' scrutiny. 'Inspiration vs. Substance' was the dichotomy proposed in another *Time* article: Obama may have 'flights of rhetoric' but Clinton 'simply knows more'.[101] Obama's inspiration factor could be interpreted as a weakness as well as a strength, if the 'maddeningly vague' rhetoric of his speeches could be revealed as lacking substance.[102] Obama's 'buckets of charisma and charm' were also thought to engender a 'cult-like following', which was noted by some analysts as a potentially troubling 'mass messianism'.[103]

The association of Barack Obama with John F. Kennedy as bearer of political charisma reached its culmination in January 2008 when Obama was endorsed by Senator Edward Kennedy and other members of the Kennedy family. The journalist Suzanne Goldenberg wrote that this endorsement was, in the American political context, 'as close as it

Figure 9.8   Barack Obama, 2008. During the US presidential campaign, Obama's message of change was propelled by the 'charisma of rhetoric' of his speeches.

gets to a coronation'. This passing of the Kennedy mantle onto Obama was performed in front of 'a rapturous, chanting crowd', as Senator Kennedy 'drew a clear line of succession from the Democratic hero of the past to a younger generation'. Obama was thereby appointed 'the rightful political heir' to Kennedy, as designated by members of his family.[104] The Obama campaign team quickly capitalised on this symbolic gesture, releasing a TV advertisement underlining the Kennedy comparison. This advertisement opened with images of John F. Kennedy and closed with Obama flanked by two generations of the Kennedy family. The voice-over by Caroline Kennedy (daughter of John F. Kennedy) declared: 'Once we had a President who made people feel hopeful about America and brought us together to do great things. Today, Barack Obama gives us that same chance. He makes us believe in ourselves again'.[105] Ensuing media headlines termed Obama 'The JFK of a New Generation'.[106] The anointing of Obama by the Kennedy family was satirised by Garry Trudeau in a *Doonesbury* comic strip, which referred to Obama as 'the first black Kennedy', who will

Figure 9.9   Garry Trudeau, *Doonesbury*, 14 February 2008.

'have to offer *twice* as much hope as a white Kennedy, have *twice* the charisma'.[107]

Obama's 'coronation' was celebrated at the Democratic convention in August 2008, with speeches linking Obama and John F. Kennedy: 'Leaders like them come along rarely. But once or twice in a lifetime, they come along just when we need them most'.[108] Declarations such as these elevated Obama's standing within the party to lofty heights; the Democratic nominee himself, however, was more circumspect. Obama defused hopes that his acceptance speech at the convention would reach levels of 'high rhetoric', promising instead a 'more workmanlike' speech. This decision was part of a strategy to counter claims by the Republican nominee, John McCain, that Obama's inspiring rhetoric 'masks naivete and inexperience'.[109] McCain, who did not have 'an obvious, room-filling charisma', in the words of one journalist, periodically mocked the 'messiansim' around Obama, calling him 'The Deliverer'.[110]

The Republican strategy was to attack Obama's 'cult of personality' as a poor substitute for substantial, experienced leadership. This attack was led at the Republican convention in September by Sarah Palin, newly unveiled as the Republican vice-presidential nominee. Palin criticised Obama for authoring two memoirs but no significant legislation, thereby attributing both narcissism and lack of substance to the Democratic candidate. She ridiculed as a dangerous diversion the quasi-religious aura of salvation surrounding Obama: when he was 'done turning back the waters and healing the planet', she claimed, he would 'enlarge government and take more of the people's money'.[111] Palin's selection as McCain's running mate was itself regarded by commentators as 'a counter to Barack Obama's own television-lit charisma juggernaut'.[112] Palin's appeal as a 'folksy outsider'[113] resounded with large sections of the electorate, at least in the initial stages of her campaign, bringing an element of personality politics to the Republican cause. She was frequently described as charismatic by her supporters, thrilled by her ability to galvanise audiences. Media analysts, however, were more reserved: critics such as Naomi Wolf dismissed Palin as the latest in a line of 'glossy faux-populists' like Eva Peron.[114] Even conservative commentators, supportive of Palin, described her as charismatic but within a restricted range: one remarked on Palin's 'middle-class charisma' during the vice-presidential debate, so that middle-class America was said to be 'charmed by [the] charisma of one of its own'.[115]

The danger for the Republicans' highlighting of Palin's popular appeal, however, was that the very charges levelled against Obama – inexperience and lack of substance – were also levelled against her. As the campaign wore on, engulfed by a global financial crisis, opinion polls regularly found that a majority of voters considered Palin unprepared for high office. The long and arduous campaign – stretching back almost two years and with total expenditure far exceeding previous presidential campaigns – appeared to take its toll on Obama as well. It was observed that he seemed 'a shadow of the charismatic reformer as he carefully tip-toes towards November'.[116] As the election neared, media commentary focused on the severity of the financial crisis and the need for responsible leadership. One academic commentator warned in the *Wall Street Journal* of the danger of 'the politics of charisma'. In this article, Fouad Ajamai adopted the perspective of Durkheim concerning the 'projection of a collectivity' onto its leader. Observing the vast crowds of adoring Obama supporters, Ajami described Obama as 'a blank slate' for 'devotees' to 'project on to him what they wish'. For Ajami, the huge Obama crowds recalled 'the politics of charisma that wrecked Arab and Muslim societies'. He predicted that an Obama victory would deliver 'the sobering verdict that our troubles won't be solved by a leader's magic'.[117]

Obama's victory in the November election, however, generated much more positive responses. The euphoria with which Democratic supporters greeted Obama's victory speech suffused much of the journalistic coverage of the election result. The words 'inspirational' and 'transformational' were frequently used: one journalist observed that the 'stunning transformational victory' was 'reminiscent of that of Jack Kennedy in its emotional tone – rare is the politician inspiring enough to draw this many tears'.[118] Obama was praised – with reference to his disciplined campaign, which raised unprecedented levels of funding – as '[p]art prophet, part money machine' by another commentator.[119] E. J. Dionne of *The Washington Post* encapsulated the transformative nature of Obama's success by describing it as a 'post-everything candidacy': Obama 'broke with almost every category we have been used to',[120] including race.

Various articles in a commemorative issue of *Time* touched on aspects of Obama's victory, in ways unwittingly redolent of Weber's theorising of charismatic leadership. Michael Grunwald, observing the economic 'mess' inherited by the new President, remarked that 'mess-inheriting is almost a pre-requisite for presidential greatness'[121] (Weber's assertion that charismatic leaders arise at times of great crisis). Nancy Gibbs, musing on the transformational aspect of the victory, declared that 'by design or default, the past now loses power'[122] (Weber's contention that charismatic authority 'repudiates the past'). The general air of excitement and great change echoed Weber's belief that charisma was '*the* great revolutionary force'. Even a conservative politician, acknowledging that 'Obama's charisma has captured global attention', looked forward to the dwindling of this energy in a way suggestive of Weber's 'routinisation of charisma': 'As time wears on ... grievances accumulate. Life is more humdrum, more tawdry than the utopia promised by apostles of change'.[123] The religious dimension, acknowledged by Weber as the source of his conception of charisma, was conveyed by an Obama campaign volunteer, who was reported as claiming that 'Barack Obama rejuvenated me'. The volunteer linked Obama with Martin Luther King, Jr: 'They both have the light in them. God within them. The word "hope" is powerful'.[124] Finally, Beverley Gage in *Time* composed a typology of 'rookie Presidents': military heroes, technocrats and 'charismatic youngsters'. Obama was installed in the third category along with Teddy Roosevelt, John F. Kennedy and Bill Clinton: all in their 40s when assuming office, all 'ambitious, championing transformative programs for national change', all with 'outsize personal traits'. Gage made the qualification, however, that Obama 'seems to have far more self-control' than the previous Presidents considered 'charismatic youngsters'.[125]

Barack Obama's success demonstrates the continued relevance of Weber's analysis of the political process. The operation of party politics has reached extraordinary levels of rationalisation and control, yet a candidate was able to attract wide support – and media coverage – based on his perceived charismatic qualities. The momentum of Obama's campaign was maintained at his frequent stump speeches, in which his 'charisma of rhetoric' was repeatedly exhibited. The 'emotional effect' and the 'charismatic hero worship' described by Weber emerged largely from these stump speeches; the 'charisma of rhetoric' was amplified and extended by Obama's media appearances. Even the criticisms levelled at Obama by his opponents and some journalists targeted the perceived hazards of charismatic expression: its elevation of inspiration over substance, its emotional nature and the tendency to attract an irrational, 'cult-like' following. In all this, Weber's prediction of the endurance of charisma as a significant factor in the democratic political system has been validated.

10
That Elusive Something Called Charisma

In this final chapter I return to some of the issues raised in Chapter 1. The relationship between charisma of the first century and that of the twenty-first is reconsidered, as is the connection – if any – between the two charismas of contemporary culture: the secular and the Christian. A re-examination of these questions may illuminate the cultural role currently played by charisma.

Continuity/Discontinuity: Giftedness

The current meaning of charisma has been moulded by the flux of social, economic and technological factors informing the media-saturated cultures of the West. The contemporary emphasis on individuality, and the relatively secular nature of Western societies, are immediately relevant. The force of these two factors alone yields a current version of charisma which is markedly different to the religious, collectivist vision of charisma articulated by Paul. Paul spoke of charisma as a miraculous spiritual gift, entailing supernatural powers; it was a gift from God to be shared with all members of the new Christian community. Twenty-first-century charisma, by contrast, pertains to individuals – whether politicians or entertainment figures – thought to have 'drawing power' or 'personal magnetism'. It is not bestowed by divine grace, and it does not manifest itself in diverse forms, to be used primarily for communal benefit.

There is a strong case, then, for rendering the history of charisma in the terms of radical disjuncture. If we consider this history as the 'career of a term', we trace a singular career indeed. It is a career marked by a profound break, when the term all but disappeared completely. On its re-emergence this word, of Greek origin, took on a new meaning, as determined by a new epistemological configuration. 'Charisma' thus embarked on a second career, but in a radically new social and cultural context. As a result of this new environment, it signified something altogether different to its earlier manifestation. The term may have survived its extended eclipse, but – like those other terms whose meanings have altered profoundly over centuries – 'charisma' in the twenty-first century is shaped by its new world. It owes much more to the political, economic, social and cultural determinants of twenty-first-century Western culture than it does to any ancient forebear, to which it is linked by nothing more than a name.

This argument would be entirely persuasive if it could demonstrate that there is no continuity of meaning between the ancient 'charisma' and the contemporary version. It can be argued, however, that there is a thread, however slender, linking 'charisma' then and now. The key may lie in the hazy semantic status of contemporary charisma. References to charisma in the mass media continually invoke the elusive character of this entity, the great difficulty in defining it with any precision. The contrast with celebrity is instructive. Charisma differs from celebrity in its mysterious nature: celebrity may be manufactured by mass media, but charisma is thought to be different. One either has charisma or one doesn't; it can't be made or bought. It is considered intrinsic to a person, whereas celebrity is extrinsic, in that it can be fabricated for an individual. Even fame or prestige differs from charisma, in that the former attributes are earned by achievement (or inherited social position). Charisma, by contrast, is thought simply to inhere in one.

Charisma is understood as an innate quality vested in certain individuals, but it remains baffling as to its origin. A person is somehow endowed with charisma, in a way that defies rational analysis. It is still spoken of as a 'gift'. A person gifted with charisma will attract attention, possibly followers. This extraordinary quality may prove dangerous, in the manner of cult leaders and their fanatical followers. Or it may generate thrilling political leadership, or even a more intense form of entertainment (charismatic actors or rock stars stand out from their peers, who are merely celebrities). This mysterious aspect of charisma suggests a persistence, however modified, of the mystical-religious dimension of the idea as elaborated by Paul. The meanings attached to the word two millennia apart are not identical, but they are similar enough to allow some form of continuity. This idea has travelled 2000 years, preserving its core meaning: that is, an extraordinary gift.

It is important not to overstate this continuity. The contemporary usage of 'charisma', following Weber, is shorn of the explicit religious-mystical connotations of the word as used in the first century. When media commentators speak of a politician's charisma, they are not normally referring to a gift from God, or to supernatural capacities. Charisma is still considered a gift, but in the sense of a 'gifted' individual, without reference to divine origins. The contemporary sense of charisma as a head-turning, eye-catching appeal is indeed closer to the Homeric description of Telemachus than it is to Paul's Christian construction: 'Athene endowed him with such supernatural grace (*charis*) that all eyes were turned on him in admiration when he came up'.[1] Attraction is the main element, magnetic pulling power. Yet charisma today, like charisma in the first century, and even as prefigured in Homer as 'supernatural grace', is understood as a remarkable and rare attribute possessed by some individuals. While the term is stripped of its religious meaning, it nevertheless conveys a meaning of 'giftedness', shrouded in a degree of mystery.

The mystique surrounding giftedness is evident in popular culture, which displays a fascination with gifted individuals. TV talent shows delight in unearthing a prodigy exhibiting a gift of the highest level, while science fiction extends this idea to the supernatural, embodied in those heroes possessing superhuman abilities. The comic-styled TV series *Heroes*, for example, features a band of extravagantly gifted individuals; their special gifts, some miraculous, have descended on them for reasons that remain mysterious. Entertainments such as this extend the idea of giftedness into fiction, delighting in the unexplained, baffling nature of exceptional gifts.

Two charismas?

Siegfried Schatzmann, writing on the Pauline charismata, perceives 'little parallelism' between contemporary popular usage of 'charisma' – in the Weberian sense – and the New Testament meaning of the term.[2] As noted in Chapter 7, Christian theologians and historians of religion writing in the late twentieth century maintained a strict distinction between charismatic Christianity and the secular notion of charisma. In the early twenty-first century, the Christian Charismatic movement has a lower profile – both within the church and within the general community – than it enjoyed in the 1960s and 1970s. If charismatic Christianity receives any mainstream media attention, it is usually associated with millionaire showman televangelists or fringe cults, both considered disreputable manifestations of contemporary religion. The charismata remain the subject of religious historical scholarship and are mentioned in sermons – but generally with reference to the very early church. Given the mainstream ubiquity of the secular version of charisma, and the restricted usage of the Christian version, it would appear that there are two charismas, one of a much higher profile than the other, and with little or no connection between them.

If there are links between these two charismas, they are implicit rather than explicit. Perhaps secular charisma enjoys such prevalence in contemporary culture because of the secularisation of Western thought, which has devalued religious explanations for social realities such as hierarchical relations. In previous centuries, social authority and hierarchy received explanation – and justification – with recourse to religion, as in the divine right of monarchs. The 'royal charisma' of the healing touch was held by the church to reside in the person of the monarch until the eighteenth century. A secular culture requires a secular explanation for social relationships, including that of leader and followers: the idea of charisma is mobilised to perform that function.

Another connection between the secular and the religious concerns the common notion of giftedness that has survived – in however altered a form – from the first century to the present. Charismatic speakers and leaders are frequently described as 'gifted'. Various enterprises – both secular and religious – have concerned themselves with 'empowering' individuals by enhancing their innate gifts. The charisma self-help books surveyed in Chapter 9 and the Christian charismatic guides to identifying charismata (discussed in Chapter 7) advocate a similar approach. Both seek to develop the potential of latent charisma; both assume that charisma is an innate gift that needs to be identified and cultivated within each individual.

There are overlaps between the secular and the religious even in the media descriptions of charismatic individuals. Barack Obama's rapturous audiences in 2008 conjured images of 'mass messianism' for some commentators, while Obama's inspirational speech-making was grounded in the uplifting tradition of Martin Luther King, Jr. Dr King, commonly identified along with John F. Kennedy as one of the most charismatic leaders of the twentieth century, incorporated both the religious and the political in his resounding oratory. His galvanising force as a speaker drew on the power of the oral tradition of communication, which is significant in the context of charisma. In early Christianity, charismatic prophecy flourished when the faith was fundamentally oral, with no written texts and a tradition transmitted by the spoken word. As described in Chapter 4, the prominence of prophets receded

Figure 10.1   Dr Martin Luther King, Jr. Dr King, frequently mentioned as one of the most charismatic figures of the twentieth century, fused the religious and the political in his inspiring oratory.

as the church developed a canon of sacred texts. In the twentieth century, charismatic politicians, including Kennedy and King, attained eminence for their rhetoric as broadcast by the audio-visual means of TV. Indeed, the impact of television should not be underestimated in the imprinting on the popular mind of enduring images of charismatic individuals. In the first half of the 1960s, Kennedy, King, Fidel Castro and Muhammad Ali – all brilliant verbal practitioners in their respective fields – reached vast international audiences via television; all are widely considered charismatic performers of the highest order. In the twenty-first century, the oral tradition continues to be associated with charisma, in the form of inspiring stump speeches made by those rare politicians – such as Barack Obama – deemed charismatic. Even if these speeches are thoroughly scripted and read from autocues, their delivery in person and as broadcast conveys the attributes of the charismatic performer and leader.

'That Elusive Something'

It is perfectly possible to argue that charisma does not exist. A plausible argument, based on rational and materialist grounds, can be made that there is no such thing as 'charisma', that what has been mistaken for charisma has in reality been the confidence, attractiveness, boldness, oratorical skill, manipulation or exhibitionism displayed by some individuals. Further, it could be argued that 'charisma' has functioned as a mystification, an ideological charade, used to justify instances of authority by apologists for certain forms of power relations; this charge, as we have seen, has indeed been levelled against Max Weber. Yet this argument needs to be set against the persistent belief in charisma within Western culture. The quality called charisma is prominent in the discourses of the twenty-first century – in media analysis of politics, in popular culture, in discussions of celebrity. There is constant discussion of which public figures possess charisma and which do not. In all these discourses, charisma retains an indefinable aspect. It is consistently referred to as 'that elusive something', the x-factor, the It-factor, the unknown factor, the I-don't-know-what, the indefinable, the intangible, the mysterious, the indescribable, the irreducible, the enigmatic.

Charisma is an idea that has been used and adapted by culture – or, rather, by different cultures at different times. The idea has shifted to meet cultural demands. In all likelihood, the term 'charisma' would not exist without the invention and reinvention of the idea by Paul and Weber. Yet Paul did not intend charisma to apply to anyone beyond the small Christian communities addressed in his letters. Weber did not intend charisma to refer to celebrities. The authors' intentions, as always, are of limited relevance when set against the long and complex sweep of cultural history.

In the contemporary Western milieu, 'charisma' responds to a cultural need that is not fulfilled by other terms such as 'celebrity' or 'prestige'. The rational analysis proffered by Bourdieu, Kotter and other theorists does not satisfy this need, as it is experienced by the general public. The irrational aspect of charisma – as theorised by Weber and as disparaged by Weber's critics – is a significant factor. In its common everyday usage, charisma is considered unpredictable and unmeasurable. It cannot be bottled, destroyed or manufactured. Celebrity is at best a synthetic substitute. Charisma is thought to touch individuals without warning or reason; it simply lights on them.

The elusive, indefinable character of charisma holds the clue to its persistence in contemporary culture. There is something mystical about charisma. It was a mystical concept in Paul's theology, expounded in the first century. It was a semi-mystical concept in Weber's sociology of the twentieth century. Charisma in Weber retained traces of its mystical-religious roots; indeed, the irrational nature of charisma appealed to Weber as he sought a theoretical counter to the arch-rationalisation of Modernity. The survival – indeed the flourishing – of charisma as an idea in Western culture is a vindication of Weber's belief that the modern world is not entirely disenchanted.

Charisma has a presence in the contemporary world – in even the most bureaucratic regimens of politics and management – because of its enchanted nature. It denotes something of the mystery, the inexplicable, in human relations. As a concept it hovers in the space between reason and belief. It signifies the unfathomable, explaining why certain very rare individuals seem to exert a spell on their contemporaries. It is used as an index of authenticity in a world of artifice, in which anything can be manufactured, including fame. It explains, in the words of one newspaper article, 'why some people will always stand out from the crowd'. How does this happen? Can it be rationally dissected and satisfactorily explained, or is it the result of some inner gift? The culture isn't sure, or it doesn't want to decide: that is why it uses the word 'charisma'.

Notes

1 The History of a Word

1. Pierre Bourdieu, 'Legitimation and Structured Interests in Weber's Sociology of Religion', p. 129.
2. John Kotter, *What Leaders Really Do*, p. 51.
3. Len Oakes, *Prophetic Charisma: The Psychology of Revolutionary Religious Personalities*. Oakes's study of charisma, analysed in Chapter 6, is less a rejection of Weberian charisma than a modification of it.
4. Susie Tucker, *Enthusiasm: A Study in Semantic Change*; P. N. Furbank, *Reflections on the Word 'Image'*; Neil Kenny, *The Uses of Curiosity in Early Modern Germany and France*; John Lyons, *Before Imagination: Embodied Thought from Montaigne to Rousseau*.
5. Tucker, *Enthusiasm*, p. 5.
6. Ibid., p. 165.
7. Terence Ball, 'Political Theory and Conceptual Change', p. 41.
8. Edward Said, *The World, the Text, and the Critic*, p. 35.
9. David Spadafora, *The Idea of Progress in Eighteenth-Century Britain*, p. 423.
10. Ibid., p. 423.
11. Ibid., p. 422.
12. Lovejoy outlines his method in *The Great Chain of Being* (1936). The historian of ideas breaks up philosophical doctrines into their 'component elements', which he calls 'unit-ideas' (p. 3). Lovejoy accounts for evolutionary change in the history of thought by pointing to the shifting compound of intellectual elements clustered around the 'unit-idea', but the fundamental 'prior idea' or unit remains constant (pp. 5–6).
13. The methodological validity of tracing the history of 'unit-ideas' was assailed by Skinner in an essay originally published in 1969. Skinner criticised Lovejoy's method for its neglect of social agents, and for its assumption that an idea could retain an essential and unchanging meaning (*Visions of Politics* Vol. 1, pp. 84–5). Foucault's critique was not localised to Lovejoy, but embraced a rejection – in *The Order of Things* (1970) and *The Archaeology of Knowledge* (1972) – of the practice of tracing the 'empirical progress of ideas' pursued in the conventional history of ideas (*Archaeology of Knowledge*, p. 63).
14. Ian Maclean, 'The Process of Intellectual Change: A Post-Foucauldian Hypothesis', p. 166.
15. Mark Bevir makes the point that a contextualist history need not preclude the ability of individual authors to 'act creatively in any given social context'. Bevir defends 'a space for conscious and rational human agency' within such intellectual histories: *The Logic of the History of Ideas*, pp. 33 and 311.
16. The social historical approach emerging in the 1970s was to a large extent triggered by Edwin Judge's *The Social Pattern of the Christian Groups in the*

First Century, originally published in 1960. This analysis of the social constituency of the early Christian groups opened – or rather reopened – the social question for historical scholarship of Christianity. James Harrison discusses this work and its scholarly impact in his introduction to Judge's *The First Christians in the Roman Empire: Augustan and New Testament Essays.*
17. James Harrison, *Paul's Language of Grace in Its Graeco-Roman Context*, p. 13.

2   The Roots of Charisma

1. Ceslas Spicq, *Theological Lexicon of the New Testament*, p. 500.
2. Ibid., pp. 500–3.
3. *The Iliad*, trans. Richard Lattimore, p. 385.
4. Liddell and Scott, *Greek–English Lexicon*, p. 883.
5. *The Odyssey*, trans. E. V. Rieu, p. 17.
6. James Harrison, *Paul's Language of Grace in Its Graeco-Roman Context*, p. 108.
7. Ibid., p. 8.
8. Ibid., pp. 209 and 174.
9. Ibid., p. 184.
10. Liddell and Scott, *Greek–English Lexicon*, pp. 882–3.
11. Edward Campbell, 'Grace', p. 260.
12. Harrison, *Paul's Language of Grace*, p. 108.
13. Revised standard version. All other quotations from the Old and New Testaments are from this version unless otherwise stated.
14. Harrison, *Paul's Language of Grace*, p. 108.
15. Hippolytus, *Discourse on the Holy Theophany*, trans. S. D. F. Salmond, Ante-Nicene Christian Library Vol. IX.
16. R. N. Whybray, 'Prophets: Ancient Israel', p. 621, citing 1 Sam 10: 10–13; 1 Kings 17: 17–24; 1 Kings 22.
17. David Aune, *Prophecy in Early Christianity and the Ancient Mediterranean World*, p. 83.
18. Ibid.
19. Ibid., p. 85.
20. Whybray, 'Prophets', p. 621.
21. Aune, *Prophecy*, p. 126.
22. Quoted in James Dunn, *Jesus and the Spirit: A Study of the Religious and Charismatic Experience of Jesus and the First Christians as Reflected in the New Testament*, p. 304.
23. *De Migratione Abrahami* 35, quoted Aune, *Prophecy*, p. 147.
24. Aune, *Prophecy*, p. 86.
25. Ibid.
26. This definition, originating in M. Eliade's 1964 study *Shamanism: Archaic Techniques of Ecstasy*, is endorsed and paraphrased by James McLenon, 'How Shamanism Began' and Michael Winkelman, 'Spirits as Human Nature', both essays published in 2004.
27. McLenon, 'How Shamanism Began', p. 21.
28. Winkelman, 'Spirits as Human Nature', p. 72, posits the universality of shamanism in hunter-gatherer societies; McLenon, 'How Shamanism Began',

drawing on Winkelman's previous studies, observes that shamans were the only such practitioners in these societies, p. 21.

29. Winkelman, 'Spirits as Human Nature', pp. 59–60, citing works in neurophenomenology by Laughlin, McManus, d'Aquili and himself, that 'seek linkages between the neurological functions of the brain and phenomenal experiences, particularly those manifested in universal and cross-cultural patterns'.

30. Winkelman, 'Spirits as Human Nature', p. 72.

31. Aune, *Prophecy*, p. 83.

32. Dunn, *Jesus and the Spirit*, p. 68.

33. E. R. Dodds, *The Greeks and the Irrational*, p. 146.

34. Ibid., p. 144.

35. Ibid., p. 146.

36. John Ashton, *The Religion of Paul the Apostle*, p. 33, quoting a study of shamanism in Japan by Carmen Blacker, *The Catalpa Bow*.

37. I. M. Lewis, *Religion in Context*, p. 121.

38. Ashton, *Religion of Paul the Apostle*, p. 33.

39. Martin Hengel, *The Charismatic Leader and His Followers*, pp. 21–2.

40. Ibid., p. 35.

41. Jack Sanders, *Charisma, Converts, Competitors*, p. 17, paraphrases the argument of Geza Vermes, *Jesus the Jew*, in these terms.

42. Sanders, ibid., pp. 17–18, rejecting Vermes's claimed charismatic lineage of Galilean Hasid holy men. Sanders supports his argument with the distinction made by Theodore Long between 'just any old charisma' and prophecy, which is seen to conform to Weber's definition.

3   Paul Invents Charisma

1. While the word 'supernatural' – 'above nature' – is an apt descriptor, from a modern perspective, of the miraculous powers described in Paul and in Acts, it should be remembered that Paul himself does not use a word equivalent to 'supernatural'. For Paul, the miraculous is simply one form of the demonstration of divine power. Bengt Holmberg, *Paul and Power*, p. 103, uses 'super-human' rather than 'supernatural' to describe the 'pneumatic endowments' detailed by Paul in his letters.

2. There is a degree of uncertainty surrounding this Council, due in part to differences between the account in Acts 15 and Paul's account in Galatians 2: 1–10. Holmberg, *Paul and Power*, p. 21, finds it prudent to limit resolutions of the Council to an agreement that gentiles converting to Christianity need not be circumcised.

3. Henry Chadwick, *The Early Church*, p. 20.

4. Richard Wallace and Wynne Williams, *The Three Worlds of Paul of Tarsus*.

5. Ibid., pp. 3–7.

6. Chadwick, *The Early Church*, p. 26.

7. Chris McGillion, 'Delusions Can Be a Religious Experience', *Sydney Morning Herald*, 23 July 2002, p. 11, discusses contemporary medical interpretations of religious and mystical experience in this light. A. E. Harvey, *Jesus and the Constraints of History*, p. 99, makes the more general observation that 'what

seemed miraculous to the ancients does not necessarily seem so to us', and that 'a substantial number of incidents reported as healing miracles in the gospels may be accounted for as natural phenomena'.

8. James Dunn, *Jesus and the Spirit: A Study of the Religious and Charismatic Experience of Jesus and the First Christians as Reflected in the New Testament*, pp. 302–4.

9. Christopher Forbes, *Prophecy and Inspired Speech in Early Christianity*, p. 125.

10. John Ashton, in *The Religion of Paul the Apostle*, p. 198, states that any 'inexplicable event ... was ascribed, if you were a pagan, to the work of gods, goddesses or demons, or, if you were a Jew, either to the providential power of God or else to the malign influence of wicked spirits or the devil'. Ashton, p. 176, quotes A. N. Wilson: 'In the world of classical antiquity ... most people would have accepted the powers of the unseen; it was simply a question of which demons or gods were better than another, or, if you were Jewish, which were legitimate'.

11. Paula Friedriksen, *From Jesus to Christ*, p. 88, n. 99, quoted in Jack Sanders, *Charisma, Converts, Competitors*, p. 13.

12. Jerome Murphy-O'Connor, *Paul: A Critical Life*, p. vi. Murphy-O'Connor states that he follows the principle laid down by J. Knox in *Chapters in a Life of Paul*, published in 1950.

13. An example of this approach is provided by F. F. Bruce, in his *The Acts of the Apostles*. Commenting on an exorcism performed by Paul as described by Luke in Acts, Bruce observes: 'Such an incident was bound to make a deep impression on minds conditioned to think in magical terms, although modern readers may wonder about the quality of the faith so engendered'. Quoted in Ashton, *The Religion of Paul the Apostle*, p. 175.

14. Ashton, *The Religion of Paul the Apostle*, p. 177. Ashton offers a sketch (pp. 30–31) of the largely marginal strain of scholarship emphasising the mystical or supernatural aspects of Paul's theology. This approach includes Hermann Gunkel's *The Influence of the Holy Spirit*, first published in German in 1888, which argued that 'the concept of spirit that Paul inherited was of an undifferentiated supernatural force'; Albert Schweitzer's *The Mysticism of Paul the Apostle*, published in German in 1931; Ioan Lewis's *Ecstatic Religion* (1971), proposing a link between gifts of the Spirit and shamanism; and Michael Bourdillon's essay 'Thoughts of the Spirit' (1976), which applies anthropological insights into shamanism to the New Testament.

15. Murphy-O'Connor, *Paul*, p. 51.

16. McGillion, 'Delusions Can Be a Religious Experience', p.11.

17. 'Very commonly, as with St Paul, the road to the assumption of the shaman's vocation lies through affliction valiantly endured, and, in the end, transformed into spiritual grace'. Ioan Lewis, *Ecstatic Religion*, quoted in Ashton, *The Religion of Paul the Apostle*, p. 46.

18. Francis Gignac, 'Greek', p. 263.

19. William Arnt and Wilbur Gingrich, *A Greek-English Lexicon of the New Testament*, p. xxi.

20. Ceslas Spicq, *Theological Lexicon of the New Testament*, Vol. 3, p. 500.

21. James Harrison, *Paul's Language of Grace in Its Graeco-Roman Context*, p. 348.

22. Edward Campbell, 'Grace', p. 261.
23. Siegfried Schatzmann, *A Pauline Theology of Charismata*, p. 2, citing P. Bonnetain. Gerhard Friedrich similarly states that grace is the 'central concept' in Pauline theology, its power displayed in 'the overcoming of sin', *Theological Dictionary of the New Testament*, p. 395.
24. Schatzmann, *A Pauline Theology of Charismata*, p. 2.
25. Friedrich, *Theological Dictionary of the New Testament*, p. 376.
26. Dunn, *Jesus and the Spirit*, p. 202.
27. Harrison, *Paul's Language of Grace*, p. 2. In his book-length study of Paul's 'language of grace', James Harrison details the ways in which Paul articulated his theology of grace within the Graeco-Roman social context, specifically the system of reciprocity.
28. Seneca, *De Beneficiis*, cited in Murphy-O'Connor, *Paul*, p. 305.
29. Harrison, *Paul's Language of Grace*, p. 214.
30. Ibid., pp. 230, 212, 224.
31. Ibid., p. 324.
32. Ibid., pp. 346 and 243.
33. Schatzmann, *A Pauline Theology of Charismata*, p. 2.
34. Harrison, *Paul's Language of Grace*, remarks that 'there remains text-critical argument among scholars concerning the presence of charisma in *Leg. All*', pp. 279–80, n. 255. Harrison cites scholars who dispute 'charisma' in Philo: U. Brockhaus, J. Wobbe and H. Conzelmann. Schatzmann, *A Pauline Theology of Charismata*, states that charisma in Philo is 'questionable, at best, and may represent a late reading', p. 3, citing E. Käsemann.
35. Friedrich, *Theological Dictionary of the New Testament*, pp. 402–3.
36. Harrison, *Paul's Language of Grace*, p. 280, n. 255.
37. Schatzmann, *A Pauline Theology of Charismata*, p. 4.
38. Dunn, *Jesus and the Spirit*, p. 206.
39. Harrison, *Paul's Language of Grace*, p. 280, citing E. Nardoni.
40. Schatzmann, *A Pauline Theology of Charismata*, p. 2, citing Hasenhüttl.
41. Christopher Forbes has suggested this translation.
42. Friedrich, *Theological Dictionary of the New Testament*, p. 403.
43. E. Käsemann, quoted in Schatzmann, *A Pauline Theology of Charismata*, p. 7.
44. All cited by Schatzmann, *A Pauline Theology of Charismata*, p. 8.
45. Dunn, *Jesus and the Spirit*, pp. 254–5.
46. Schatzmann, *A Pauline Theology of Charismata*, p. 11.
47. Ibid., p. 10.
48. Ibid.
49. Schatzmann, *A Pauline Theology of Charismata*, provides a detailed exegesis of the 16 references to charisma in Paul. He cites at p. 12 n. 17 Conzelmann and Brockhaus on the Pauline 'echo' in Peter.
50. Murphy-O'Connor, *Paul*, p. 284.
51. Forbes, *Prophecy and Inspired Speech in Early Christianity*, p. 316.
52. Murphy-O'Connor, *Paul*, pp. 276 and 281.
53. Schatzmann, *A Pauline Theology of Charismata*, p. 28, citing MacGorman.
54. Schatzmann, p. 51, uses the term 'grace gift'.
55. Schatzmann, pp. 21–4. On the nature of Christian prophecy, Dunn, *Jesus and the Spirit*, p. 228, defines prophecy as 'a spontaneous utterance, a revelation given in words to the prophet to be delivered as it is given'.

Aune, *Prophecy*, p. 338, describes Christian prophetic speech as 'Christian discourse presented with divine legitimation'.

56. Dunn, *Jesus and the Spirit*, pp. 232–3.
57. Murphy-O'Connor, *Paul*, p. 332.
58. Schatzmann, *A Pauline Theology of Charismata*, p. 16, citing Käsemann.
59. Ibid., p. 17.
60. Ibid., p. 49.
61. Schatzmann, *A Pauline Theology of Charismata*, p. 49, quotes Karol Gábris finding that the charismata have been institutionalised for 'they are no longer direct gifts of the Spirit of God'. There is also scholarly debate concerning the authorship of these letters, although it is likely that they were written by Paul.
62. Ibid., p. 49.
63. Dunn, *Jesus and the Spirit*, p. 265: 'the church as charismatic community means unity in and through diversity – the unity of charis in and though the diversity of charismata'.
64. Acts 19: 40, referring to an assembly in Ephesus. Cited by Edwin Judge, *The Social Patterns of the Christian Groups in the First Century*, p. 24.
65. Harrison, *Paul's Language of Grace*, pp. 281–2.
66. Schütz, 'Charisma and Social Reality in Primitive Christianity', p. 52, quoted in Schatzmann, *A Pauline Theology of Charismata*, p. 96.
67. Dunn, *Jesus and the Spirit*, p. 291.
68. Schatzmann, *A Pauline Theology of Charismata*, p. 97.
69. Holmberg, *Paul and Power*, p. 7.
70. Ibid., p. 150.
71. Ibid., p. 160.
72. Ibid., p. 195.
73. Robert Banks, *Paul's Idea of Community*, p. 118.
74. Ibid., p. 213.
75. Ibid., p. 166.
76. Ibid., p. 21.
77. Ibid., p. 126.
78. Ibid., p. 130.
79. Ibid., p. 125.
80. Ibid., p. 159.
81. Dunn, *Jesus and the Spirit*, p. 260.
82. Schatzmann, *A Pauline Theology of Charismata*, pp. 51–2.
83. Ashton, *The Religion of Paul the Apostle*, p. 31, citing Gunkel, *The Influence of the Holy Spirit*.
84. Forbes, *Prophecy and Inspired Speech in Early Christianity*, p. 318.

4   Charisma Eclipsed

1. Christopher Forbes gives a thorough account of the differing interpretations of this passage, *Prophecy and Inspired Speech*, pp. 85–91.
2. Henry Chadwick, *The Early Church*, p. 46.
3. Dunn, *Jesus and the Spirit,* p. 346.
4. Ibid., p. 206 citing E. Schweizer, *Church Office in the New Testament*.
5. Ibid., 349.

6. Ronald Kydd, *Charismatic Gifts in the Early Church*, p. 4.

7. Ibid.

8. Stephen Patterson, 'Didache 11–13: The Legacy of Radical Itinerancy in Early Christianity', p. 315, lists several scholars who date the text 'in or near the end of the first century', citing also Jean-Paul Audet's estimate of 50–70. Chadwick, *The Early Church*, p. 47, finds the only 'plausible' niche for it to be the period 70–110.

9. Aaron Milavec, *The Didache: Text, Translation, Analysis, and Commentary*, p. ix, is 'quite certain' that the *Didache* was 'originally composed orally', pointing to 'manifest clues of orality' within the work (p. 41). These include references to teaching as speaking and listening, indicating oral training. Milavec cites Henderson that the literary modes are passed over in silence. He also cites Achtemeier and Ong on cultures of 'high residual authority' in which oral sources are given greater weight than written.

10. Kydd, *Charismatic Gifts in the Early Church*, p. 6, citing discussion by Shepherd and Adam, proposes: 'We should probably assume that the *Didache* was written in Syria'. David Aune, *Prophecy in Early Christianity and the Ancient Mediterranean World*, p. 310, sees the Didache as concerning Christian practice in Syria–Palestine.

11. Trans. Alfred Cody in Clayton Jefford (ed.) *The* Didache *in Context*. All other *Didache* translations are by Cody unless otherwise noted.

12. Milavec, *The Didache*, p. 31, translates this term as 'Christ-peddler'; C. Bigg in his earlier translation (1898) rendered it as 'Christmonger'.

13. After reviewing the debates on this issue, Kydd, *Charismatic Gifts in the Early Church*, p. 19, concludes that *The Shepherd* should be dated in 'the early second century'.

14. Trans. G. F. Snyder, *Hermas of Rome*.

15. Patterson, 'Didache 11–13', p. 328.

16. Jonathan Draper, 'Social Ambiguity and the Production of Text', p. 295.

17. Patterson, 'Didache 11–13', p. 327.

18. Ibid., p. 329.

19. Milavec, *The Didache*, p. 76.

20. Rudolf Sohm, *Outlines of Church History*, p. 36.

21. Draper, 'Social Ambiguity and the Production of Text', p. 302.

22. Ibid., p. 305.

23. Ibid., p. 306.

24. Milavec, *The Didache*, p. 41.

25. Trans. Milavec, *The Didache*.

26. Draper, 'Social Ambiguity and the Production of Text', p. 312.

27. Andrew Louth, *Early Christian Writings: The Apostolic Fathers*, p. 19.

28. Clement of Rome, trans. Staniforth and Louth, *Early Christian Writings*.

29. Trans. William Schoedel, in *Ignatius of Antioch: A Commentary on the Letters of Ignatius of Antioch*.

30. Kydd, *Charismatic Gifts in the Early Church*, p. 17, citing F. A. Schilling.

31. Ibid., p. 17.

32. *Dialogue with Trypho*, trans. Roberts and Donaldson, *The Ante-Nicene Fathers*, quoted by Kydd, *Charismatic Gifts in the Early Church*, p. 26.

33. Kydd, *Charismatic Gifts in the Early Church*, draws this conclusion from a survey on Justin scholarship, p. 91 n. 11.

34. William Tabbernee, *Montanist Inscriptions and Testimonia*, quoted in Dunn, *Jesus and the Spirit*, p. 6.
35. Dominic Unger, 'Introduction' in St Irenaeus, *Against the Heresies Book 1*, p. 1.
36. Irenaeus, *Against Heresies* trans. Roberts and Rambaut, *Ante-Nicene Christian Library*, Vol. V.
37. Cited in Forbes, *Prophecy and Inspired Speech*, p. 78. Forbes uses this passage to confirm that glossolalia was still 'a feature of Christian life' in the late second century, p. 79.
38. Sohm, *Outlines of Church History*, p. 41.
39. Hippolytus, *Refutation of All Heresies*, trans. J. H. MacMahon, *Ante-Nicene Christian Library Vol. VI*.
40. Chadwick, *The Early Church*, p. 53.
41. Tertullian, *Adversus Marcionem* trans. Ernest Evans.
42. Trans. Kydd, in *Charismatic Gifts in the Early Church*, p. 68.
43. Tertullian, *Treatises on Penance: On Penitence and on Purity*, trans. William Le Saint.
44. Le Saint, p. 281, n. 627, Tertullian, *Treatises on Penance*.
45. Augustine wrote in 388 of a sect known as the Tertullianistae, of Carthaginian origin. From this evidence it has been widely assumed that the rebellious Tertullian broke from the Montanists to form his own sect. However, Barnes, *Tertullian*, p. 258, cautions that this assumption is based on little more than the name of the sect, and should be viewed with suspicion.
46. Le Saint, *Treatises on Penance*, p. 289, n. 667.
47. Chadwick, *The Early Church*, pp. 34–5.
48. Pheme Perkins, *Gnosticism and the New Testament*, p. 91, concludes that 'systematic formalization of Gnostic theology does not appear to have existed in the first century'. Robert Grant, *Gnosticism: A Source Book*, p. 14, proposes that 'if we reserve the name "Gnostic" for adherents of [second century] systems, we have to admit that something to be called "proto-Gnostic" or "incipiently Gnostic" or "Gnosticising" was in existence at an earlier date'.
49. Grant, *Gnosticism* p. 16.
50. Ibid., pp. 160–1.
51. Ibid., p. 180.
52. Novitian, *On the Trinity*, trans. R. E. Wallis, *The Ante-Nicene Fathers*, Vol. 5, quoted by Forbes, *Prophecy and Inspired Speech*, p. 80.
53. Kydd, *Charismatic Gifts in the Early Church*, p. 62, acknowledges that Novitian's use of the present tense may be operating as an extended present; yet Forbes, *Prophecy and Inspired Speech*, p. 81, argues that Novitian's switching between past and perfect tenses in this passage shows clear differentiation between the Apostolic age and that of the writer.
54. Cyprian, *Epistulae* 16, 4, transl. Kydd, quoted Kydd, p. 72. Kydd quotes a letter written to Cyprian referring to his 'prophecy', p. 71.
55. Cecil Roebuck, 'Origen's Treatment of the Charismata', p. 113.
56. Origen, *Against Celsus*, trans. H. Chadwick, quoted Kydd, p. 78.
57. Kydd, *Charismatic Gifts in the Early Church*, p. 78.
58. Ibid., p. 79.
59. Ibid., p. 85.

60. Ibid., p. 4.
61. Forbes, *Prophecy and Inspired Speech*, p. 249.
62. Henry Chadwick, *Priscillian of Avila: The Occult and the Charismatic in the Early Church,* p. 8.
63. Ibid., p. 80.
64. John Chrysostom, *Homilies,* trans. Talbot Chambers, *Nicene and Post-Nicene Fathers* Vol. XII.
65. Forbes, *Prophecy and Inspired Speech*, p. 84.
66. William Schoedel, *Ignatius of Antioch*, p. 22 n. 111.
67. Chadwick, *The Early Church*, p. 51.
68. Forbes, *Prophecy and Inspired Speech*, p. 250.
69. Kydd, *Charismatic Gifts in the Early Church*, p. 96 n. 1.
70. Ibid., p. 87.
71. Aune, *Prophecy*, p. 189.
72. Hans Conzelmann, *History of Primitive Christianity*, p. 129.
73. Seutonius, *Nero*, 16, quoted in Conzelmann, *History of Primitive Christianity*, p. 130.
74. Tacitus, *Annals of Imperial Rome* XV.44, trans. Michael Grant, p. 365.
75. Kydd, *Charismatic Gifts in the Early Church*, p. 57.
76. Aune, *Prophecy*, p. 338.

5   Where Did Charisma Go?

1. Augustine writes in *City of God* (Book 22, Ch 8) that Ambrose was afforded 'a revelation in a dream' of a miracle performed in Carthage.
2. Trans. R. J. Defferari, quoted Christopher Forbes, *Prophecy and Inspired Speech in Early Christianity*, p. 83.
3. Forbes, *Prophecy and Inspired Speech in Early Christianity*, p. 83.
4. Henry Chadwick, *The Early Church*, p. 166, citing John Chrysostom.
5. Augustine, *Confessions*, trans. J. G. Pilkingon.
6. Augustine, *Later Works Vol. VIII*, trans. John Burnaby.
7. Quoted by Augustine in his *Retractions*, Book One 12. 7, trans. Mary Inez Bogan.
8. Augustine, *City of God*, trans. John Healey.
9. Augustine, *Retractions*, 1.12.7, trans. Mary Inez Bogan.
10. Forbes, *Prophecy and Inspired Speech in Early Christianity*, p. 82.
11. *The Ascetic Works of St Basil*, quoted in Christopher Brooke, *The Rise and Fall of the Medieval Monastery*, p. 9.
12. Chadwick, *The Early Church*, p. 182.
13. John Ashton, *The Religion of Paul the Apostle*, p. 35. Peter Brown, in *Society and the Holy in Late Antiquity*, also discusses the 'power of the holy man' with reference to the exorcisms performed by Theodore. Brown likens the holy man's function in this regard to 'the shaman of Siberian tribes', pp. 124–5.
14. William Le Saint, *Tertullian, Treatises on Penance*, pp. 289–2, n. 667.
15. Paul Meyendorff, 'Eastern Liturgical Theology', p. 356.
16. Gregory of Nazianzus, *Oration* 39.14; Gregory of Nyssa, *de Spiritu sancto contra Macedonianos* 19. Quoted in G. W. H. Lampe (ed.) *A Patristic Greek Lexicon*, p. 1518.

17. Hannah Hunt, 'Byzantine Christianity', p. 81.
18. *Orations* 41.16, 8.15. Quoted in Lampe (ed.) *A Patristic Greek Dictionary*, pp. 1518–19.
19. *de virginitate* 17. Lampe, *A Patristic Greek Lexicon*, p. 1519.
20. Jean Gribomont, 'Monasticism and Asceticism', p. 101.
21. Ibid., p. 103.
22. Theodoret, Commentary on the First Epistle to the Corinthians 240, 243 in Gerald Bray (ed.) *Ancient Christian Commentary on Scripture: New Testament VII: 1–2 Corinthians*, pp. 117 and 121.
23. Hunt, 'Byzantine Christianity', p. 74.
24. Ibid., p. 82.
25. Ibid., p. 86.
26. Symeon the New Theologian, *Hymns of Divine Love*, trans. George A. Maloney, p. 145.
27. John Meyendorff, 'Christ as Saviour in the East', p. 248.
28. R. A. Knox, *Enthusiasm*, p. 1.
29. Ibid.
30. Ibid., p. 2.
31. Ibid.
32. Ibid.
33. Ibid., p. 11.
34. Ibid., p. 4.
35. Ibid., p. 21.
36. Ibid., p. 22.
37. Ibid., p. 23.
38. Ibid., p. 25.
39. Ibid., p. 82, citing Stephen Runciman, *The Medieval Manichee*.
40. Ibid., p. 72.
41. Brooke, *The Rise and Fall of the Medieval Monastery*, pp. 107–9.
42. Hunt, 'Byzantine Christianity', p. 91.
43. Thomas Aquinas, *Summa Theologia*, trans. Fathers of the English Dominican Province.
44. J. F. Gallagher, 'Charism: For the Church' in *The New Catholic Encyclopedia* Vol. 3 p. 462.
45. Ibid., p. 462.
46. Keith Thomas, *Religion and the Decline of Magic*, p. 45.
47. John Browne, *Adenochoiradelogia, or, An anatomick-chirurgical treatise of glandules and strumaes …*, 1684.
48. William Tooker, *Charisma suie Donum sanationis …*, 1597. Title translated by Greg Fox.
49. Thomas, *Religion and the Decline of Magic*, p. 195.
50. Ibid., pp. 190–1. Marc Bloch's *The Royal Touch* (1924) was an early study of 'the supernatural character that was long attributed to the royal power' (p. 3) of healing through touch.
51. Knox, *Enthusiasm*, p. 5.
52. Timothy George, 'The Spirituality of the Radical Reformation', p. 336.
53. Ibid., p. 334.
54. Knox, *Enthusiasm*, p. 134, quoting Rufus Jones, *Spiritual Reformers*.
55. Ibid., p. 138.

56. Ibid., p. 356 quoting Turner, *History of Providences*.
57. Bishop Gibson quoted in Knox, *Enthusiasm*, p. 450.
58. Edwards's 'Thoughts on the Revival' quoted in Knox, *Enthusiasm*, p. 526.
59. Stuart Piggin, *Firestorm of the Lord: The History of and Prospects for Revival in the Church and the World*, p. 49.
60. Ibid., p. 94, citing Edwards's *Distinguishing Marks*.
61. W. R. Ward, *The Protestant Evangelical Awakening*, p. 292.
62. Ibid., p. 561, quoting Caswall, *Prophet of the Nineteenth Century.*
63. Knox, *Enthusiasm*, p. 554.
64. Ashton, *The Religion of Paul the Apostle*, p. 241.

6 Weber Reinvents Charisma

1. The 1947 translation of *Wirtschaft und Gesellschaft* by R. A. Henderson and Talcott Parsons was entitled *Theory of Social and Economic Organisation* and was a translation of only Part One. The 1968 English edition of Parts One and Two, edited by Guenther Roth and Claus Wittich, translated by E. Fischoff et al., was published as *Economy and Society: An Outline of Interpretive Sociology.*
2. *OED*, 2nd edition, 1989, Vol. 3, p. 41, 'Charisma'.
3. Wolfgang J. Mommsen, *The Age of Bureaucracy: Perspectives on the Political Sociology of Max Weber*, p. 78.
4. Siegfired Schatzmann, *The Pauline Theory of Charismata*, p. 1, is critical of those religious historians such as Schütz who 'argue back to Paul from Weber's contemporary usage', seeing a conceptual anachronism at play when Weberian notions of charisma are applied to the New Testament. I discuss of the hazards of this approach more fully in Chapters 2 and 3.
5. Charles Lindholm, *Charisma*, pp. 5 and 24.
6. P. David Marshall, *Celebrity and Power*, p. 20.
7. Lewis A. Coser, 'Preface' in Arthur Mitzman, *The Iron Cage: An Historical Interpretation of Max Weber*, 1985 [1969], p. xxv.
8. Irvine Schiffer, *Charisma: A Psychoanalytical Look at Mass Society*, p. 3.
9. *Webster's Third New International Dictionary*, 1981, Vol. 1 p. 377.
10. *OED*, Vol. 3, p. 41.
11. R. Mayhew, *Charisma Patrikon, a Paternal Gift ...*, 1676.
12. *OED*, Vol 3, p. 41.
13. Mitzman, *The Iron Cage*, p. 23.
14. *The Barnhart Dictionary of Etymology*, 1988, p. 160.
15. *OED*, Vol 3, p. 41.
16. P. David Marshall, *Celebrity and Power*, p. 20, citing S. Moscovici, *The Age of the Crowd: A Historical Treatise of Mass Psychology.*
17. *OED*, 2nd edition, 1989, Vol. 12, p. 426, 'Prestige'.
18. *OED*, Vol. 12, p. 426 cites usage from 1937: 'We have a status and a prestige to keep. We can't lower ourselves unduly', and from 1955: 'The prestige-conscious descendants of the ancien régime'.
19. Theodore Abel, *Why Hitler Came into Power*, p. 181.
20. Mommsen, *The Age of Bureaucracy*, p. 78, quoting Reinhard Bendix, *Max Weber: An Intellectual Portrait*, p. 112.

21. Mommsen, *The Age of Bureaucracy*, p. 95, citing Talcott Parsons in Otto Stammer (ed.) *Max Weber and Sociology Today*.
22. Arthur Mitzman's 1969 biographical study of Weber, *The Iron Cage*, makes a great deal of the pressure felt by Weber in choosing between his parents, with particular emphasis on Weber's guilt following an altercation with his father (who died soon afterwards), shortly before Weber's own breakdown. But Mitzman's attempt to map this personal relationship onto Weber's thought is severely overdetermined by an unmitigated Freudian interpretation.
23. H. Gerth and C. Wright Mills, 'Introduction: The Man and His Work', p. 23.
24. Mommsen, *The Age of Bureaucracy*, pp. 103–4; Mitzman, *The Iron Cage*, p. 182.
25. Gerth and Mills, 'Introduction', p. 49.
26. Weber, *Gesammelte Politische Schriften*, quoted in Mitzman, *The Iron Cage*, p. 184.
27. Weber, 'Der Sozialismus', quoted in Gerth and Mills, 'Introduction', p. 50.
28. Friedrich Nietzsche, *The Anti-Christ*, 4, p. 116.
29. Nietzsche, *Thus Spake Zarathustra*, I, 4, p. 16.
30. Charles Lindholm, *Charisma*, pp. 25–6.
31. Weber quoted in Gerth and Mills, 'Introduction', p. 25.
32. Mitzman, *The Iron Cage*, p. 144.
33. Weber, 'Gesammelte Aufsätze zur Soziologie und Sozialpolitik', quoted in Mitzman, *The Iron Cage*, p. 178
34. Weber, 'Science as a Vocation' in Gerth and Mills (eds) *From Max Weber*, p. 155.
35. Weber, 'Politics as a Vocation' in *From Max Weber*, p. 79.
36. W. E. H. Lecky, *History of Rationalism*, quoted in Gerth and Mills, 'Introduction', p. 53.
37. Mommsen, *The Age of Bureaucracy*, p. 20.
38. Mitzman, *The Iron Cage*, p. 177.
39. Wilhelm Dilthey, 'Hermeneutics and the Study of History', quoted in Burns and Rayment-Pickard, *Philosophies of History*, p. 155.
40. Weber acknowledged Jellinek's work as 'a crucial stimulus ... to investigate the impact of religion in areas where one might not otherwise look'. Quoted in Guenther Roth, 'Introduction', *Economy and Society*, p. LXXVII.
41. Mommsen, *The Age of Bureaucracy*, p. 110.
42. Gerth and Mills, 'Introduction', p. 51.
43. Lewis A. Coser, 'Preface', in Mitzman, *The Iron Cage*, p. xxvi.
44. Weber, *The Protestant Ethic and the Spirit of Capitalism*, p. 178.
45. Ibid., n. 105, p. 281.
46. Ibid., p. 181.
47. Ibid., p. 182.
48. Roth, 'Introduction' to *Economy and Society*, p. LXIV.
49. Jack Sanders, *Charisma, Converts, Competitors*, p. 21. Mommsen, *The Age of Bureaucracy*, pp. 73–5, also notes the confusion generated across the two parts, one dealing with 'pure types' of domination, including charisma, the other more historically based.
50. Weber, *Economy and Society*, p. 241.
51. Ibid., p. 215. There has been much debate concerning the appropriate English translation of *Herrschaft*, the term used by Weber. Mommsen,

The Age of Bureaucracy, p. 72 n. 1, argues that 'domination' is the most accurate English equivalent, following the precedent of Aron and Runciman. The 1968 English translation of *Economy and Society* edited by Roth and Wittich prefers to alternate between 'domination' and 'authority', depending on the context.

52. Weber, *Economy and Society*, p. 212.
53. Ibid., p. 215.
54. Ibid., pp. 215–216.
55. Ibid., p. 216 n. 1.
56. Ibid., p. 1112.
57. Ibid., p. 216.
58. F. C. Bauer, *Paul the Apostle of Jesus Christ: A Contribution to the Critical History of Primitive Christianity* (published in German in 1845, English translation 1876) cited in Schatzmann, *A Pauline Theology of Charismata*, p. 13 n. 42.
59. Rudolf Sohm, *Outlines of Church History*, p. 33.
60. Ibid., p. 40.
61. Weber, *Economy and Society*, p. 241.
62. Ibid.
63. Ibid., p. 242.
64. Ibid., p. 244.
65. Ibid., p. 245.
66. Ibid., p. 216 n. 2.
67. Ibid., p. 246.
68. Ibid., p. 248.
69. These studies, originally published as essays in the *Archiv* journal in 1916–17, were reworked by Weber in 1920 as two volumes – *The Religion of China* and *The Religion of India* – to accompany *The Protestant Ethic* in a Sociology of Religion series. Weber died before he could complete revision of the essays on religion in India.
70. Weber, *The Religion of China*, p. 35, *The Religion of India*, p. 54. Reinhard Bendix, *Max Weber: An Intellectual Portrait*, proposes the translation 'familial charisma' in preference to 'gentile charisma' to convey Weber's sense of 'charisma attributed to kinship' with regard to China and India, p. 146 n. 9.
71. Weber, *Economy and Society*, p. 249.
72. Ibid., p. 400.
73. Ibid.
74. Ibid., pp. 439–40.
75. Ibid., p. 440.
76. Ibid., p. 445.
77. Ibid., p. 631.
78. Ibid., pp. 1111–12.
79. Ibid., p. 1121.
80. Ibid., p. 1113.
81. Ibid., p. 1116.
82. Ibid., p. 1121.
83. Ibid., pp. 1119–1121.
84. Ibid., p. 1122.

85. Ibid., pp. 1122–3.
86. Ibid., p. 1133.
87. Ibid., pp. 1133–4.
88. Ibid., pp. 1135–6.
89. Ibid., p. 1148.
90. Ibid., p. 1156.
91. Ibid., p. 1130.
92. Ibid., pp. 1130 and 1132.
93. Ibid., pp. 1129–30.
94. Ibid., p. 1132.
95. Weber, *From Max Weber*, p. 79.
96. Ibid., p. 155.
97. Albert Salamon, 'Max Weber', *Die Gesellschaft*, quoted in Mitzman, *The Iron Cage*, p. 5.
98. *Social Research* II. 72, quoted *OED*, Vol. 3, p. 41, 'Charisma'.
99. Theodore Abel, *Why Hitler Came into Power*, p. 67.
100. *The Barnhart Dictionary of Etymology*, p. 160.
101. *OED*, Vol. 3, p. 41.
102. Geoffrey Parrinder, 'Charisma' in *The Encyclopedia of Religion* (ed.) Mircea Eliade, 1987, Vol 3, p. 218.
103. *OED*, Vol. 3, p. 41.
104. Roger Eatwell, 'The Concept and Theory of Charismatic Leadership', p. 5.
105. Abel, *Why Hitler Came into Power*, p. 181.
106. Karl Löwith, *Mass und Wert*, 1939, quoted by Wolfgang Mommsen, *Max Weber and German Politics 1890–1920*, p. 410 n. 73.
107. Mommsen, 'Preface to the English Edition', *Max Weber and German Politics*, p. viii.
108. Mommsen, *Max Weber and German Politics*, p. 410 n. 73.
109. Ibid., p. 410.
110. Guenther Roth, 'Introduction to the New Edition', Reinhard Bendix, *Max Weber: An Intellectual Portrait*, p. xxviii.
111. Mommsen, 'Preface to the Second German Edition', *Max Weber and German Politics 1890–1920*, p. xii.
112. Mommsen, *Max Weber and German Politics*, p. 410.
113. Ibid., p. 409.
114. Ibid., p. 411 n. 73.
115. Ibid., p. 410,
116. Schlesinger quoted in Mommsen, *The Age of Bureaucracy*, p. 92.
117. Arthur Schlesinger, *The Politics of Hope*, pp. 9–10.
118. Ibid., p. 11.
119. Cited by Roger Eatwell, 'The Concept and Theory of Charismatic Leadership', p. 4.
120. Roth, 'Introduction to the New Edition', p. xviii.
121. Ibid., p. xxxi.
122. Mommsen, *Max Weber and German Politics*, p. 104.
123. Roth, 'Introduction to the New Edition', p. xvi.
124. Talcott Parsons, *The Structure of Social Action*, Vol. II, p. 669.
125. Ibid., p. 564, p. 564 n. 5.
126. Ibid., p. 662.

127. Roth, 'Introduction to the New Edition', p. xvi.
128. Ibid., p. xvi.
129. Mommsen, *The Age of Bureaucracy*, p. 86 n. 12, p. 92.
130. 'De-Parsonizing Weber: A Critique of Parsons' Interpretation of Weber's Sociology' was the title of a 1975 article in *American Sociological Review*, cited by Roth, 'Introduction to the New Edition', p. xvi.
131. Anthony Giddens, *Capitalism and Modern Social Theory*, pp. vii and ix.
132. Irvine Schiffer, *Charisma*, p. 7.
133. Ibid., pp. 5 and 7.
134. Ibid., pp. 3 and 4.
135. Ibid., p. 6, p. xi.
136. Sanders, *Charisma, Converts, Competitors*, pp. 25–6.
137. Robert Tucker, 'The Theory of Charismatic Leadership' in *Daedalus*, quoted by Sanders, *Charisma, Converts, Competitors*, p. 26.
138. Sanders, *Charisma, Converts, Competitors*, p. 26 quoting Durkheim, *The Elementary Forms of Religious Life*; Lindholm, *Charisma*, p. 32.
139. Roy Wallis, 'The Social Construction of Charisma', quoted by Sanders, *Charisma, Converts, Competitors*, p. 26.
140. Roy Wallis, 'Charisma and Explanation', quoted in Sanders, *Charisma, Converts, Competitors*, p. 27.
141. Sanders, *Charisma, Converts, Competitors*, p. 27.
142. Bryan Wilson and Robert Tucker quoted by Sanders, *Charisma, Converts, Competitors*, p. 27.
143. Pierre Bourdieu, 'Legitimation and Structured Interests in Weber's Sociology of Religion', p. 129.
144. Ibid., pp. 129–130.
145. Ibid., p. 131.
146. Len Oakes, *Prophetic Charisma*, p. 2.
147. Ibid., p. 2
148. Ibid., pp. 6–16.
149. Ibid., p. 31.
150. Ibid., pp. 30 and 32.
151. Ibid., pp. 21–2.
152. Ibid., p. 25.
153. Philip Rieff, *Charisma*, pp. 3, 5, 6.
154. Ibid., pp. 82 and 37.
155. Ibid., p. 122.
156. Ibid., p. x.
157. Ann Ruth Willner, *The Spellbinders*, p. 12.
158. Ibid., p. 3.
159. Doris McIlwain, 'The Charisma of Fallible Leaders and the Limits of Self-Help', p. 2, *Australian Review of Public Affairs* at http://www.australianreview.net/digest/2006/05/mcilwain.html.
160. William Clark, *Academic Charisma*, pp. 14 and 3.
161. Tom Griiifiths, *Hunters and Collectors*, quoted in Gelder and Jacobs, *Uncanny Australia*, p. 83.
162. Gelder and Jacobs, *Uncanny Australia*, pp. 82–96.
163. Roger Eatwell, 'The Concept and Theory of Charismatic Leadership', p. 6.

7 Twentieth-Century Charismatics

1. Edith Blumhofer, 'The Christian Catholic Apostolic Church', p. 141 n. 2, citing Dowie's *Leaves of Healing*, published in 1904.
2. Dowie quoted in Blumhofer, 'The Christian Catholic Apostolic Church', p. 129.
3. Dowie quoted in Barry Chant, 'The Nineteenth and Early Twentieth Century Origins of the Australian Pentecostal Movement', p. 107.
4. Blumhofer, 'The Christian Catholic Apostolic Church', pp. 132–3, citing Dowie on 'Apostolic Powers' in his *Leaves of Healing*.
5. Ibid., p. 132.
6. Ibid., pp. 134–5, citing Philip Cook, 'Zion City, Illinois: Twentieth Century Utopia', PhD dissertation.
7. Dowie, *Leaves of Healing*, quoted by Blumhofer, 'The Christian Catholic Apostolic Church', p. 140.
8. Chant, 'The Nineteenth and Early Twentieth Century Origins of the Australian Pentecostal Movement', p. 107, quotes Dowie's itemised listing of the 'nine gifts of the Holy Spirit'.
9. Blumhofer, 'The Christian Catholic Apostolic Church', p. 144 n. 45, quotes J. R. Flower, whose parents worked with Dowie, in Bernice Lee, *Bread of Life*.
10. William Arthur, *The Tongue of Fire; or, the True Power of Christianity* (1856), quoted in Steven J. Land, 'Pentecostal Spirituality', p. 479.
11. Blumhofer, 'The Christian Catholic Apostolic Church', p. 136, citing Sarah Parham, *The Life of Charles Parham*.
12. Ibid., p. 137.
13. Land, 'Pentecostal Spirituality', pp. 480–1.
14. C. Peter Wagner, 'Foreword', p. 15.
15. Harold D. Hunter, 'Two Movements of the Holy Spirit in the 20th Century', p. 1.
16. John Ashton, *The Religion of Paul the Apostle*, p. 241.
17. Rudolf Bultmann, 'New Testament and Mythology' quoted in Andrew Walker, 'Miracles, Strange Phenomena, and Holiness'.
18. Andrew Walker, 'The Devil You Think You Know', p. 90.
19. Oral Roberts, *My Story*, quoted in Ashton, *The Religion of Paul the Apostle*, p. 27.
20. Ashton, *The Religion of Paul the Apostle*, p. 37.
21. Land, 'Pentecostal Spirituality', p. 483, writing in 1988, estimated the global membership of Pentecostals and charismatics at 21 per cent with an annual growth of 19 million. Harvey Cox, writing in 1998, referred to estimates of global Pentecostal numbers of 410 million (*Fire from Heaven*, p. xv). *The World Christian Encyclopedia*, edited by David Barrett, attempted to enumerate all Christian groups. Its first edition, published in 1982, estimated the global Pentecostal-Charismatic population at over 100 million (p. 838); the second edition, 2001, put the 2000 numbers of Pentecostals/Charismatics at 523 million (p. 4).
22. Peter Hocken, 'Charismatic Movement', p. 404.
23. John MacArthur, *Charismatic Chaos*, p. 19, citing Bennett's book *Nine O'Clock in the Morning*.

24. Ibid., p. 19.
25. Hocken, 'Charismatic Movement', p. 404.
26. Dennis Bennett, 'God's Strength for This Generation', p. 2.
27. *OED*, 2nd edition, Vol. 3 p. 41, 'Charisma'.
28. Ibid.
29. Bennett, 'God's Strength for This Generation', p. 2.
30. Hocken, 'Charismatic Movement', p. 404.
31. Ibid., p. 404.
32. *OED*, 2nd edition, Vol. 3 p. 41, 'Charisma'.
33. Bruce Shelley, *Church History in Plain Language*, pp. 459–60.
34. Harvey Cox, *Fire from Heaven*, p. 107.
35. Hocken, 'Charismatic Movement', p. 405.
36. Shelley, *Church History*, p. 459.
37. Tom Smail, 'In Spirit and in Truth: Reflections on Charismatic Worship', p. 112.
38. Ibid., p. 109.
39. Daniel Radosh, 'The Good Book Business', p. 55.
40. Cox, *Fire from Heaven*, pp. 152 and 106.
41. James Dunn, 'Ministry and the Ministry', p. 82, p. 99 n. 3.
42. Gary Greig and Kevin Springer, 'Introduction', p. 21.
43. Land, 'Pentecostal Spirituality', p. 483.
44. Hocken, 'Charismatic Movement', p. 404.
45. MacArthur, *Charismatic Chaos*, p. 109, quotes Roberts in *Time* (July 13, 1987, p. 52): 'I can't tell you about [all] the dead people I've raised. I've had to stop a sermon, go back and raise a dead person'.
46. Walker, 'Miracles, Strange Phenomena, and Holiness', p. 126.
47. Paul G. Hiebert, 'Discerning the Work of God', p. 148.
48. Tom Smail, 'A Renewal Recalled', p. 19.
49. Nigel Wright, 'A Pilgrimage in Renewal', p. 27.
50. Ibid., p. 29.
51. Tom Smail, Andrew Walker and Nigel Wright, 'From "The Toronto Blessing" to Trinitarian Renewal', p. 157.
52. Smail, 'A Renewal Recalled', p. 19.
53. Ibid.
54. Walker, 'Miracles, Strange Phenomena and Holiness', p. 126.
55. Andrew Walker, 'Notes From a Wayward Son', p. 37.
56. Smail, 'A Renewal Recalled', p. 19.
57. Reverend Bill L. Williams in the *Los Angeles Times*, 1987, quoted by MacArthur, *Charismatic Chaos*, p. 221.
58. MacArthur, *Charismatic Chaos*, p. 227.
59. The psychologist John Kildahl, *The Psychology of Speaking in Tongues* (1972), concluded that glossolalia is a learned skill, a conclusion supported by other studies, including Nicholas Spanos et. al., 'Glossolalia as Learned Behaviour: An Experimental Demonstration', published in *Journal of Abnormal Psychology* (1987). Cited by MacArthur, *Charismatic Chaos*, pp. 240–2.
60. Charles R. Smith, *Tongues in Biblical Perspective* (1972), cited by MacArthur, *Charismatic Chaos*, p. 243.
61. Dunn, 'Ministry and the Ministry', p. 83.

62. www.agts.edu/community/wagner_modified_houts.pdf   (accessed   14 October 2007).

63. Smail, Walker and Wright, discussing the charismatic ministries of several evangelists within the 'faith movement', conclude that some of the 'central tenets' of this movement 'offend against the dogmatic heart of historic orthodoxy' and that such teaching 'functions as heresy even if its teachers are not de jure heretics'. '"Revelation Knowledge" and Knowledge of Revelation: The Faith Movement and the Question of Heresy', p. 135.

64. Hiebert, 'Discerning the Work of God', pp. 152–3.

65. MacArthur, *Charismatic Chaos*, pp. 47–50.

66. Walker, 'Miracles, Strange Phenomena, and Holiness', pp. 126–7, cites Dr Peter May, who has investigated alleged healings for 20 years and has not found a single occurrence justifying the epithet 'miracle'. Similarly, MacArthur, *Charismatic Chaos*, cites investigations of miraculous healings by Dr Philip Selden, Dr William Nolen and James Randi, all of which found no evidence of permanent healing (p. 133, pp. 205–9).

67. MacArthur, *Charismatic Chaos*, p. 21.

68. Mark Evans discusses the crucial role of music, especially singing, in creating Pentecostal fervour in *Open Up the Doors: Music in the Modern Church*.

69. Walker, 'Miracles, Strange Phenomena and Holiness', pp. 126–8; MacArthur, *Charismatic Chaos*, p. 206, citing Dr William Nolen on the power of suggestion in effecting minor cures: 'Such cures are not miraculous but result from the functioning of the patient's own automatic nervous system'.

70. David Lewis, 'A Social Anthropologist's Analysis of Contemporary Healing', p. 323, cites a study by Dr Rex Gardner of 'half a dozen medically documented cases of otherwise inexplicable healings'.

71. MacArthur, *Charismatic Chaos*, p. 132.

72. David Millikan, 'God, Power and Money', *Sydney Morning Herald*, 3 March 2008, p. 13.

73. Ibid.

74. http://bennyhinn.org, 10 March 2008.

75. Millikan, 'God, Power and Money', p. 13.

76. John Zizioulas, *Eucharist, Bishop, Church*, Preface to 2nd Edition, p. 7.

77. Ibid., p. 7: 'Never in the past, throughout the long history of the Orthodox Church, was it possible to exercise spiritual fatherhood without express Episcopal permission in writing'.

78. Smail, 'In Spirit and in Truth', p. 112.

79. Ibid., p. 114. Mark Evans makes a similar observation in *Open Up the Doors*, p. 105, when he remarks of the 'glory movement' in Pentecostal worship: 'What is common about [such] movements ... is the sheer hype and intensity of experience on offer, the superlative descriptions that surround it, and, ultimately, their fleetingness'.

80. MacArtur, *Charismatic Chaos*, p. 295.

81. Ibid., p. 292.

82. Ibid., p. 75, citing Larry Christenson, 'Penetecostalism's Forgotten Forerunner'.

83. Ibid., p. 117.

84. Ibid., p. 21, pp. 57–8.

85. Arthur L. Johnson, *Faith Misguided: Exposing the Dangers of Mysticism*, p. 113, quoted by MacArthur, *Charismatic Chaos*, p. 221.

86. MacArthur, *Charismatic Chaos*, p. 27.
87. Hiebert, 'Discerning the Work of God', p. 148, p. 161 n. 2.
88. Walker, 'Miracles, Strange Phenomena, and Holiness', p. 128.

8   The Age of Media: Charisma and Celebrity

1. P. G. W. Glare (ed.) *Oxford Latin Dictionary*, p. 294, 'Celebritas'; p. 674, 'Fama'.
2. Andrew Anthony, 'It Could Be You: Celebrity Exposed' in *The Observer Magazine*, 27 January 2002, p. 9.
3. Samantha Barbas, *Movie Crazy: Fans, Stars, and the Cult of Celebrity*, p. 37.
4. Leo Braudy, *The Frenzy of Renown: Fame and Its History*, p. 598.
5. Ibid., p. 29.
6. Ibid., pp. 42–3.
7. Ibid., p. 56.
8. Ibid., p. 60.
9. Ibid., pp. 73–4.
10. Ibid., pp. 123 and 75.
11. Ibid., p. 105.
12. Ibid., p. 162.
13. Ibid., pp. 236 and 238.
14. Ibid., p. 242.
15. Ibid., p. 255, quoting Petrarch, *The Fates of Illustrious Men*.
16. Ibid., p. 265.
17. Ibid., p. 355, quoting Milton's *Lycidas*.
18. Ibid., pp. 361 and 364.
19. *OED* 2nd Edition, 1989, Vol. II, p. 1019, 'Celebrity'.
20. Braudy, *The Frenzy of Renown*, p. 372.
21. Ibid., p. 373, quoting Rousseau, *Confessions*.
22. Ibid., p. 374, quoting Hume, *Letters*.
23. Ibid., p. 375.
24. Ibid., p. 405.
25. Ibid., p. 445.
26. Ibid., p. 447.
27. *OED* 2nd Edition, 1989, Vol. II, p. 1019, 'Celebrity'.
28. Braudy, *The Frenzy of Renown*, pp. 491–2.
29. Ibid., p. 499.
30. *OED* Vol. XVI, p. 523, 'Star'.
31. Barbas, *Movie Crazy*, p. 19.
32. Edgar Morin, *The Stars*, p. 6.
33. *OED* Vol. X, p. 36, 'Movie'; Vol. V, p. 914, 'Film'.
34. Richard de Cordova, 'The Emergence of the Star System in America', p. 26.
35. David Robinson, *History of World Cinema*, p. 31.
36. Robinson, *History of World Cinema*, p. 122.
37. Morin, *The Stars*, p. 135.
38. Quoted in Morin, *The Stars*, p. 136.
39. Joshua Gamson, 'The Assembly-Line of Greatness: Celebrity in Twentieth-Century America'; David Denby, 'Fallen Idols: Have Stars Lost Their Magic?', p. 107.

40. Gamson, 'The Assembly-Line of Greatness', p. 114.
41. Robinson, *History of World Cinema*, p. 179.
42. Thomas Schatz, in *The Genius of the System: Hollywood Filmmaking in the Studio Era*, p. 70, regards the 'watershed period from the coming of sound into the early Depression' as the period in which the studio system fully coalesced.
43. Ellis Cashmore, *Celebrity/Culture*, p. 62.
44. Morin, *The Stars*, p. 57.
45. Barbas, *Movie Crazy*, p. 144.
46. Denby, 'Fallen Idols', p. 104.
47. Barbas, *Movie Crazy*, p. 143.
48. Morin, *The Stars*, p. 59.
49. Cashmore, *Celebrity/Culture*, p. 60. There were certainly exceptions to this general rule, as Samantha Barbas notes: the occasional press or magazine article that 'slipped by the studios and caused a near-scandal', and the probings of high-profile gossip columnists such as Louella Parsons. However, the studios were able to control publicity to their satisfaction, so that fan magazines 'almost never contradicted the studios' (Barbas, *Movie Crazy*, p. 99).
50. Morin, *The Stars*, p. 90.
51. Barbas, *Movie Crazy*, p. 36.
52. *New York Times*, 1926, quoted in Barbas, *Movie Crazy*, p. 171.
53. Barbas, *Movie Crazy*, p. 171.
54. Morin, *The Stars*, pp. 75 and 90.
55. Ibid., pp. 102, 103, 105.
56. Walter Benjamin, 'The Work of Art in the Age of Mechanical Reproduction', p. 226.
57. Ibid., p. 223.
58. Ibid., p. 233.
59. Morin, *The Stars*, pp. 137–8.
60. Ibid., p. 141.
61. Barbas, *Movie Crazy*, p. 42.
62. Ibid., p. 44.
63. Ibid., p. 45.
64. Ibid., quoting *Photoplay*, 1927.
65. Ibid., p. 54, quoting *Photoplay*, 1929 and Alice Williamson, *Alice in Movieland*, 1928.
66. Gamson, 'The Assembly-Line of Greatness', p. 147, quoting *Photoplay Treasury*, 1919.
67. Ibid., quoting *American Magazine*, 1940.
68. Ibid., p. 147.
69. Morin, *The Stars*, p. 51.
70. Goldwyn quoted in Richard Dyer, *Stars*, p. 18.
71. Molly Haskell, *From Reverence to Rape*, quoted in Dyer, *Stars*, p. 18.
72. Dyer, *Stars*, p. 36.
73. Denby, 'Fallen idols', p. 105.
74. Cashmore, *Celebrity/Culture*, p. 64.
75. Denby, 'Fallen idols', p. 105.
76. Joel Stein argues that George Clooney is 'maybe the only one [star] we have now' in 'Guess Who Came to Dinner? A Visit from George Clooney, Home Handyman and the Last True Movie Star', *Time*, 3 March 2008, pp. 36–41.

77. Ibid., p. 19, quoting B. King, 'Stardom as an Occupation'.
78. Richard Schickel, *Common Fame: The Culture of Celebrity*, p. 23.
79. George Cukor dir., *It Should Happen To You!*, Columbia Pictures, 1954.
80. Daniel Boorstin, *The Image: A Guide to Pseudo-Events in America* 2nd edition, p. 58.
81. Ibid., p. 57.
82. Ibid., p. 60.
83. Ibid., p. 47.
84. Ibid., p. 59. Boorstin cites a study of the *Saturday Evening Post* and *Collier's*.
85. Ibid., pp. 48 and 58.
86. Ibid., p. 61.
87. Ibid., p. 64.
88. Ibid., p. 75.
89. Ibid., p. 74.
90. Ibid., p. viii.
91. Braudy, *The Frenzy of Renown*, p. 3.
92. Cashmore, *Celebrity/Culture*, p. 193.
93. Wannabe Famous website quoted in Bernard Zuel, 'Everyone is Falling for Fame's Big Lie', *Sydney Morning Herald*, 15 January 2005, p. 11.
94. http://iwannabefamous.com, accessed 23 January 2008.
95. Denby, 'Fallen Idols', p. 105.
96. Ibid., p. 105.
97. Ibid., p. 112.
98. Damien Woolnough, 'Dead Gorgeous', *The Australian, Wish Magazine*, 3 August 2007, p. 24.
99. 'Finally! Stars Show Their Age!', *New Weekly*, 24 December 2007, p. 30.
100. Denby, 'Fallen Idols', p. 105.
101. Examples of this scholarship may be found in the edited collections *Framing Celebrity* (eds Holmes and Redmond) and *The Celebrity Culture Reader* (ed. P. David Marshall).
102. Graeme Turner, in 'Celebrity, the Tabloid and the Democratic Public Sphere', refers to the 'demotic turn' in the media industry from the mid-1990s with the opening of media access to a much wider range of individuals. A 'demotic turn' can also be identified, from around the same period, in media and cultural studies, as researchers read 'democratic political possibilities' (Turner, p. 497) into this new access for 'ordinary' citizens to the media as well as the 'self-determination' achieved by web users. Turner (p. 492) quotes two scholars, Ian Connell (1992) and John Hartley (1996) who rejected the elitism and 'snobbery' of critiques of tabloid journalism and popular culture. This theoretical perspective, which found more to celebrate than to disdain in the growth of celebrity within an expanded public sphere, became well established in media studies by the end of the 1990s.
103. Bernard Zuel, 'Everyone is Falling for Fame's Big Lie', *Sydney Morning Herald*, 15 January 2005, p. 11.
104. Rachel Weisz quoted in the *Sydney Morning Herald*, 15 November 2007, p. 17.
105. The analysis of media coverage on this issue is drawn from a periodical – and unsystematic – study of British, American and Australian media, primarily newspapers and magazines, from 1999 to 2008.

106. Liz Porter and Sue Williams, 'The It Factor', *The Sun-Herald, Sunday Life!*, 7 November 1999, p. 8.
107. Ibid., p. 8.
108. Bernard Zuel, 'Pleasant, Sure, But ...', *The Sydney Morning Herald*, 9 October 2001, p. 12.
109. Robert Lusetich, 'Karrie's Battle Out in the Open', *The Weekend Australian*, 27 April, 2002, p. 50.
110. Michael Millett and Mike Seccombe, 'The Charisma Game', *Sydney Morning Herald*, 29 June 2002, p. 27.
111. Andrew Anthony, 'It Could Be You', *The Observer Magazine*, 27 January 2002, p. 12.
112. Laura Demasi, 'Kiss and Swell: Britney Unveils Her Trout Pout', *Sydney Morning Herald*, 30 October 2007, p. 18.
113. Terry Smyth, 'The Fame Game, frame by Frame', *The Sun-Herald*, 4 November 2007, pp. 54–5. The book is Richard Simpkin, *Richard & Famous*.
114. Christine Sams, 'ARIAs: Inside Gossip', *Sun-Herald, S*, 4 November 2007, p. 10; Bernard Zuel, 'Scarlet Letters', *Sydney Morning Herald, Metro*, 6 September 2007, p. 4.
115. Ruth Ritchie, 'Idol Worship's Hollow Ring', *Sydney Morning Herald, Spectrum*, 3 November 2007, p. 10.
116. Richard Jinman, 'A Rock God Remembered', *Sydney Morning Herald*, 22 November 2007, p. 16.
117. Porter and Williams, 'The It Factor', p. 10.
118. Ibid., p. 8.
119. Ibid.
120. Corrie Perkin, 'Hitting His Heights', *The Weekend Australian Magazine*, 15 December 2007, p. 37.

9 Charisma Past, Present and Future

1. *China Daily*, 16 November 2005, p. 8, 'University Must Focus on Intellect' is an English version of a news item previously published in *Qilu Evening News*. *Charisma* is a 1999 film directed by Kiyoshi Kurosawa.
2. Since Chinese tends to avoid direct borrowings from other languages (in contrast to Japanese) the Western 'charisma' is used in China, especially when the technical, Weberian, sense is intended. The popular Chinese press, however, uses *mei li* – meaning 'attractiveness, allure, charm' – as a Chinese equivalent to charisma. *Mei li* is a recent construction (unknown in the 1930s), forged by combining *mei* (evil spirit) with *li* (charm, enchantment), giving the word a hint of the mysterious or magical. The recent invention of the word indicates that it is a response, using the resources of the Chinese language, to 'charisma'. Daniel Kane has provided this translation.
3. Glynnis Chantrell (ed.) *Oxford Dictionary of Word Histories* (2002), p. 92.
4. Charles Lindholm, *Charisma*, p. 5.
5. These references to charisma have been drawn from Australian, British and American press and magazines over the period 1999–2008.
6. Liz Porter and Sue Williams, 'The "It" Factor' in *The Sun-Herald, SundayLife!*, 7 November 1999, pp. 6–10.

7. Ibid., p. 7.
8. Ibid., pp. 7–10, quoting interviewees Anne Morrison, Harry M. Miller, and an unnamed political staffer.
9. Michael Millett and Mike Seccombe, 'The Charisma Game', in *The Sydney Morning Herald*, 29 June 2002, p. 27.
10. Garry Maddox, 'Another Shot at Justice for Ned Kelly', *The Sydney Morning Herald, The Guide* supplement, 15 April 2002, p. 14.
11. Matt Buchanan, preview of the documentary *Fassbinder's Women*. 'The power of charisma is frightening and Fassbinder's was apparently all-devouring', *The Sydney Morning Herald, Guide*, 15 April 2002, p. 24.
12. Nina L. Khrushcheva, 'Project Syndicate', *The Australian*, 22 January 2007, p. 14; Richard Hinds, 'Open and Shut: Why We Can't Produce a Champion', *The Sydney Morning Herald, Sport*, 22 January 2007, p. 2.
13. Letter by Marc Hendricks, *Sydney Morning Herald*, 31 December 2007, p. 10; Valerie Lawson, 'Chance for Fans to See Charismatic Cuban Dancer', *Sydney Morning Herald*, 8 October 2007, p. 13.
14. Sheila Fitzpatrick, 'Charmer', *London Review of Books*, 1 November 2007, p. 27; Thomas Jones, 'Short Cuts', *London Review of Books*, 1 November 2007, p. 25.
15. Richard Beeston, 'Terrorist Leader with Charm and Charisma', *The Times*, 4 September 2004, p. 6.
16. John Lanchester, 'Walled Off: Can Burma Escape from Its History?', *The New Yorker*, 1 December 2006, p. 106.
17. Maggie Alderson, 'It's a Kind of Magic', *Sydney Morning Herald, Good Weekend*, 6 October 2007, p. 53.
18. Ibid.
19. Arthur Schlesinger, *The Politics of Hope*, p. 12.
20. Jacqueline Lunn, 'Don't Give Up On Her, Dad', *Sydney Morning Herald, Spectrum*, 6 January 2007, p. 21, quoting Michael Carr-Gregg, *The Princess Bitchface Syndrome: Surviving Adolescent Girls*.
21. Elizabeth Farrelly, 'Applying Soul to Cities Is a Hit and Miss Affair', *Sydney Morning Herald*, 20 February 2008, p. 11.
22. *The Sun-Herald, Travel* supplement 24 August 2008, front page: 'Sheer Charisma: In Love with Lake Como'.
23. John Lahr, 'Demolition Man: Harold Pinter and "The Homecoming"', *The New Yorker*, 24 & 31 December 2007, pp. 54–6.
24. *London Review of Books*, 18 October 2007, p. 14. Advertisement for new titles from Reaction Books, featuring an excerpt from a review in the *Times Higher Education Supplement* of the book *A History of the Heart* by Ole M. Haystad.
25. Andrew McConnell, 'The Iceberg Cometh', *Sydney Morning Herald, Good Weekend*, 6 January 2007, p. 32.
26. Bernard Zuel, 'Because the Night Belonged to Her', *Sydney Morning Herald*, 17 October 2008, p. 11.
27. Doe Lang, *The New Secrets of Charisma: How to Discover and Unleash Your Hidden Powers*, p. xi.
28. Ibid., p. ix.
29. Ibid., p. 6.
30. Ibid., pp. 7, 10, 18.
31. D. A. Benton, *Executive Charisma*, p. x.
32. Ibid., pp. xv, xi, xiv.

33. These sacred steps are, in summary: be the first to initiate; expect and give acceptance to maintain self-esteem; ask questions, and ask favours; stand tall, straight and smile; be human, humorous and hands-on; slow down, shut up and listen.
34. Tony Alessandra, *Charisma: Seven Keys to Developing the Magnetism That Leads to Success*, p. i, excerpt from review by Robert Kriegel.
35. Ibid., p. 11, quoting Charles Lindholm, *Charisma*.
36. Ibid., pp. 23 and p. 29.
37. Ibid., pp. 10–11.
38. Ibid., p. 2.
39. These seven elements are your silent message; your ability to speak well; your listening skills; your persuasive talent; your use of pace and time; your ability to adapt to others; your vision, your ideas.
40. Ibid., pp. 21, 20, 24.
41. Desmond Guilfoyle, *The Charisma Effect*, p. 314.
42. Ibid., p. 11.
43. Ben Macintyre and James Landale, 'A Master of Charisma to Pep Up Peers', *The Times*, 30 June 1999, p. 13.
44. Jay Conger and Rabindra Kanungo, *Charismatic Leadership in Organizations*, p. 3. The authors, p. 4, provide a survey of the empirical studies of charismatic leadership since 1988, including field surveys and samples of managers, executives and military leaders; laboratory experiments; content analyses of interviews and observation; and historical archival information.
45. Ibid., p. 4.
46. Ibid., p. 47.
47. Key texts in the development of these conceptual models, as surveyed by Conger and Kanungo, included Robert House, 'A 1976 Theory of Charismatic Leadership' (1977); James McGregor Burns, *Leadership* (1978), which posited the transformational/transactional distinction; and Bernard Bass, *Leadership and Performance beyond Expectations* (1985), which incorporated charisma as one component within the transformational leadership model in the business organisation context.
48. Conger and Kanungo, *Charismatic Leadership in Organizations*, p. 65, associate these dominant models with their originators and developers as follows: transformational leadership – Bass and Avolio; charismatic leadership – House and Shamir; visionary leadership – Sashkin. The attributional model is proposed by Conger and Kanungo themselves.
49. Ibid., p. 48.
50. Ibid., p. 70.
51. Ibid., p. 108.
52. Ibid., pp. 115–16.
53. Ibid., p. 207.
54. Bernard M. Bass, *Transformational Leadership: Industry, Military, and Educational Impact*, p. 5.
55. Ibid., p. 166.
56. Ibid., p. 14.
57. Jane M. Howell and Peter J. Frost, 'A Laboratory Study of Charismatic Leadership', p. 211. Howell and Frost note that M. Sashkin had previously (1977) argued for this irreducible nature of charisma.

58. Ibid., p. 211.
59. These three leadership styles were given the following traits by Howell and Frost, 'A Laboratory Study of Charismatic Leadership', p. 198: charismatic – captivating, engaging voice tone, energetic delivery, pacing etc.; considerate – exhibiting concern and two-way participation; structuring – providing detailed and careful explanation of the task.
60. Ibid., p. 209.
61. Ibid., p. 211.
62. Nancy C. Roberts and Raymond Trevor Bradley, 'Limits of Charisma', p. 86.
63. Ibid., p. 90. Roberts and Bradley draw the data for their study from multiple sources, including archival material; participant observation of meetings; and interviews with teachers, parents, students and others (p. 89).
64. Ibid., pp. 96–9.
65. Ibid., p. 101.
66. Ibid., p. 102.
67. Ibid., pp. 102–3.
68. Ibid., p. 103.
69. John P. Kotter, *John P. Kotter on What Leaders Really Do*, p. 51.
70. Ibid., pp. 54–75.
71. Bernieri quoted in Mark Greer, 'The Science of Savoir Faire', p. 1, *Monitor on Psychology*, http://www.apa.org/monitor/jan05/savoir.html, accessed 24 September 2007.
72. Bernieri quoted in Carlin Flora, 'The X-Factors of Success', p. 2, *Psychology Today* at http://psychologytoday.com/articles/pto-3751.html, accessed 24 September 2007.
73. Riggio quoted in Mark Greer, 'The Science of Savoir Faire', pp. 1–2.
74. Anne Davies and Andrew Clennell, 'Debnam Out of Focus in Battle for Hearts and Minds', *Sydney Morning Herald*, 15 March 2007, p. 9.
75. Helen Thomas quoted in Carlin Flora, 'The X-Factors of Success', p. 1.
76. Rauschenberg quoted in Roni Feinstein, *Robert Rauschenberg: The Silkscreen Paintings 1962–64*, pp. 82–3.
77. Feinstein, *Robert Rauschenberg*, p. 83.
78. Robert Hughes, *The Shock of the New: Art and the Century of Change*, p. 346.
79. Christopher Kremmer, 'Forever Stalked by Shadow of Violence', *Sydney Morning Herald*, 29 December 2007, p. 18.
80. Neil Tweedie, 'Brother in the Shadows a Diligent Executor', *Sydney Morning Herald*, 21 February 2008, p. 8 (reprinted from the *Telegraph*, London).
81. Tim Padgett, 'Cuba's Chance', *Time*, 3 March 2008, p. 23.
82. Donald T. Phillips, *The Clinton Charisma: A Legacy of Leadership*, 2008.
83. Patrick Wintour, 'Brown Insists: Labour "Must Change the Way It Governs"', *The Guardian Weekly*, 18 May 2007, p. 13.
84. David Barnet quoted in Porter and Williams, 'The "It" Factor', p. 8.
85. Paul Ginsborg, *The Politics of Everyday Life: Making Choices, Changing Lives*, quoted in the book review by Stephen Bennetts, 'Put Citizens in the Frame', *The Australian*, *Review*, 24 September 2005, pp. 12–13.
86. Greg Sheridan, 'Liberals Again Fail to Honour a Party Hero, Unlike Labor', *The Australian*, *Inquirer*, 1 December 2007, p. 24.

87. Karl Galinsky, 'Fortuna Teller: A Biography of Caesar Reflects His Age and Ours', *Book Forum*, December/January 2007, p. 46.
88. Quoted in Porter and Williams, 'The "It" Factor', p. 10.
89. Millett and Seccombe, 'The Charisma Game', *The Sydney Morning Herald*, 29 June 2002, p. 27.
90. Alan Ramsey, 'Passionate Words Forge Great Nations', *Sydney Morning Herald*, 8 November 2008, p. 35, quoting from *Advancing Australia*, a book of speeches by Paul Keating.
91. Hugh Mackay, 'How a Lack of Charisma Helped the PM to Seduce Us', *Sydney Morning Herald*, 21 February 2006, p. 9.
92. Gary Younge, 'We Dream That the Good Guy Will Win But Then Vote for Someone Else', *The Guardian Weekly*, 26 October 2007, p. 9.
93. Joshua Meyrowitz, *No Sense of Place: The Impact of Electronic Media on Social Behavior*, p. 281.
94. Ibid., pp. 268–304.
95. Gerard Wright, '$100 m Just to Get Started in This Game', *Sydney Morning Herald*, 9 February 2008, p. 28.
96. Anne Davies, 'A Season for Primary Colours', *Sydney Morning Herald*, 29 December 2007, p. 21.
97. Tom Krauze, 'A New Dream', *The Australian, Review*, 12 May 2007, p. 13.
98. Anne Davies, 'Something's Happening Here', *Sydney Morning Herald*, 12 January 2008, p. 19.
99. Dan Balz, 'Magic v Muscle – and the Rest', *Sydney Morning Herald*, 20 January 2007, p. 40. Reprinted from *The Washington Post*.
100. Joe Klein, 'How Hillary Learned to Trust Herself', *Time*, 21 January 2008, p. 17.
101. Joe Klein, 'Inspiration vs. Substance', *Time*, 18 February 2008, p. 16.
102. Ibid.
103. Geoff Elliott, 'Obama's First Coming', *The Australian, Inquirer*, 9 February 2008, p. 22; Joe Klein, 'Inspiration vs. Substance', p. 16.
104. Suzanne Goldenberg and Ewen MacAskill, 'Democrats Face Fighting on Past Super Tuesday', *The Guardian Weekly*, 1 February 2008, p. 1.
105. *Sydney Morning Herald*, 31 January 2008, p. 7. The advertisement can be viewed at http://www.youtube.com/watch?v=vVlnL1_xXJM.
106. Alan Mascarenhas, 'The JFK of a New Generation', *The Sun-Herald*, 3 February 2008, pp. 24–5.
107. Garry Trudeau, *Doonesbury*, *The Australian*, 14 February 2008, p. 22.
108. Ian Munro, 'Kennedy Plea: Believe Again', *Sydney Morning Herald*, 27 August 2008, p. 7, quoting Senator Edward Kennedy at the Democratic convention.
109. Ibid., p. 7, including material reprinted from the *Los Angles Times*.
110. Nicholas Lemann, 'Worlds Apart: Obama, McCain and the Future of Foreign Policy', *The New Yorker*, 13 October 2008, p. 116; Peter Hartcher, 'Hopes and Hurdles', *Sydney Morning Herald*, 8 November 2008, p. 31.
111. David Nason, '"Rocky" Palin Weighs in for a Fight', *The Australian*, 5 September 2008, p. 9.
112. Steve Coll, 'The Get', *The New Yorker*, 22 September 2008, pp. 31–2.
113. Gerard Baker, 'Folksy Outsider Scores Points by Not Losing', *The Australian*, 4 October 2008, p. 13. Reprinted from *The Times*.

114. Naomi Wolf, 'Don't Be Fooled, Palin Is Bush in Pumps', *Sydney Morning Herald*, 4 October 2008, p. 37.
115. Janet Albrechtsen, 'Middle-Class America Charmed by Charisma of One of Their Own', *The Australian*, 4 October 2008, p. 13.
116. Robert Lusetich, 'McCain the Worst Offender as Duo Ditch Their Idealism', *The Australian*, 23 September 2008, p. 8.
117. Fouad Ajami, 'Looking for Mr Right', *The Australian*, 1 November 2008, p. 26. Reprinted from the *Wall Street Journal*.
118. Robert Lusetich, 'Message of Hope for Weary Nation', *The Australian*, 6 November 2008, p. 13.
119. David Nason, 'Rival Let Ground Slip Away Early On', *The Australian*, 6 November 2008, p. 13.
120. E. J. Dionne quoted in Peter Hartcher, 'A New Race for the White House', *Sydney Morning Herald*, 6 November 2008, p. 11.
121. Michael Grunwald, 'The New Agenda', *Time*, 17 November 2008, p. 48.
122. Nancy Gibbs, 'Yes He Did', *Time*, 17 November 2008, p. 28.
123. Peter Costello, 'The Heads Keep Rolling in a World Hungry for Change', *Sydney Morning Herald*, 12 November 2008, p. 15. Peter Costello is a former treasurer of Australia.
124. Melvin Nelson quoted in Michelle Cazzulino, 'Obama Realises King's Dream', *Daily Telegraph*, 6 November 2008, p. 5.
125. Beverley Gage, 'Do Rookies Make Good Presidents?', *Time*, 17 November 2008, p. 62.

10   That Elusive Something Called Charisma

1. *The Odyssey*, trans. E. V. Rieu, p. 17.
2. Siegfried Schatzmann, *The Pauline Theory of Charismata*, p. 1.

Bibliography

Abel, Theodore, *Why Hitler Came into Power* (New York: AMS Press, 1938).

Alessandra, Tony, *Charisma: Seven Keys to Developing the Magnetism That Leads to Success* (New York: Warner Business Books, 2000).

Aquinas, Thomas, *Summa Theologica* trans. Fathers of the English Dominican Province (New York: Benziger Brothers, 1947).

Arnt, William F. and Gingrich, F. Wilbur, *A Greek–English Lexicon of the New Testament and Other Early Christian Literature* (Chicago: University of Chicago Press, 1957).

Ashton, John, *The Religion of Paul the Apostle* (New Haven: Yale University Press, 2000).

Augustine, *City of God* trans. John Healey, *Everyman's Library* ed. Ernest Rhys (London: J. M. Dent, 1945).

Augustine, *Later Works* Vol. VIII, trans. John Burnaby, *The Library of Christian Classics* (London: SCM Press, 1955).

Augustine, *The Retractions* trans. Mary Inez Bogan, *The Fathers of The Church* Vol. 60 (Washington: The Catholic University of America Press, 1968).

Augustine, *Confessions* trans. J. G. Pilkington, revised Justin Lovill (London: Folio Society, 2006).

Aune, David E., *Prophecy in Early Christianity and the Ancient Mediterranean World* (Grand Rapids: William B. Eerdmans, 1983).

Ball, Terence, 'Political Theory and Conceptual Change' in Andrew Vincent (ed.) *Political Theory: Tradition and Diversity* (Cambridge: Cambridge University Press, 1997).

Banks, Robert, *Paul's Idea of Community: The Early House Churches in Their Historical Setting* (Sydney: Anzea Books, 1979).

Barbas, Samantha, *Movie Crazy: Fans, Stars, and the Cult of Celebrity* (Basingstoke: Palgrave Macmillan, 2002).

Barnes, Timothy, *Tertullian: A Historical and Literary Study* (Oxford: Clarendon Press, 1971).

Barnhart, Robert K. (ed.), *The Barnhart Dictionary of Etymology* (New York: H. W. Wilson Co., 1988).

Barrett, David B. (ed.), *World Christian Encyclopedia* (Oxford: Oxford University Press, 1982).

Barrett, David B., Kurian, George T. and Johnson, Todd M., *World Christian Encyclopedia*, 2nd Edition (Oxford: Oxford University Press, 2001).

Bass, Bernard M., *Transformational Leadership: Industry, Military, and Educational Impact* (Mahvah: Lawrence Erlbaum Associates, 1998).

Bendix, Reinhard, *Max Weber: An Intellectual Portrait* 2nd edition (Berkeley: University of California Press, 1977).

Benjamin, Walter, *Illuminations* ed. Hannah Arendt (London: Fontana, 1982).

Bennett, Dennis, 'God's Strength for This Generation', from 'The Charismatic Revival' issue, *Mission & Ministry* magazine, Trinity Episcopal School for

Ministry, at http://www.emotionallyfree.org/dennis-strength.htm accessed 24 October 2007.

Benton, D. A., *Executive Charisma* (New York: McGraw-Hill, 2005).

Bevir, Mark, *The Logic of the History of Ideas* (Cambridge: Cambridge University Press, 1999).

Bloch, Marc, *The Royal Touch: Sacred Monarchy and Scrofula in England and France* trans. J. E. Anderson (London: Routledge & Kegan Paul, 1973 [1924]).

Blumhofer, Edith L., 'The Christian Catholic Apostolic Church and the Apostolic Faith: A Study in the 1906 Pentecostal Revival' in Cecil Robeck (ed.) *Charismatic Experiences in History* (Peabody, MA: Hendrickson Publishers, 1985).

Boorstin, Daniel J., *The Image: A Guide to Pseudo-Events in America* 2nd edition (New York: Vintage, 1987).

Bourdieu, Pierre, 'Legitimation and Structured Interests in Weber's Sociology of Religion' in Scott Lash and Sam Whimster (eds) *Max Weber, Rationality and Modernity* (Boston: Allen & Unwin, 1987).

Braudy, Leo, *The Frenzy of Renown: Fame and Its History* (New York: Oxford University Press, 1986).

Bray, Gerald (ed.), *Ancient Christian Commentary on Scripture: New Testament VII: 1–2 Corinthians* (Downers Grove, IL: InterVarsity Press, 1999).

Brooke, Christopher, *The Rise and Fall of the Medieval Monastery* (London: Folio, 2006).

Brown, Peter, *Society and the Holy in Late Antiquity* (London: Faber and Faber, 1982).

Browne, John, *Adenochoiradelogia, or, An anatomick-chirurgical treatise of glandules and strumaes ...* (London: Tho. Newcomb for Sam. Lowndes, 1684).

Bruce, F. F., *The Acts of the Apostles: The Greek Text with Introduction and Commentary* (Michigan: William B. Eerdmans, 1951).

Burns, Robert M. and Rayment-Pickard, Hugh (eds), *Philosophies of History: From Enlightenment to Postmodernity* (Oxford: Blackwell, 2000).

Campbell, Edward F., 'Grace', in Bruce M. Metzger and Michael D. Coogan (eds), *The Oxford Companion to the Bible* (New York: Oxford University Press, 1993).

Cashmore, Ellis, *Celebrity/Culture* (New York: Routledge, 2006).

Chadwick, Henry, *Priscillian of Avila: The Occult and the Charismatic in the Early Church* (Oxford: Oxford University Press, 1976).

Chadwick, Henry, *The Early Church* revised edition (London: Penguin, 1993).

Chant, Barry, 'The Nineteenth and Early Twentieth Century Origins of the Australian Pentecostal Movement' in Mark Hutchinson and Stuart Piggin (eds) *Reviving Australia: Essays on the History and Experience of Revival and Revivalism in Australian Christianity* (Sydney: Centre For the Study of Australian Christianity, 1994).

Chantrell, Glynnis (ed.), *The Oxford Dictionary of Word Histories* (Oxford: Oxford University Press, 2002).

Chrysostom, John, *The Homilies of Saint John Chrysostom on the Epistles of Paul to the Corinthians* trans. Talbot W. Chambers, *Nicene and Post-Nicene Fathers* Vol. XII (Grand Rapids: Wm. B. Eerdmans, 1969).

Clark, William, *Academic Charisma and the Origins of the Research University* (Chicago: University of Chicago Press, 2007).

Cody, Alfred, 'The *Didache*: An English Translation' in Clayton N. Jefford (ed.) *The* Didache *in Context: Essays on Its Text, History and Transmission* (Leiden: E. J. Brill, 1995).

Conger, Jay A. and Kanungo, Rabindra N., *Charismatic Leadership in Organizations* (London: Sage, 1998).

Conzelmann, Hans, *History of Primitive Christianity* trans. John Steely (London: Darton, Longman & Todd, 1973).

Coser, Lewis A., 'Preface' in Arthur Mitzman (ed.), *The Iron Cage: An Historical Interpretation of Max Weber* (New Brunswick: Transaction Inc., 1985 [1969]).

Costa Pinto, A., Eatwell, R., and Larsen, S. (eds), *Charisma and Fascism in Interwar Europe* (London: Routledge, 2007).

Cox, Harvey, *Fire from Heaven: The Rise of Pentecostal Spirituality and the Reshaping of Religion in the Twenty-First Century* (London: Cassell, 1996).

De Cordova, Richard, 'The Emergence of the Star System in America' in Christine Gledhill (ed.) *Stardom: Industry of Desire* (London: Routledge, 1991).

Denby, David, 'Fallen Idols: Have Stars Lost Their Magic?', *The New Yorker*, 22 October 2007, pp. 104–12.

Dodds, E. R., *The Greeks and the Irrational* (Berkeley: University of California Press, 1951).

Draper, Jonathan A., 'Social Ambiguity and the Production of Text: Prophets, Teachers, Bishops and Deacons and the Development of the Jesus Tradition in the Community of the *Didache*' in Clayton N. Jefford (ed.) *The Didache in Context: Essays on Its Text, History and Transmission* (Leiden: E. J. Brill, 1995).

Dunn, Geoffrey D., *Tertullian* (London: Routledge, 2004).

Dunn, James D. G., *Jesus and the Spirit: A Study of the Religious and Charismatic Experience of Jesus and the First Christians as Reflected in the New Testament* (London: SCM Press, 1975).

Dunn, James D. G., 'Ministry and the Ministry: The Charismatic Renewal's Challenge to Traditional Ecclesiology' in Cecil Robeck (ed.) *Charismatic Experiences in History* (Peabody, MA: Hendrickson Publishers, 1985).

Dyer, Richard, *Stars* 2nd edition (London: BFI, 1986).

Eatwell, Roger, 'The Concept and Theory of Charismatic Leadership' in A. Costa Pinto, R. Eatwell and S. Larsen (eds) *Charisma and Fascism in Interwar Europe* (London: Routledge, 2007).

Eliade, Mircea (ed.), *The Encyclopedia of Religion* (New York: Macmillan, 1987).

Emerson, J. A., (ed.), *Prophecy: Essays Presented to Georg Fohrer* (Berlin: Walter to Gruyter, 1980).

Evans, Mark, *Open Up the Doors: Music in the Modern Church* (London: Equinox, 2006).

Feinstein, Roni, *Robert Rauschenberg: The Silkscreen Paintings 1962–64* (New York: Whitney Museum of American Art, 1990).

Forbes, Christopher, *Prophecy and Inspired Speech in Early Christianity and Its Hellenistic Environment* (Tübingen: J. C. B. Mohr, 1995).

Foucault, Michel, *The Archaeology of Knowledge* trans. A. M. Sheridan Smith (New York: Pantheon, 1972).

Foucault, Michel, *The Order of Things: An Archaeology of the Human Sciences* (New York: Vintage, 1973 [1970]).

Friedrich, Gerhard (ed.), *Theological Dictionary of the New Testament* translated and edited Geoffrey W. Bromiley (Grand Rapids: Wm. B. Eerdmans, 1974).

Friedriksen, Paula, *From Jesus to Christ: The Origins of the New Testament Images of Jesus* (New Haven: Yale University Press, 1988).

Furbank, P. N., *Reflections on the Word 'Image'* (London: Secker & Warburg, 1970).

Gallagher, J. F., 'Charism: For the Church' in *The New Catholic Encyclopedia* (New York: McGraw-Hill, 1967) Vol. 3 pp. 462–3.

Gamson, Joshua, 'The Assembly Line of Greatness: Celebrity in Twentieth-Century America' in Sean Redmond and Su Holmes (eds) *Stardom and Celebrity: A Reader* (London: Sage, 2007).

Gelder, Ken and Jacobs, Jane M., *Uncanny Australia: Sacredness and Identity in a Postcolonial Nation* (Melbourne: Melbourne University Press, 1998).

George, Timothy, 'The Spirituality of the Radical Reformation' in Bernard McGinn and John Meyendorff (eds) *Christian Spirituality* Vol. 2 (London: Routledge & Keegan Paul, 1987).

Gerth, H. H. and Mills, C. Wright, 'Introduction: The Man and His Work' in Gerth and Mills (trans. and eds) *From Max Weber: Essays in Sociology* (New York: Galaxy, 1958 [1946]).

Giddens, Anthony, *Capitalism and Modern Social Theory: An Analysis of the Writings of Marx, Durkheim and Max Weber* (Cambridge: Cambridge University Press, 1971).

Gignac, Francis, 'Greek' in B. Metzger and M. Coogan (eds) *The Oxford Companion to the Bible* (New York: Oxford University Press, 1993).

Glare, P. G. W., *Oxford Latin Dictionary* (Oxford: Clarendon Press, 1982).

Gledhill, Christine (ed.), *Stardom: Industry of Desire* (London: Routledge, 1991).

Grant, Robert M. (ed.), *Gnosticism: A Source Book of Heretical Writings from the Early Christian Period* (New York: Harper & Brothers, 1978).

Greig, Gary S. and Springer, Kevin N., 'Introduction' in Greig and Springer (eds) *The Kingdom and the Power: Are Healing and the Spiritual Gifts Used by Jesus and the Early Church Meant for the Church Today?* (Ventura: Regal Books, 1993).

Gribomont, John, 'Monasticism and Asceticism' in Bernard McGinn and John Meyendorff (eds) *Christian Spirituality Vol. 1* (London: Routledge & Keegan Paul, 1986).

Guilfoyle, Desmond, *The Charisma Effect* (Sydney: McGraw-Hill, 2002).

Harrison, James R., *Paul's Language of Grace in Its Graeco-Roman Context* (Tübingen: Mohr Siebeck, 2003).

Harvey, A. E., *Jesus and the Constraints of History* (London: Duckworth, 1982).

Hengel, Martin, *The Charismatic Leader and His Followers* trans. J. C. G. Greig (Edinburgh: T. & T. Clark, 1996 [1968]).

Hermas of Rome, trans. G. F. Snyder, *The Apostolic Fathers* Vol. 6 (Camden: Thomas Nelson and Sons, 1968).

Herodotus, *The Histories* trans. Aubrey de Sélincourt (Harmondsworth: Penguin, 1976).

Hiebert, Paul G., 'Discerning the Work of God' in Cecil Robeck (ed.) *Charismatic Experiences in History* (Peabody, MA: Hendrickson Publishers, 1985).

Hippolytus, *The Refutation of All Heresies* trans. J. H. MacMahon, *Ante-Nicene Christian Library Vol. VI* (Edinburgh: T. & T. Clark, 1911).

Hippolytus, *The Extant Works and Fragments of Hippolytus* trans. S. D. F. Salmond *Ante-Nicene Christian Library Vol. IX* (Edinburgh: T. & T. Clark, 1911).

Hocken, Peter, 'Charismatic Movement' in *Encyclopedia of Christianity* Vol. 1 trans. and ed. Geoffrey W. Bromiley (Grand Rapids, MI: Wm. B. Eerdamns, 1999).

Holmberg, Bengt, *Paul and Power: The Structure of Authority in the Primitive Church as Reflected in the Pauline Epistles* (Philadelphia: Fortress Press, 1980).

Holmes, Su and Redmond, Sean (eds), *Framing Celebrity: New Directions in Celebrity Culture* (London: Routledge, 2006).

Homer, *The Iliad* trans. Richard Lattimore (Chicago: University of Chicago Press, 1961).

Homer, *The Odyssey*, trans. E. V. Rieu (London: Penguin, 1991).

Howell, Jane M. and Frost, Peter J., 'A Laboratory Study of Charismatic Leadership' in Jeffrey A. Sonnenfeld (ed.), *Concepts of Leadership* (Aldershot: Dartmouth, 1995).

Hughes, Robert, *The Shock of the New: Art and the Century of Change* 2nd edition (London: Thames & Hudson, 1991).

Hunt, Hannah, 'Byzantine Christianity' in Ken Parry (ed.) *The Blackwell Companion to Eastern Christianity* (Oxford: Blackwell, 2007).

Hunter, Harold D., 'Two Movements of the Holy Spirit in the 20th Century: A Closer Look at Global Pentecostalism and Ecumenism' in *European Pentecostal Charismatic Research Association* Papers, www.epcra.ch/papers_pdf/hunter_1999.pdf accessed 8 October 2007.

Irenaeus of Lyons, *Against the Heresies* Book 1 trans. Dominic J. Unger (New York: Paulist Press, 1992).

Irenaeus of Lyons, *The Writings of Irenaeus Vol. 1* trans. Alexander Roberts and W. H. Rambaut in *Ante-Nicene Christian Library Vol. V* (Edinburgh: T. & T. Clark, 1910).

Jefford, Clayton N. (ed.), *The Didache in Context: Essays on Its Text, History and Transmission* (Leiden: E. J. Brill, 1995).

Judge, E. A., *The Social Pattern of the Christian Groups in the First Century: Some Prolegomena to the Study of New Testament Ideas of Social Obligation* (London: The Tyndale Press, 1960).

Judge, E. A., *The First Christians in the Roman Empire: Augustan and New Testament Essays* ed. James R. Harrison (Tübingen: Mohr Siebeck, 2008).

Kenny, Neil, *The Uses of Curiosity in Early Modern France and Germany* (Oxford: Oxford University Press, 2004).

Knox, J., *Chapters in a Life of Paul* (New York: Abingdon-Cokesbury, 1950).

Knox, R. A., *Enthusiasm: A Chapter in the History of Religion* (Oxford: Oxford University Press, 1950).

Kotter, John P., *John Kotter on What Leaders Really Do* (Harvard: Harvard Business Review Books, 1999).

Kydd, Ronald A. N., *Charismatic Gifts in the Early Church* (Peabody, MA: Hendrickson Publishing, 1984).

Lampe, G. W. H. (ed.), *A Patristic Greek Lexicon* (Oxford: Oxford University Press, 1961).

Land, Steven J., 'Pentecostal Spirituality: Living in the Spirit' in Louis Dupré and Don Sauers (eds) *Christian Spirituality Vol. 3: Post-Reformation and Modern* (London: SCM Press, 1990).

Lang, Doe, *The New Secrets of Charisma: How to Discover and Unleash Your Hidden Powers* (Chicago: Contemporary Books, 1999).

Lewis, David C., 'A Social Anthropologist's Analysis of Contemporary Healing' in Gary Greig and Kevin Springer (eds) *The Kingdom and the Power: Are Healing and the Spiritual Gifts Used by Jesus and the Early Church Meant for the Church Today?* (Ventura: Regal Books, 1993).

Lewis, I. M., *Ecstatic Religion: A Study of Shamanism and Spirit Possession* 2nd edition (London: Routledge, 1989).

Lewis, I. M., *Religion in Context: Cult and Charisma* 2nd edition (Cambridge: Cambridge University Press, 1996).

Liddel, H. G. and Scott, R., *Greek–English Lexicon*, Intermediate Version (Oxford: Oxford University Press, 1975).

Lindholm, Charles, *Charisma* (Oxford: Blackwell, 1990).

Long, Theodore E., 'Prophecy, Charisma and Politics: Reinterpreting the Weberian Thesis' in J. Hadden and A. Shupe (eds) *Prophetic Religions and Politics: Religion and the Political Order* Vol. 1 (New York: Paragon House, 1986).

Louth, Andrew (ed.), *Early Christian Writings: The Apostolic Fathers* trans. Maxwell Stanforth and Andrew Louth (London: Penguin, 1987).

Lovejoy, Arthur O., *The Great Chain of Being: A Study of the History of an Idea* (Cambridge: Harvard University Press, 1936).

Lyons, John, *Before Imagination: Embodied Thought from Montaigne to Rousseau* (Stanford: Stanford University Press, 2005).

MacArthur, John F. Jr, *Charismatic Chaos* (Grand Rapids: Zondervan Publishing, 1992).

Maclean, Ian, 'The Process of Intellectual Change: A Post-Foucauldian Hypothesis' in John Neubauer (ed.) *Cultural History After Foucault* (New York: Aldine De Gruyter, 1999).

Marshall, P. David, *Celebrity and Power* (Minneapolis: University of Minnesota Press, 1997).

Marshall, P. David (ed.), *The Celebrity Culture Reader* (New York: Routledge, 2006).

Mayhew, R., *Charisma patrikon, a paternal gift, or, The legacie of a dying father, to his living children wherein there is a taste of the childs duty of heart-keeping to be hard keeping ...* (London: Printed for John Hancock, 1676).

McGinn, Bernard and Meyendorff, John (eds), *Christian Spirituality* three volumes (London: Routledge & Keegan Paul, 1986, 1987, 1988).

McLenon, James, 'How Shamanism Began: Human Evolution, Dissociation, and Anomalous Experience' in James Houran (ed.) *From Shaman to Scientist: Essays on Humanity's Search for Spirits* (Lanham: Scarecrow Press, 2004).

McIlwain, Doris, 'The Charisma of Fallible Leaders and the Limits of Self-Help', *Australian Review of Public Affairs* at http://www.australianreview.net/digest/2006/05/mcilwain.html.

Meyendorff, John, 'Christ as Saviour in the East' in Bernard McGinn and John Meyendorff (eds) *Christian Spirituality* Vol. 1 (London: Routledge & Keegan Paul, 1986).

Meyendorff, Paul, 'Eastern Liturgical Theology' in Bernard McGinn and John Meyendorff (eds) *Christian Spirituality* Vol. 1 (London: Routledge & Keegan Paul, 1986).

Meyrowitz, Joshua, *No Sense of Place: The Impact of Electronic Media on Social Behavior* (New York: Oxford University Press, 1985).

Milavec, Aaron, *The Didache: Text, Translation, Analysis, and Commentary* (Collegeville: Liturgical Press, 2003).

Mitzman, Arthur, *The Iron Cage: An Historical Interpretation of Max Weber* (New Brunswick: Transaction Inc., 1985 [1969]).

Mommsen, Wolfgang J., *The Age of Bureaucracy: Perspectives on the Political Sociology of Max Weber* (Oxford: Basil Blackwell, 1974).

Mommsen, Wolfgang J., *Max Weber and German Politics 1890–1920* trans. Michael S. Steinberg (Chicago: Chicago University Press, 1984 [1959]).

Morin, Edgar, *The Stars* trans. Richard Howard (New York: Grove Press, 1960).

Moxnes, Halvor, 'The Quest for Honor and the Unity of the Community in Romans 12 and the Orations of Dio Chrysotom' in Troels Engber-Pederson (ed.) *Paul in His Hellenistic Context* (Edinburgh: T & T Clark, 1994).

Murphy-O'Connor, Jerome, *Paul: A Critical Life* (Oxford: Clarendon Press, 1996).

Nietzsche, Friedrich, *Twilight of the Idols and the Anti-Christ* trans. R. J. Hollingdale (Hammondsworth: Penguin, 1978).

Nietzsche, Friedrich, *Thus Spake Zarathustra* trans. Walter Kaufmann (Hammondsworth: Penguin, 1981).

Oakes, Len, *Prophetic Charisma: The Psychology of Revolutionary Religious Personalities* (Syracuse: Syracuse University Press, 1997).

Ong, Walter J., *The Presence of the Word: Some Prolegomena for Cultural and Religious History* (Minneapolis: University of Minnesota Press, 1967).

Oxford English Dictionary (OED) 2nd edition (Oxford: Oxford University Press, 1989).

Parsons, Talcott, *The Structure of Social Action* (New York: The Free Press, 1968 [1937]).

Patterson, Stephen J., 'Didache 11–13: The Legacy of Radical Itinerancy in Early Christianity' in Clayton N. Jefford (ed.) *The* Didache *in Context: Essays on Its Text, History and Transmission* (Leiden: E. J. Brill, 1995).

Perkins, Pheme, *Gnosticism and the New Testament* (Minneapolis: Fortress Press, 1993).

Phillips, Donald T., *The Clinton Charisma: A Legacy of Leadership* (Basingstoke: Palgrave, 2008).

Piggin, Stuart, *Firestorm of the Lord: The History of and Prospects for Revival in the Church and the World* (Carlisle: Paternoster Press, 2000).

Radosh, Daniel, 'The Good Book Business' in *The New Yorker* 26 December 2006 pp. 54–9.

Redmond, Sean and Holmes, Su, (eds), *Stardom and Celebrity: A Reader* (London: Sage, 2007).

Rieff, Philip, *Charisma: The Gift of Grace and How It Has Been Taken Away from Us* (New York: Pantheon, 2007).

Robeck, Cecil M. Jr, (ed.), *Charismatic Experiences in History* (Peabody, MA: Hendrickson Publishers, 1985).

Robeck, Cecil M. Jr, 'Origen's Treatment of the Charismata in 1 Corinthians 12: 8–10' in Cecil M. Robeck (ed.) *Charismatic Experiences in History* (Peabody, MA: Hendrickson Publishers, 1985).

Roberts, Nancy C. and Bradley, Raymond Trevor, 'Limits of Charisma' in Jeffrey A. Sonnenfeld (ed.) *Concepts of Leadership* (Aldershot: Dartmouth, 1995).

Robinson, David, *The History of World Cinema* 2nd edition (New York: Stein and Day, 1981).

Roth, Guenther, 'Introduction' in Max Weber *Economy and Society: An Outline of Interpretive Sociology* in Guenther Roth and Claus Wittich (eds) trans. E. Fischoff et al. (New York: Bedminster Press, 1968).

Roth, Guenther, 'Introduction to the New Edition' in Reinhard Bendix (ed.) *Max Weber: An Intellectual Portrait* 2nd edition (Berkeley: University of California Press, 1977).

Said, Edward, *The World, the Text, and the Critic* (London: Faber and Faber, 1984).

Sanders, Jack T., *Charisma, Converts, Competitors: Societal and Sociological Factors in the Success of Early Christianity* (London: SCM Press, 2000).

Schatz, Thomas, *The Genius of the System: Hollywood Filmmaking in the Studio Era* (New York: Pantheon, 1988).

Schatzmann, Siegfried, *A Pauline Theology of Charismata* (Peabody, MA: Hendrickson Publishers, 1989).

Schickel, Richard, *Common Fame: The Culture of Celebrity* (London: Pavilion Books, 1985).

Schiffer, Irvine, *Charisma: A Psychoanalytical Look at Mass Society* (Toronto: University of Toronto Press, 1973).

Schlesinger, Arthur M. Jr., *The Politics of Hope* (London: Eyre & Spottiswoode, 1964).

Schoedel, William R., *Ignatius of Antioch: A Commentary on the Letters of Ignatius of Antioch* (Philadelphia: Fortress Press, 1985).

Shelley, Bruce L., *Church History in Plain Language*, 2nd edition (Dallas: Word Publishing, 1995).

Sica, Alan, *Weber, Irrationality, and Social Order* (Berkeley: University of California Press, 1988).

Skinner, Quentin, *Visions of Politics Volume 1: Regarding Method* (Cambridge: Cambridge University Press, 2002).

Smail, Tom, 'A Renewal Recalled' in Tom Smail, Andrew Walker and Nigel Wright (eds) *Charismatic Renewal: The Search for a Theology* (London: SPCK, 1995).

Smail, Tom, 'In Spirit and in Truth: Reflections on Charismatic Worship' in Tom Smail, Andrew Walker and Nigel Wright (eds) *Charismatic Renewal: The Search for a Theology* (London: SPCK, 1995).

Smail, Tom, Walker, Andrew and Wright, Nigel, 'From "The Toronto Blessing" to Trinitarian Renewal: A Theological Conversation' in Walker Smail and Wright (eds) *Charismatic Renewal: The Search for a Theology* (London: SPCK, 1995).

Smail, Tom, Walker, Andrew and Wright, Nigel, '"Revelation Knowledge" and Knowledge of Revelation: The Faith Movement and the Question of Heresy' in Walker Smail and Wright (eds) *Charismatic Renewal: The Search for a Theology* (London: SPCK, 1995).

Sohm, Rudolf, *Outlines of Church History* trans. May Sinclair (London: Macmillan, 1895).

Sonnenfeld, Jeffrey A. (ed.), *Concepts of Leadership* (Aldershot: Dartmouth, 1995).

Spadafora, David, *The Idea of Progress in Eighteenth-Century Britain* (New Haven: Yale University Press, 1990).

Spicq, Ceslas, *Theological Lexicon of the New Testament* trans. James D. Ernest (Peabody, MA: Hendrickson, 1994).

Stendhal, Krister, *Paul among Jews and Gentiles* (Philadelphia: Fortress Press, 1976).

Symeon the New Theologian, *Hymns of Divine Love* trans. George A. Maloney (Denville: Dimension Books, 1976).

Tabbernee, William, *Montanist Inscriptions and Testimonia: Epigraphic Sources Illustrating the History of Montanism* (Macon, GA: Mercer University Press, 1997).

Tacitus, *The Annals of Imperial Rome* trans. Michael Grant (Hammondsworth: Penguin, 1975).

Tertullian, *Treatises on Penance: On Penitence and on Purity* trans. and annotated William P. Le Saint (Westminster, MD: The Newman Press, 1959).

Tertullian, *Adversus Marcionem*, trans. Ernest Evans (Oxford: Oxford University Press, 1972).

Thomas, Keith, *Religion and the Decline of Magic* (London: Weidenfeld & Nicolson, 1971).

Tooker, William, *Charisma siue Donum sanationis Seu explicatio totius quaestionis de mirabilium sanitatum gratia ...* (London: John Windet, 1597).

Tucker, Susie I., *Enthusiasm: A Study in Semantic Change* (Cambridge: Cambridge University Press, 1972).

Turner, Graeme, 'Celebrity, the Tabloid and the Democratic Public Sphere' in P. David Marshall (ed.) *The Celebrity Culture Reader* (New York: Routledge, 2006).

Unger, Dominic J., 'Introduction' in St Irenaeus of Lyons *Against the Heresies Book 1* trans. Dominic J. Unger (New York: Paulist Press, 1992).

Vermes, Geza, *Jesus the Jew: A Historian's Reading of the Gospels* (London: SCM Press, 1973).

Wagner, C. Peter, 'Forward' in Gary Greig and Kevin Springer (eds) *The Kingdom and the Power: Are Healing and the Spiritual Gifts Used by Jesus and the Early Church Meant for the Church Today?* (Ventura: Regal Books, 1993).

Waldman, David A., Bass, Bernard M. and Yammarino, Francis J., 'Adding to Contingent-Reward Behavior: The Augmenting Effect of Charismatic Leadership' in Jeffrey A. Sonnenfeld (ed.) *Concepts of Leadership* (Aldershot: Dartmouth, 1995).

Walker, Andrew, 'The Devil You Think You Know: Demonology and the Charismatic Movement' in Tom Smail, Andrew Walker and Nigel Wright (eds) *Charismatic Renewal: The Search for a Theology* (London: SPCK, 1995).

Walker, Andrew, 'Miracles, Strange Phenomena, and Holiness' in Tom Smail, Andrew Walker and Nigel Wright (eds) *Charismatic Renewal: The Search for a Theology* (London: SPCK, 1995).

Walker, Andrew, 'Notes from a Wayward Son' in Tom Smail, Andrew Walker and Nigel Wright (eds) *Charismatic Renewal: The Search for a Theology* (London: SPCK, 1995).

Wallace, Richard and Williams, Wynne, *The Three Worlds of Paul of Tarsus* (London: Routledge, 1998).

Wallis, Roy, 'The Social Construction of Charisma' in Roy Wallis and Steve Bruce (eds) *Sociological Theory, Religion and Collective Action* (Belfast: The Queen's University, 1986).

Wallis, Roy, 'Charisma and Explanation' in Eileen Barker, James A. Beckford and Karel Dobbelaere (eds) *Secularization, Rationalism, and Sectarianism: Essays in Honour of Bryan R. Wilson* (Oxford: Clarendon Press, 1993).

Ward, W. R., *The Protestant Evangelical Awakening* (Cambridge: Cambridge University Press, 1992).

Weber, Max, *From Max Weber: Essays in Sociology* (trans. and eds) H. Gerth and C. Wright Mills (New York: Galaxy, 1958 [1946]).

Weber, Max, *The Religion of China: Confucianism and Taoism* trans. Hans H. Gerth (New York: The Free Press, 1964 [1951]).

Weber, Max, *Economy and Society: An Outline of Interpretive Sociology* (eds) Roth, Guenther and Wittich, Claus, trans. E. Fischoff et al. (New York: Bedminster Press, 1968).

Weber, Max, *The Protestant Ethic and the Spirit of Capitalism* trans. Talcott Parsons (London: Unwin University Books, 1971 [1930]).

Weber, Max, *The Religion of India: The Sociology of Hinduism and Buddhism* trans. H. Gerth and D. Martindale (New York: The Free Press, 1992 [1958]).

Whybray, R. N., 'Prophets: Ancient Israel' in Bruce M. Metzger and Michael D. Coogan (eds) *The Oxford Companion to the Bible* (New York: Oxford University Press, 1993).

Willner, Ann Ruth, *The Spellbinders: Charismatic Political Leadership* (New Haven: Yale University Press, 1984).

Wilson, A. N., *Paul: The Mind of the Apostle* (London: W.W. Norton, 1997).

Wilson, Bryan R., *The Noble Savages: The Primitive Origins of Charisma and Its Contemporary Survival* (Berkeley: Quantum Books, 1975).

Winkelman, Michael, 'Spirits as Human Nature and the Fundamental Structures of Consciousness' in James Houran (ed.) *From Shaman to Scientist: Essays on Humanity's Search for Spirits* (Lanham: Scarecrow Press, 2004).

Zizioulas, John D., *Eucharist, Bishop, Church* (Brookline, MA: Holy Cross Orthodox Press, 2001).

Index